LABOR
AND
EMPLOYMENT
LAW DESK BOOK
Second Edition

◆━━━━━━━━━━━━━━━━━◆

Gordon E. Jackson

1996 Cumulative Supplement

PRENTICE HALL
Englewood Cliffs, New Jersey 07632

Prentice-Hall International (UK) Limited, *London*
Prentice-Hall of Australia Pty. Limited, *Sydney*
Prentice-Hall of Canada, Inc., *Toronto*
Prentice-Hall Hispanoamericana, S.A., *Mexico*
Prentice-Hall of India Private Limited, *New Delhi*
Prentice-Hall of Japan, Inc., *Tokyo*
Simon & Schuster Asia Pte. Ltd., *Singapore*
Editora Prentice-Hall do Brazil, Ltda. *Rio de Janeiro*

©1996 by
Gordon E. Jackson

All rights reserved. No part of this book
may be reproduced in any form or
by any means, without permission
in writing from the publisher.

This publication is designed to provide accurate and
authoritative information in regard to the subject matter
covered. It is sold with the understanding that the publisher
is not engaged in rendering legal, accounting, or
other professional service. If legal advice or other
expert assistance is required, the services of a competent
professional person should be sought.

*. . . From the Declaration of Principles jointly adopted by a
Committee of the American Bar Association and a Committee of
Publishers and Associations.*

10 9 8 7 6 5 4 3 2 1

Library of Congress Cataloging-in-Publication Data
(Revised for Suppl.)
Jackson, Gordon E.
    Labor and employment law desk book.
    Kept up to date by supplements.
    Includes index.
    1. Labor laws and legislation—United
States 2. Labor laws and legislation—
United States—States—Outlines, syllabi, etc.
I. Title.
KF3319.J33   1996   93-28069

ISBN 0-13-228537-1

PRENTICE HALL
Englewood Cliffs, NJ 07632

A Simon & Schuster Company

Printed in the United States of America

Preface

The *1996 Cumulative Supplement* to the *Labor and Employment Law Desk Book, Second Edition,* has been developed and written with several purposes in mind.

The most important purpose is its use as a means of updating the Second Edition of the main volume, which was published in 1993.

The second purpose of this *1996 Cumulative Supplement* is to share with the reader a more comprehensive insight into the developing trends of labor and employment law. For example, this Supplement discusses, more comprehensively, developments in the Americans with Disabilities Act and the Family and Medical Leave Act.

Third, the *1996 Cumulative Supplement* contains coverage of recent OSHA regulations and the new Uniform Services Employment and Reemployment Rights statute.

Additionally, the *1996 Cumulative Supplement* discusses the FMLA final rule and the EEOC's guidance on pre-employment inquiries.

Finally, the *1996 Cumulative Supplement* augments and updates the labor and employment laws in all fifty states and the District of Columbia.

Acknowledgments

This Supplement would not have been possible without the assistance and support of some very special people. The author therefore expresses his gratitude to Carol Gatlin who so patiently and diligently prepared the final manuscript for publishing.

A special note of thanks is extended to Tim Bland who devoted countless hours of time and energy in assisting the author in the completion of this *1996 Cumulative Supplement.*

Next, the author extends his gratitude to his law partners, Steve Shields, Ted Yeiser, Jr., Frank Cantrell, Bill Harvey and Jim Holt, Jr. who provided support and insight as well as to associates Beth Stengel, Valerie Speakman and Robin Rasmussen.

Writers know better than anyone the importance of family support in such efforts as writing articles, books and supplements. Therefore, a special note of love and thanks are expressed to my beloved wife, Sandy, as well as to Angela, Celeste, Eric, Amanda, Alex and Peyton for all their encouragement, support, and patience relative to this effort.

How to Use This Supplement

The *1996 Cumulative Supplement* to the *Labor and Employment Law Desk Book, Second Edition,* is divided into the same seven parts as was the main volume:

Part I covers the NLRA, as amended;
Part II addresses the various federal EEO laws;
Part III discusses various federal wage and hour laws, particularly the FLSA;
Part IV covers the federal OSHA statutes and related laws;
Part V addresses ERISA and other pension and welfare laws; and
Part VI discusses state statutory laws and court decisions relative to labor and employment matters within the various states.

The substantial advantage the reader has in utilizing the *Labor and Employment Law Desk Book* and its cumulative supplements as a research source over other such books is that the main volume and cumulative supplements provide notes and citations to each statute or decision referenced and, with the use of its contents, index and decimalized references and format, the reader is provided with a quick, easy and friendly means of accessing the exact law in question.

This supplement's index is cumulative. References are to pages in the main volume and supplement. Supplement entries are preceded by an "S."

Contents

Part One
National Labor Relations Act
and Related Laws

Part Two
Federal Anti-Discrimination Laws
and Executive Orders

Part Three
Federal Wage and Hour Laws

Part Four
Federal Safety and Health Laws

Part Five
Federal Retirement,
Welfare, and Privacy Laws

Part Six
State Labor Laws

PART ONE

NATIONAL LABOR RELATIONS ACT AND RELATED LAWS

1

Introduction to the
Labor Management Relations Act

[1.01]–[1.05]—NO SIGNIFICANT CHANGES SINCE MAIN VOLUME.

2

Jurisdiction of the
National Labor Relations Board

[2.02]–[2.04]—NO SIGNIFICANT CHANGES SINCE MAIN VOLUME.

3

LMRA Coverage

[3.01]–[3.06]—NO SIGNIFICANT CHANGES SINCE MAIN VOLUME.

4

LMRA—
Preemption
and Conflicts

[4.01]–[4.06]—NO SIGNIFICANT CHANGES SINCE MAIN VOLUME.

5

Employer Interference
with Protected Activities—
Section 8(a)(1) Violations

[5.02] EMPLOYER INTERFERENCE WITH UNION ACTIVITY

The United States Supreme Court has granted certiorari in a case that should resolve the current conflict between the Circuit Courts over whether an employer is required to hire paid union organizers.[1]

[5.04] NONEMPLOYEE SOLICITATION AND DISTRIBUTION RULES

In two recent cases the NLRB has held that nonemployee union representatives are prohibited from conducting area standards picketing on an employer's private property.[2]

SUPPLEMENTAL NOTES TO CHAPTER 5

1. *Town & Country Electric, Inc. v. NLRB*, 34 F3rd 625 (8th Cir., 1995), c. granted, Sup. Ct. (1995).
2. *Leslie Homes, Inc.*, 316 NLRB No. 29 (1995); *Makro, Inc. & Renaissance Properties Co.*, 316 NLRB No. 24 (1995).

6

Employer Domination and Retaliation— Sections 8(a)(2) and 8(a)(4) Violations

[6.03] "GRIEVANCE COMMITTEES" AS EMPLOYER UNIONS

The NLRB has held that an employee involvement committee may be a labor organization regardless of:

- employee motive in setting up the committee;
- employee perception of the employee committee;
- formal structure, because a labor organization may exist even though it lacks a constitution or bylaws, elected officials, or formal meetings.[1]

Joint employer/employee safety committees have been found to be labor organizations, where the committees discussed subjects such as safety, incentive awards, employee picnics, and jogging tracks.[2]

"Action Committees" created by an employer in response to employees' dissatisfaction with unilaterally implemented changes in working conditions were found to be labor organizations, despite the employees' claim that they were merely communications devices.[3] The Third Circuit Court of Appeals has upheld the NLRB's *Electromation* decision.[4]

SUPPLEMENTAL NOTES TO CHAPTER 6

1. NLRB General Counsel Memorandum 93-4 (4-15-93).
2. *E.I. Dupont de Neumours*, 311 NLRB No. 88, 143 1121 (1993).
3. *Electromation, Inc.*, 309 NLRB No. 163, 142 LRRM 1001 (1992).
4. *Electromation v. NLRB*, 147 LRRM 2257 (Third Cir. 1994).

7

Employer Discrimination and Discharge— Section 8(a)(3) Violations

[7.01]–[7.06]—NO SIGNIFICANT CHANGES SINCE MAIN VOLUME.

8

Protected Concerted Activities

[8.01]–[8.05]—NO SIGNIFICANT CHANGES SINCE MAIN VOLUME.

9

Union Restraint of Employee Rights— Section 8(b)(1) Violations

[9.02] FAILURE TO REPRESENT EMPLOYEES FAIRLY

Union security clauses are devices within a collective bargaining agreement that require union membership in good standing. A union security clause requiring membership in good standing does not constitute unlawful union action, but failure to clarify to the employee that "good standing" is at most an obligation to pay initiation fees and dues constitutes a violation of the union's duty of fair representation.[1] If an employee with a disability files an 8(b)(1)(A) charge, claiming that the union has failed to fairly represent him or her and the employee has also filed an ADA charge with the EEOC, the NLRB may:

- dismiss the case if it lacks merit; or
- defer processing of the charge for a reasonable period of time, pending the completion of the EEOC's investigation and determination of whether there is reasonable cause to believe that a violation has occurred.

Furthermore:

- If the EEOC negotiates a settlement of a charge after finding for the charging party, the NLRB will obtain a withdrawal or dismiss the charge if further processing is not necessary to effectuate the purposes of the Act.
- If the EEOC does not reach a settlement after finding for the charging party, the NLRB will determine whether to resume processing of the charge or continue to defer processing.
- If the EEOC finds no violation has occurred, the NLRB will resume processing the ULP charge.
- If the person with a disability files a ULP charge claiming failure to represent and has not filed an ADA charge, the NLRB will follow its normal procedures for processing the charge and notify the employee how to file a charge with the EEOC.
- The agencies will share investigative files.[2]

SUPPLEMENTAL NOTES TO CHAPTER 9

1. *Paramex Systems Corp.*, 311 NLRB No. 105 (5-28-93).
2. (Memorandum of Understanding Between the General Counsel of the NLRB and EEOC 11/16/93).

10

Coercion to Entice
Employer Discrimination—
Section 8(b)(2) Violations

[10.01]–[10.06]—NO SIGNIFICANT CHANGES SINCE MAIN VOLUME.

11

Secondary Boycotts—
Section 8(b)(4)(a), (b) and (c)
Violations

[11.01]–[11.08]—NO SIGNIFICANT CHANGES SINCE MAIN VOLUME.

12

Jurisdictional Disputes,
Informational Picketing,
and Other 8(b) Violations

[12.01]–[12.09]—NO SIGNIFICANT CHANGES SINCE MAIN VOLUME.

13

Introduction to
Collective Bargaining

[13.01] CONDITIONS PRECEDENT TO DUTY TO BARGAIN

An employer's obligation to bargain with a union runs from the date on which the employer receives the union's request for recognition rather than from the later date on which the union won a representation election.[1]

[13.05] UNION'S LOSS OF MAJORITY STATUS

The Ninth Circuit Court of Appeals has held that an employer's final and best offer to a union remained in effect even after the employer's unlawful withdrawal of recognition from the unions with which it was negotiating a collective bargaining contract.[2] The court noted that the offer contained no express time limits or conditions for acceptance.[3] Thus, the employer could not reasonably be led to believe that its offer had been terminated.[4]

SUPPLEMENTAL NOTES TO CHAPTER 13

1. *Power, Inc. v. NLRB*, 147 LRRM 2833 (DC Cir. 1994).
2. *Ivaldi v. NLRB*, 148 LRRM 2649 (Ninth Cir. 1995).
3. *Ibid.*
4. *Ibid.*

14

Duty to Bargain: Employer's Obligations

[14.01] REFUSAL TO NEGOTIATE MANDATORY BARGAINING SUBJECTS

The Board has held that an employer violates § 8(a)(1) and (5) of the Act when, while negotiating its initial contract with a union, the company changes insurance carriers with the result that its employees' benefits are changed although their contributions toward coverage remain the same.[1]

The Board has held that an employer is not permitted to negotiate directly with its employees and offer them retirement and/or separation incentives in order to "buy out" their rights under lifetime employment agreements without union participation.[2]

In order to waive the right to bargain there must be a clear and unmistakable waiver of the rights and not just a management rights clause with general language. A company unilaterally reduced the hours of its bargaining unit employees, causing them to be reclassified as part-time workers who, under the contract, received lower wages and were ineligible for health insurance benefits. It justified its action under the management rights clause in the most recently expired agreement, which gave the employer the "right to schedule hours of employment (or) to relieve employees of duties because of lack of work." The Board held that such generalized language was not sufficient to establish the union's waiver of its right to bargain over changes in hours.[3] If an employer presents a proposal to the union as a *fait accompli,* the union will not be deemed to have waived its right to bargain over the proposal by inaction.[4]

However, if a union has sufficient notice of a proposed action, but does not request bargaining, a waiver by inaction will be found.[5]

[14.06] FAILURE TO FURNISH INFORMATION TO UNION

An employer may not refuse to comply with an ambiguous or overbroad request for information from a union, but must request clarification and/or comply with the request to the extent it encompasses necessary and relevant information.[6]

SUPPLEMENTAL NOTES TO CHAPTER 14

1. *Josten Concrete Products Co., Inc.,* 303 NLRB No. 16.
2. *Toledo Blade Co.,* 301 NLRB No. 70.
3. *Control Serv.,* 303 NLRB No. 83.
4. *Chrissy Sportswear, Inc.,* 304 NLRB No. 124; 8 *The Labor Lawyer* 413.
5. *Haddon Craftsmen, Inc.,* 300 NLRB No. 100.
6. *Stanley E. Stein,* 303 NLRB 367, 138 LRRM 1159.

15

Collective Bargaining: Union's Obligations

[15.01]

During negotiation, a union must clearly intend, express, and manifest a conscious relinquishment of its right to bargain before relinquishment will be found.[1]

SUPPLEMENTAL NOTES TO CHAPTER 15

1. *Intermountain Rural Electrical Assn. v NLRB*, 305 NLRB 783, 139 LRRM 1003 (1991).

16

How to Process an
Unfair Labor Practice Charge

[16.01]–[16.06]—NO SIGNIFICANT CHANGES SINCE MAIN VOLUME.

17

The Unfair Labor Practice Hearing

[17.01]–[17.09]—NO SIGNIFICANT CHANGES SINCE MAIN VOLUME.

18

Unfair Labor Practices:
Post-Hearing Proceedings

[18.01]–[18.06]—NO SIGNIFICANT CHANGES SINCE MAIN VOLUME.

19

Representation Petitions
for Certification

[19.06] ELECTION BAR/CERTIFICATION BAR

The NLRB has modified one of its prior rulings by holding that a recognition agreement does not bar an election petition if, as of the date of recognition, thirty percent or more of the recognized unit consists of employees that have been previously represented by the petitioning non-stranger union.[1] Thus, under this rule, it is necessary to determine whether the petitioning non-stranger union had opportunity to demonstrate the extent of its interest.[2]

SUPPLEMENTAL NOTES TO CHAPTER 19

1. Custom Deliveries, 315 NLRB, No. 152 (1994).
2. *Ibid.*

20

Pre-election
Representation Hearings

[20.04] APPROPRIATE BARGAINING UNITS

The Eighth Circuit Court of Appeals has held that the NLRB is incorrect in presuming that single-plant units are appropriate bargaining units in refusing to consider changed circumstances in determining whether bargaining orders should be issued.[1]

[20.09] PRE-ELECTION NOTICES

The NLRB has held that employers must inform the NLRB's regional office at least five full working days prior to 12:01 a.m. of the day of an election that the pre-election notices prescribed by the NLRB have not been received.[2]

SUPPLEMENTAL NOTES TO CHAPTER 20

1. *NLRB v. Cell Agricultural Manufacturing Co.*, 147 LRRM 2961 (Eighth Cir. 1994).
2. Club Demonstration Services, 317 NLRB No. 52 (1995).

21

The NLRB
Election Process

[21.01]–[21.08]—NO SIGNIFICANT CHANGES SINCE MAIN VOLUME.

22

Interference with
NLRB Elections

[22.09] SPEECHES WITHIN 24 HOURS

The NLRB has held that a union was free to play union songs from a sound truck parked outside the plant on the day of a representation election even though the broadcasts were heard at many work stations inside the plant during working time.[1] The Board held that such a broadcast did not constitute a campaign speech.[2]

SUPPLEMENTAL NOTES TO CHAPTER 22

1. Bro-Tech Corp., 315 NLRB No. 151 (1994).
2. *Ibid.*

23

Objections and Challenges to NLRB Elections

[23.01]–[23.10]—NO SIGNIFICANT CHANGES SINCE MAIN VOLUME.

24

Decertification, Deauthorization, and Unit Clarification Petitions

[24.01]–[24.09]—NO SIGNIFICANT CHANGES SINCE MAIN VOLUME.

25

The Labor Management
Reporting and Disclosure Act

[25.01]–[25.10]—NO SIGNIFICANT CHANGES SINCE MAIN VOLUME

26

Labor Arbitration

[26.02] CONTRACTUAL OBLIGATIONS

The Ninth Circuit Court of Appeals has held that an interest arbitration clause in a prehire contract survived the expiration of the contract even though the employer refused to negotiate after the contract expired.[1] This view has also been upheld by the Sixth and Seventh Circuits.[2]

SUPPLEMENTAL NOTES TO CHAPTER 26

1. *Beach Air Conditioning v. Sheet Metal Workers Local 102*, 149 LRRM 2391 (Ninth Cir. 1995).
2. *Ibid.*

27

Railway Labor Act

[27.01]–[27.08]—NO SIGNIFICANT CHANGES SINCE MAIN VOLUME

28

Federal Service
Labor-Management
Relations Act

[28.01]–[28.11]—NO SIGNIFICANT CHANGES SINCE MAIN VOLUME.

29

Miscellaneous
Labor Relations Act

[29.01]–[29.06]—NO SIGNIFICANT CHANGES SINCE MAIN VOLUME.

PART TWO

FEDERAL ANTI-DISCRIMINATION LAWS AND EXECUTIVE ORDERS

30

Civil Rights Act
of 1964, Title VII

[30.08] RETALIATION PROHIBITED

A District Court in Pennsylvania has held that an employer may not retaliate against an employee for untruthful statements that the employee makes in connection with an EEOC charge.[1] The Court said that the idea that an employer may not retaliate against an employee for filing an EEOC charge, but can retaliate for allegedly untruthful statements in the charge, creates a distinction that is too narrow to be meaningful.[2] The Court further reasoned that, except in the most blatant of cases, employers will have perceived the events forming the basis of the charge differently than the employee.[3] Thus, the risk that an employer might retaliate for a statement that is wrongfully perceived as being untrue is too great.

The Third Circuit Court of Appeals has held that an employer may be found liable for retaliation under Title VII for actions it takes against an employee after the employee has been discharged.[4] The Court reasoned that the need for protection against retaliatory conduct does not end when the employment relationship is concluded.[5] An employee's fear that his former employer might take actions against him after the employee has been discharged would chill potential claims for discriminatory discharge.[6]

SUPPLEMENTAL NOTES TO CHAPTER 30

1. *EEOC v. Snyder Doors*, 63 FEP Cases 1292 (DC E.Pa., 1994).
2. *Ibid.*
3. *Ibid.*
4. *Charlton v. Paramus Board of Education*, 64 FEP Cases 1474 (3rd Cir. 1994)
5. *Ibid.*
6. *Ibid.*

31

Civil Rights Act of 1991

[31.01] BACKGROUND AND COVERAGE

The United States Supreme Court has held that the compensatory and punitive damages provisions of the Civil Rights Act of 1991 do not apply retroactively. The Supreme Court reasoned that federal statutes affecting substantive rights, liabilities, or duties are not retroactive unless there is clear congressional intent to the contrary. The Court limited its prior ruling that courts are to apply the law in effect at the time they render their opinions to purely procedural matters. The Court did not find sufficient intent on the part of Congress in passing the CRA to overcome the presumption against retroactivity.[1]

The District of Columbia Circuit Court of Appeals held that "testers" did not have standing to sue an unemployment agency under Section 1981 because their conscious, material misrepresentation and false credentials would have rendered any contract void.[2] Further the court held that the "testers" could not sue under Title VII as it existed prior to the 1991 Amendments because at that time it provided only equitable remedies.[3]

[31.04] EXPANDED DAMAGES AND JURY TRIALS

The United States Supreme Court has held that the after-acquired evidence doctrine goes to damages rather than liability.[4] The court held that as a general rule, in cases where after-acquired evidence is proffered, neither reinstatement nor front pay are appropriate.[5] Further, the court held that in determining the appropriate amount of backpay, the beginning and ending dates of the calculation would be from the date of the unlawful discharge to the date the after-acquired evidence is discovered.[6]

[31.06] STATUTES OF LIMITATIONS

A Federal District Court has held that the Civil Rights Act of 1991 did not alter the time for bringing suit under the ADEA.[7] The Court held that the revised ADEA continues to incorporate the Fair Labor Standards Act's two-year and three-year limitations periods. The new ADEA provision stating that an action "may" be brought within 90 days after receipt of the right to sue letter was not intended to require that the suit be brought within that time. The Court noted that the purpose of the notice is not to reduce the time period within which claimants may sue, but to assist them in filing on time by requiring the EEOC to notify them concerning the handling of their charges.

A Federal District Court in Kansas has held that the ADEA, as revised by the CRA, does not require claimants to obtain a right to sue letter from the EEOC prior to filing suit.[8] The Court stated that the provision of the CRA requiring claimants to file an action within 90 days of receipt of the notice of the right to sue was enacted to establish when the statute of limitations will run. This provision did not change the right of claimants to file suit at any time after 60 days had passed since they filed the charge with the EEOC.[9]

SUPPLEMENTAL NOTES TO CHAPTER 31

1. *Landgraf v. USI Film Products* (U.S. S. Ct., No. 92-757, 1994); *Rivers v. Roadway Express, Inc.*, (U.S. S. Ct., No. 92-938, 1994).

2. *Fair Employment Council of Greater Washington, Inc. v. BMC Makering Corp.*, 28 F.3d 1268 (DC Cir. 1994).

3. *Ibid.*

4. *McKennon v. Nashville Banner Publishing Co.*, 66 FEP Cases 1192 (1995).

5. *Ibid.*

6. *Ibid.*

7. *Simmons v. Al Smith Buick Co.*, 63 FEP Cases 958 (DC NC 1993).

8. *Adams v. Burlington Northern R.R. Co.*, 63 FEP Cases 679 (DC Kan 1993).

9. *Ibid.*

32

Unfair
Employment Practices

[32.02] JOB RELATEDNESS STANDARD—PREGNANCY

A Federal District Court in Michigan has held that a pregnant employee's claim that she was terminated because she revealed that she was contemplating having an abortion is covered by the Pregnancy Discrimination Amendment to Title VII, since the amendment includes the right to an abortion.[1] Further, the fact that some of her co-workers were disturbed by her consideration of an abortion does not establish a business justification for firing her.[2]

[32.04] TESTING

The Eighth Circuit Court of Appeals has held that a black applicant may not prove that a supervisor's explanation for picking a white job applicant rather than the black applicant is discriminatory under Title VII merely by showing that the supervisor destroyed the test results. Nonetheless, the Court held that the destruction of the results violated federal regulations. For this reason, the black applicant was entitled to a presumption that the results would have bolstered her case.[3] However, the Court found persuasive the supervisor's testimony that he destroyed the results because he wanted to use the test again, and because he had not been informed of the federal regulation.[4]

[32.09] REVERSE DISCRIMINATION

The Court of Appeals for the District of Columbia has held that an allegation properly supported by facts that a white applicant had superior qualifications for a job which was given to a minority establishes a prima facie case of reverse discrimination.[5]

SUPPLEMENTAL NOTES TO CHAPTER 32

1. *Turic v. Holland Hospitality, Inc.*, 63 FEP Cases 1267 (DC W.Mich. 1994).
2. *Ibid.*
3. *Favors v. Fischer*, 63 FEP Cases 977 (8th Cir. 1994).
4. *Ibid.*
5. *Harding v. Gray*, 63 FEP Cases 475 (DC Cir. 1993).

33

Protected
Characteristics Discrimination

[33.01] RACE AND COLOR

The Fourth Circuit Court of Appeals has held that an employee who was discharged for violation of a work rule did not establish a prima facie case of race discrimination by presenting evidence that a white employee who had a worse disciplinary record was treated better by the employer.[1] The Court noted that instances existed in which the employer had treated other white employees even more severely than it had treated the black employee. The Fourth Circuit stated that in order for the black employee to establish a prima facie case of racial discrimination in the enforcement of disciplinary measures, the black employee must show that his misconduct and the misconduct of white employees was of comparable seriousness. The black employee in this case was unable to do so.[2]

The Ninth Circuit Court of Appeals has held that a black employee may strengthen her claim of race discrimination by presenting evidence of racial tension in her office place.[3]

The Fourth Circuit Court of Appeals has held that a black plaintiff may not establish a prima facie case of race discrimination by simply showing that there were no black employees in management.[4] Rather, the plaintiff must make a comparison to the qualified applicant pool.[5]

[33.03] SEX DISCRIMINATION

In direct contrast to EEOC regulations, the Eleventh Circuit Court of Appeals has ruled that a finding by a jury that the Equal Pay Act has been violated does not mean that the employer is automatically liable for sex discrimination under Title VII.[6] The Court reasoned that Title VII and the Equal Pay Act require different burdens of proof.[7] Under Title VII, a plaintiff must demonstrate that she occupies a job similar to those held by higher paid males.[8] Then, the defendant must offer a legitimate reason for the pay disparity.[9] If the defendant does so, the plaintiff may prove by a preponderance of the evidence that the employer had a discriminatory intent.[10] In contrast, under the Equal Pay Act, once a disparity in pay is proven, the defendant has the burden of proving that a factor other than sex is responsible for the difference. The Fifth and Seventh Circuit Courts of Appeals have reached similar conclusions.[11]

The 11th Circuit Court of Appeals has held that it is a violation of the Pregnancy Discrimination Act for an employer to discharge a pregnant employee for using benefits (here, sick leave) that are commonly offered to employees temporarily disabled for other reasons.[12]

[33.05] SEXUAL ORIENTATION

A Federal District Court in Pennsylvania has held that an employee who was allegedly discriminated against for being a transsexual does not state a claim for sex discrimination under Title VII.[13]

[33.07] RELIGION

The Sixth Circuit Court of Appeals has ruled that it was not a reasonable accommodation of a Seventh-day Adventist's religious beliefs to require her to use all of her accrued vacation time in order to avoid the necessity of working on Saturday.[14]

Although requiring an employee to use some vacation time can be a reasonable accommodation, requiring the employee to use all of her vacation time is not permissible. Doing so would require a religious employee to lose vacation time as a benefit. Therefore, the religious employee has been discriminated against with respect to a condition of employment.[15]

SUPPLEMENTAL NOTES TO CHAPTER 33

1. *Cook v. CSX Transp. Corp.*, 61 FEP Cases 458 (4th Cir. 1993).
2. *Ibid.*
3. *Washington v. Garrett*, 63 FEP Cases 540 (9th Cir. 1993).
4. *Carter v. Ball*, 33 F.3d 450 (4th Cir. 1994).
5. *Ibid.*
6. *Meeks v. Computer Associates International*, No. 92-2926 (11th Cir. 3/7/94).
7. *Ibid.*
8. *Ibid.*
9. *Ibid.*
10. *Ibid.*
11. *Byrd v. Lakeshore Hosp.*, 30 F.3rd 1380 (11th Cir. 1994).
12. *Peters v. City of Shreveport*, 818 F.2d 1148 (5th Cir. 1987); *Fallon v. Illinois*, 882 F.2d 1206 (7th Cir. 1989).
13. *Dobre v. National R.R. Passenger Corp.*, 2 AD Cases 1567 (DC Pa. 1993).
14. *Cooper v. Oak Rubber Co.*, 64 FEP Cases 48 (6th Cir. 1994).
15. *Ibid.*

34

Sexual Harassment Legislation and Litigation

[34.01] INTRODUCTION

Federal Rule of Evidence 412 has been amended to extend the "Rape Shield" protections to civil cases.[1] This amendment to the Rule will provide added protection for plaintiffs in cases where they allege sexual harassment.

[34.02] QUID PRO QUO SEXUAL HARASSMENT

The Second Circuit Court of Appeals has ruled that proof of actual economic loss is not necessary for establishing a valid claim of quid pro quo sexual harassment.[2] Thus, the Court held that an employer is automatically liable if terms of employment are conditioned on an employee submitting to unwelcome sexual advances. Further, the Court held that an employer may be held liable for an abusive work environment created by one of its supervisors if the supervisor uses actual or apparent authority to further the harassment or if the performance of the harassment was aided by the supervisor's agency relationship with the employer. The employer would be liable under this theory even if it had no notice of the harassment and even if it had reasonable complaint procedures in place.[3]

A valid claim of quid pro quo sexual harassment was found where a female employee working for the police department alleged that she was told by the police chief that she would have to submit to his sexual demands in order to be promoted as his secretary, where she was replaced permanently while out on leave by an employee who was having sexual relations with the chief.[4] The Court noted that this was an indication that women were required to submit to sexual demands as a condition of receiving tangible employment benefits.[5]

[34.03] HOSTILE WORK ENVIRONMENT SEXUAL HARASSMENT

The United States Supreme Court has held that tangible psychological injury is not a necessary element of a hostile work environment sexual harassment claim.[6] Instead, the plaintiff need only show that a reasonable person would find the environment hostile or abusive, and that the plaintiff had the subjective perception that it was so. Factors that courts may consider in determining whether a work environment is hostile include:

- the frequency of the conduct;
- the severity of the conduct;
- whether the conduct was physically threatening or humiliating, or a mere offensive utterance; and,
- whether the conduct unreasonably interferes with the employee's work performance.

Although psychological harm may still be considered, neither it, nor any specific other factor is required.[7]

The promotion of an alleged sexual harasser to a position in the chain of command over an alleged victim of sexual harassment may be evidence of a hostile work environment.[8] The court held that such a promotion is legally significant if the alleged harasser is more than simply an annoying presence, but rather is in a position to affect the alleged victim's job.[9]

[34.04] LIABILITY OF EMPLOYERS FOR SEXUAL HARASSMENT BY SUPERVISORS AND EMPLOYEES

A Federal Circuit Court has held that an employee could not sue her supervisors and other employees in their individual capacities under Title VII of the Civil Rights Act for sexually harassing actions that they took on their own.[10] The Fifth Circuit Court of Appeals, following the view of the Ninth Circuit, has held that there is no individual liability of an alleged harasser for sexual harassment under Title VII.[11]

The Ninth Circuit Court of Appeals has held that sexual harassment claims are not required to be arbitrated regardless of an arbitration clause in a securities dealer's contract.[12] The Court held that Congress intended that there be at least a knowing agreement to arbitrate employment disputes before employees can be deemed to have waived their statutory rights under Title VII to have their cases heard in court.[13] In this case, the court held that the contract the plaintiffs had signed could not have alerted them to the fact that they were agreeing to arbitrate sexual harassment suits.[14]

At least one Federal Court has held that an employer cannot seek indemnity against one of its supervisors to recover damages for sexual harassment that the employer has had to pay because of the supervisor's conduct.[15]

[34.05] DEFENSES

The Fifth Circuit Court of Appeals has held that an employer that took prompt and appropriate remedial action in responding to an employee's sexual harassment claim was not liable for sex bias under Title VII.[16]

The Seventh Circuit Court of Appeals has held that the words and conduct of the victim of alleged sexual harassment cannot be compared with or used to justify severe harassment where the victim has made it clear that the offensive conduct is unwelcome.[17]

The Third Circuit Court of Appeals has held that the lack of a written grievance policy regarding sexual harassment is not dispositive of the issue of employer liability where the company has a verbal open door policy for reporting grievances that is known to all employees and the company has verbally stated that sexual harassment would not be tolerated.[18]

[34.07] DAMAGES

The Seventh Circuit Court of Appeals has ruled that damages for psychological distress are available under the Civil Rights Act of 1964 in sexual harassment cases if the distress causes the employee to stop working. The Court found that although damages are not available under the 1964 Act for purely psychological distress, if the distress caused the employee to lose work and wages, the employee may recover those lost wages.[19]

[34.08] CLASS-WIDE SEXUAL HARASSMENT

A Federal District Court has found an employer liable for sexual harassment by engaging in a pattern of exposing its female employees to a hostile work environment.[20] The Court noted that the areas in which the women worked were pervaded with sexually explicit photographs, graffiti, and cartoons. Furthermore, employees in the workplace often used sexual language that indicated a male-dominated, anti-female atmosphere.

In contrast to earlier decisions by other courts where female workers in situations such as this were presumed to have been injured by the sexual harassment, the District Court held that each claimant would be required to prove that she was reasonably affected by the sexual harassment. The Court ruled that this showing by each claimant was necessary since sexual harassment claimants must prove that they were subjectively affected by the harassment.[21]

A Federal District Court in Kentucky has held that a male employee who claims to have been a victim of quid pro quo sexual harassment need not prove reverse discrimination.[22] Instead, he may present direct evidence of discrimination, such as retaliation by his supervisor for his refusal to submit to her sexual advances.[23]

SUPPLEMENTAL NOTES TO CHAPTER 34

1. Bup. L. 103–322, 108 Stat. 1796.
2. *Karibian v. Columbia University*, 63 FEP Cases 1039 (2nd Cir. 1994).
3. *Ibid.*

4. *Dirksen v. Springfield*, 64 FEP Cases 116 (CDIll. 1994)

5. *Ibid.*

6. *Harris v. Forklift Systems, Inc.*, U.S. Sup. Ct, No. 92-1168 (11- 29-93).

7. *Ibid.*

8. *King v. Hillen*, 64 FEP Cases 753 (DC Cir. 1994.)

9. *Ibid.*

10. *Stefanski v. RaZehetner & Assocs.*, 855 F. Supp. 1030 (E.D. Wis. 1994).

11. *Grant v. Lone Star Co.*, 23 F. 3d 649 (5th Cir.) cert. denied 115S. Court Ct., 574 (1994).

12. *Prudential Insurance Co. v. Lai*, 66 FEP Cases 933 (9th Cir. 1994).

13. *Ibid.*

14. *Ibid.*

15. *Gilmore v. List & Clark Construction Co.*, 866 F. Supp. 1310 (D. Kan. 1994).

16. *Carman v. Lubrizal Corp.*, 64 FEP Cases 481 (5th Cir. 1994).

17. *Carr v. Allison Turbine Div.*, 32 F.3rd 1007 (7th Cir. 1994).

18. *Bouton v. BMW of North America*, 29 F3rd 103 (3rd Cir. 1994).

19. *Townsend v. Indiana University*, 61 FEP Cases 1481 (7th Cir. 1993).

20. *Jenson v. Eveleth Taconite Co.*, 61 FEP Cases 1252 (DC Minn. 1993).

21. *Ibid.*

22. *Gardinella v. General Electric To.*, 63 FEP Cases 284 (DC Ky 1993).

23. *Ibid.*

34A

Harassment in the Workplace

[34A.01] INTRODUCTION

Although sexual harassment has come to the forefront of employment litigation, harassment in the workplace can be based on any protected characteristic, including harassment based on race, color, religion, gender, national origin, age, or disability. These alternative forms of harassment are discussed in this chapter.

[34A.02] HARASSMENT DEFINED

Proposed EEOC guidelines define harassment as verbal or physical conduct that denigrates a person or shows hostility or aversion towards the person due to the person's race, color, religion, gender, national origin, age, or disability.[1] This same conduct that is directed towards the person's relatives, friends, or associates is also defined as harassment.[2]

More specifically, the guidelines state that the following conduct in regard to race, color, religion, gender, national origin, age, or disability constitutes harassment:

- epithets;
- slurs;
- negative stereotypes;
- threats;
- intimidation;
- hostile acts; or,
- denigrating or hostile written or graphic material that is posted or circulated in the workplace.[3]

The guidelines provide that harassing conduct can be challenged even if the complaining employees were not the intended targets of the conduct.[4]

[34A.03] REASONABLE PERSON STANDARD

The guidelines state that the appropriate standard for making the determination of harassment is whether a reasonable person under the same or similar circumstances would find the conduct hostile, intimidating, or abusive.[5]

In applying the reasonable person standard, due regard may be given to the perspective of persons who share the victim's race, color, religion, gender, national origin, age, or disability.[6]

[34A.04] EMPLOYER LIABILITY FOR CONDUCT OF SUPERVISORS OR AGENTS

According to the guidelines, an employer is liable for the conduct of its agents or supervisors when it knows or should know that the harassing conduct is taking place, and fails to take immediate and appropriate corrective action to halt it.[7] The employer is also liable for harassment irrespective of whether it knew or should have known of the conduct, if the supervisor who is performing the harassing conduct is acting as the agent of the employer.[8] Agency will be determined by the circumstances and job functions of the employment relationship of the harassing person.[9]

If an employer does not implement an explicit policy prohibiting harassment that is clearly and regularly communicated to its employees, or does not create a reasonably accessible procedure for employees to complain of harassment to appropriate officials in a position to act on them, the employer will be liable under the doctrine of apparent authority.[10]

[34A.05] METHODS FOR AVOIDING LIABILITY

The guidelines indicate that employers should take all steps necessary to prevent harassment, including:

- establish an explicit policy against harassment;
- clearly and regularly communicate the policy to employees, including sanctions for harassment;
- develop methods for sensitizing all employees on harassment issues;
- inform employees of their right to complain of harassment, and the procedures for doing so; and,
- provide effective complaint procedures that enable employees to complain to appropriate officials who can take action based on the complaint.[11]

SUPPLEMENTAL NOTES TO CHAPTER 34A

1. 29 CFR § 1609.
2. *Ibid.*

3. *Ibid.*
4. *Ibid.*
5. *Ibid.*
6. *Ibid.*
7. *Ibid.*
8. *Ibid.*
9. *Ibid.*
10. *Ibid.*
11. *Ibid.*

35

How to Process a Title VII Claim

[35.06] JURISDICTIONAL CONSIDERATIONS

The Tenth Circuit Court of Appeals has held that federal jurisdiction does not exist for a suit brought to enforce a Title VII settlement.[1] Rather, it is merely a contract action and must be enforced in state court.[2]

SUPPLEMENTAL NOTES TO CHAPTER 35

1. *Morris v. City of Hobart*, 39 F.3d 1105 (10th Cir. 1994).
2. *Ibid.*

36

Defenses to a
Title VII Claim

[36.07] "FOR CAUSE" DEFENSE

The United States Supreme Court has held that evidence that an employer's stated reasons for engaging in the conduct at issue were untrue does not automatically warrant a finding that the employer engaged in discrimination.[1] In order to prove pretext where an employer's stated reasons for engaging in the conduct are untrue, the plaintiff must show that the false reason is a pretext for intentional discrimination.[2]

The EEOC has issued interpretive guidance on the *Hicks* decision.[3] The EEOC states that although the decision may affect certain litigation, it will not likely have a significant affect on the EEOC's processing of charges involving circumstantial evidence of intentional discrimination. The EEOC stated that burdens of proof and production generally are not essential to EEOC processing because its investigators examine all relevant evidence prior to determining whether there is reasonable cause to believe that discrimination occurred.

According to the EEOC, even though *Hicks* explicitly holds that showing that an employer's articulated reason for its conduct is untrue does not mandate a finding of liability, it clearly permits such a finding.

SUPPLEMENTAL NOTES TO CHAPTER 36

1. *St. Mary's Honor Center v. Hicks*, 62 FEP Cases 96 (1993).

2. *Ibid.*

3. FEP Manual, Section 405:7175, *et seq.*

37

Recordkeeping and Notice-Posting Requirements Under Title VII

[37.01]–[37.07]—NO SIGNIFICANT CHANGES SINCE MAIN VOLUME.

38

Related EEO Protective Laws

[38.01]–[38.07]—NO SIGNIFICANT CHANGES SINCE MAIN VOLUME.

39

Federal Age Discrimination in Employment Act (ADEA)

[39.02] PROHIBITED PRACTICES UNDER ADEA

A Federal District Court has held that a union that violates the ADEA can be held liable for back pay.[1] Although the ADEA incorporated the remedies of the

Fair Labor Standards Act (FLSA) and unions are not liable for back pay under the FLSA, the Court decided that the FLSA restriction does not apply to the ADEA. The Court reasoned that the ADEA specifically forbids unions from engaging in age discrimination and that refusing to impose monetary penalties on unions would not further the ADEA's purpose of deterring age discrimination.[2]

A Federal District Court in Pennsylvania has held that the disparate impact theory may not be used to prove violations of the ADEA.[3] The Court reasoned that Congress has not sanctioned the disparate impact theory under the ADEA.[4] The court said that Section 703 of the Civil Rights Act of 1964 incorporates disparate impact analysis of cases based on race, color, religion, sex, and national origin, but not age.[5]

The Tenth Circuit Court of Appeals has held that stray remarks by a company's chief executive officer regarding the company's need for younger employees and his reference that long term employees have a diminishing return are insufficient to survive a Motion for Summary Judgment.[6]

[39.03] ADMINISTRATION AND ENFORCEMENT

The Eleventh Circuit Court of Appeals has ruled that the 180-day time period for filing an age discrimination charge with the EEOC may be extended where, at the time of his discharge, the plaintiff lacks notice that the employer intends to replace him.[7] In so ruling, the court held that the 180-day filing period is similar to a statute of limitations, which is subject to waiver, estoppel, and equitable tolling.[8] Therefore, the 180-day time period does not begin to run until the facts which form the basis of a discrimination charge are apparent or should be apparent to a reasonably prudent person.[9]

[39.07] OLDER WORKERS BENEFIT PROTECTION ACT

Contrary to decisions by the Seventh and Eleventh Circuit Courts of Appeals,[10] the Fifth Circuit Court of Appeals has held that former employees who did not tender back to their former employer severance benefits that they received in exchange for signing releases of liability for ADEA claims cannot maintain a suit alleging that the denial of certain benefits to them violated the ADEA, even though they claimed that the releases did not comply with the OWBPA.[11] The Court held that the plaintiffs had ratified the waivers that they signed by showing their intention to do so by keeping the benefits that they had received.[12]

The Seventh Circuit Court of Appeals has held that severance agreements that do not comply with the OWBPA cannot be ratified by the retention of benefits of the former employees.[13]

The Seventh Circuit Court of Appeals has held that a salary schedule which correlates salary to experience is not sufficient evidence of age discrimination to withstand a motion for summary judgment.[14] The court held that the statistical correlation relied upon by the EEOC which showed that salary caps adversely impact older teachers was insufficient.[15]

[39.08] WILLFULNESS STANDARD UNDER THE ADEA

The United States Supreme Court has ruled that a violation of the ADEA is willful for purposes of awarding liquidated damages if the employer knew or showed reckless disregard for whether its conduct was prohibited by the ADEA.[16] Once an employee has established that a violation of the ADEA is willful, the employee does not have to make the additional showing that the employer's conduct was outrageous. Neither does the employee have to provide direct evidence of the employer's motivation. Nor must the employee prove that age was the predominant, rather than merely a determining, factor in the employment decision.[17]

SUPPLEMENTAL NOTES TO CHAPTER 39

1. *EEOC v. Local 350, Plumbers and Pipefitters,* 63 FEP Cases 1170 (DC Nev. 1994).
2. *Ibid.*
3. *Martincic v. Urban Redevelopment Authority of Pittsburg,* 64 FEP Cases 91 (DC W.Pa. 1994).
4. *Ibid.*
5. *Ibid.*
6. *Cone v. Longmont United Hosp. Ass'n.,* 14 F3rd 526 (10th Cir. 1994).
7. *Sturniolo v. Sheaffer, Eaton Inc.,* No. 93-8135 (11th Cir. 3/7/94)
8. *Ibid.*
9. *Ibid.*
10. *Oberg v. Allied Van Lines,* 63 FEP Cases 470 (7th Cir. 1993); *Forbus v. Sears, Roebuck and Co.,* 58 FEP Cases 1019 (11th Cir. 1992), cert. denied, 60 FEP Cases 192 (U.S. S.Ct. 1992).
11. *Wamsley v. Champlin Refining & Chemicals, Inc.,* 63 FEP Cases 821 (5th Cir. 1993).

12. *Ibid.*
13. *Oberg v. Allied Van Lines, Inc.*, 11 F3d 39 (7th Cir. 1993), cert. denied, 64 FEP 1184 (1994).
14. *EEOC v. Francis W. Parker School*, 41 F.3d 1073 (7th Cir. 1994).
15. *Ibid.*
16. *Hazen Paper Co. v. Biggins*, US Sup. Ct., No. 91-1600 (1993).
17. *Ibid.*

40

How to Process and Defend an ADEA Claim

[40.08] SUPERVISORY LIABILITY

The Tenth Circuit Court of Appeals has held that an agent who fires employees due to their age pursuant to the instructions of the principal, is not liable under the ADEA.[1] In this case, a contractor discharged protected age employees because its client did not want them working on the project. The Court found that the contractor was merely complying with its client's wishes. Further, the Court stated that it could find no authority for imputing a principal's discriminatory intent to its agent, making the agent liable for its otherwise neutral business decision.[2]

SUPPLEMENTAL NOTES TO CHAPTER 40

1. *Brownlee v. Lear Siegler Mgmt. Services Corp.*, 63 FEP Cases 1193 (10th Cir. 1994).
2. *Ibid.*

41

Equal Pay Act

[41.02] EQUAL PAY WORK STANDARDS

Equal effort: If an employer does not give females the opportunity to perform extra tasks for which male employees receive premium pay, the employer cannot use the performance of the extra duties to justify unequal wages unless a finding is made that female employees are unable or unwilling to perform the extra tasks.[1]

[41.09] REMEDIES AVAILABLE IN EQUAL PAY ACTION

Double damages may be awarded for willful violations of the Equal Pay Act, unless the employer can show that it acted in good faith, reasonably believing that its conduct was not a violation of the Act.[2]

Punitive damages may not be awarded for violations of the Equal Pay Act.[3]

SUPPLEMENTAL NOTES TO CHAPTER 41

1. *Brobst v. Columbia Serv. Int'l,* 761 F.2d 148 (3rd Cir. 1985).
2. *Lowe v. Southmark Corp.,* 62 FEP Cases 1087 (5th Cir. 1993).
3. *Soto v. Adams Elevator Equipment Co.,* 941 F.2d 543 (7th Cir. 1991).

42

Veterans' Reemployment Rights

[42.07] NEWLY ENACTED VETERANS REEMPLOYMENT RIGHTS ACT

On October 13, 1994, President Clinton signed the Uniformed Services Employment and Reemployment Rights Act which replaces the Veterans' Reemployment Rights Statute.[1] The new law is basically a codification of the case law developed around the old statute over the past fifty years.

Under the new statute, employers are not required to reemploy individuals whose employment prior to their military service was for a brief, nonrecurrent period, where there was no reasonable expectation that such employment would continue indefinitely or for a significant period.[2] The affected employee or an appropriate military officer, acting on behalf of the employee, must give the employer advance oral or written notice of military service.[3] However, no notice is required if military necessity prevents giving notice, or if notification is impossible or unreasonable.[4]

The new statute expands protection for reservists against discrimination for their reservist membership.[5] The statute covers nonservice members as well as service members.[6] Furthermore, coast guard personnel are now covered equally with the other branches of the military.[7]

Unlike the old statute which allowed employees to serve in the military up to four years (plus one extra year in some situations) and still be eligible for reemployment, the new statute increases coverage to include cumulative service periods totaling up to five years.[8] However, there are certain exceptions to the five year cap on service, including such periods as service time for training, involuntary duty extensions, and longer initial obligation periods for high-technology military occupations, as well as additional service periods required by government or the President.

Unlike the former statute, which expressed the time for reemployment application based on the type of service performed, the new statute bases the application time on the amount of time that the employee is away from the employer.[9]

A specific provision of the new statute allows an employer to request documentation establishing the timeliness of the application for reemployment, and the length and character of the employee's military service.[10] An individual must be reemployed pending receipt of such documentation, if it is not immediately available.[11]

Where the individual is away from the employer less than ninety-one days, that individual must be promptly returned to the position that he or she would have attained if no military leave had been taken.[12] However, if the individual is not qualified for the new position and cannot become qualified after reasonable effort by the employer, then the individual must be reemployed in the position that he or she held prior to military leave.[13] The rights of individuals gone more than ninety-one days are much the same, except that employers may offer those individuals positions of like seniority, status, and pay.[14] If the employee does not qualify for the new position and cannot become qualified for it after reasonable effort, then the individual must be reemployed in any other position of lesser status and pay for which he or she is qualified, with full seniority.[15] On the other hand, returning military employees may be denied reemployment if the employer's circumstances have changed so much that reemployment is impossible or unreasonable.[16]

The statute provides that returning employees who suffer from service-related disabilities must be reemployed in the position that they would have attained absent military leave, as long as they are qualified for it or can become qualified for it. However, if the individual is not qualified for such a position even after reasonable efforts by the employer to accommodate the disability, then the individual must be placed in any other position of similar seniority, status, and pay for which he or she is qualified or can become qualified.[17] If there is no such position, then the individual must be placed in the next best available position that is consistent with the circumstances of each individual's case.

Upon return from military service, individuals are entitled to any seniority and benefits that they had at the time they entered the service.[18] Additionally, if an employer has a policy providing for payment of certain benefits by furloughed employees or employees on a leave of absence, then the employees returning from military service would be entitled to credit for such benefits during the term of their military service.[19]

Employers must offer employees leaving for military duty the option of continuing their health insurance, for both the employee and his or her dependents, for up to eighteen months.[20] Additionally, pension benefits are protected while an employee is performing military service.[21] No forfeiture of benefits is allowed and when returning to employment, the employee is not required to requalify for participation.[22] Furthermore, employers are required to make any contribution to a returning service person's pension plan that it would have made if the person had not performed military service.[23] Where the employer plan requires employees to make contributions to the plan before the employer has the responsibility to do the same, returning service persons may make any contributions they missed within a certain period of time, (depending on length of military service), not exceeding five years.[24] Once the returning service person makes those contributions, the employer is required to make any matching contributions provided by the plan.[25]

Any vacation or similar leave time accrued prior to leaving for military service may be used by the employee while on military leave.[26]

A reemployed service person may not be discharged from his employment, except for cause, within one year of his or her return to work if the period of military service was for more than 180 days.[27] If the service period was for more than 30 days, but less than 181 days, the employee may only be fired for cause for a period of six months. However, reemployed service persons are not protected from layoffs or downsizing that they would be included in had they not served in the military.[28] The statute provides for double damages for willful violations.[29] Furthermore, the statute provides for attorney's fees and costs.[30]

SUPPLEMENTAL NOTES TO CHAPTER 42

1. 43 U.S.C. § 2021 et seq.
2. *Ibid.*

3. *Ibid.*

4. *Ibid.*

5. *Ibid.*

6. *Ibid.*

7. *Ibid.*

8. *Ibid.*

9. *Ibid.*

10. *Ibid.*

11. *Ibid.*

12. *Ibid.*

13. *Ibid.*

14. *Ibid.*

15. *Ibid.*

16. *Ibid.*

17. *Ibid.*

18. *Ibid.*

19. *Ibid.*

20. *Ibid.*

21. *Ibid.*

22. *Ibid.*

23. *Ibid.*

24. *Ibid.*

25. *Ibid.*

26. *Ibid.*

27. *Ibid.*

28. *Ibid.*

29. *Ibid.*

30. *Ibid.*

43

The Rehabilitation Act of 1973 and Related Discrimination Bans in Federal Programs

[43.01]–[43.07]—NO SIGNIFICANT CHANGES SINCE MAIN VOLUME.

44

Americans with Disabilities Act

[44.02] DISABILITY BROADLY DEFINED

A physical or mental impairment is defined as "any physiological disorder, or condition, cosmetic disfigurement, or anatomical loss affecting one or more of the following body systems: neurological, musculoskeletal, special sense organs, respiratory including speech organs, cardiovascular, reproductive, digestive, genitourinary, hemic and lymphatic, skin, and endocrine; or any mental or physiological disorder, such as mental retardation, organic brain syndrome, emotional or mental illness, and specific learning disabilities.[1] Major life activities are defined as "functions such as caring for oneself, performing manual tasks, walking, seeing, hearing, speaking, breathing, learning, and working."[2]

The First Circuit Court of Appeals has ruled that obesity may be a disability under the Rehabilitation Act.[3] By way of implication, the ruling probably applies to the ADA as well. The Circuit Court upheld the jury's verdict that the plaintiff, who stood five feet two inches tall and weighed over 320 pounds, suffered from "morbid obesity."[4] According to the plaintiff's medical expert, morbid obesity is a physiological disorder involving a dysfunction of both the metabolic system and the neurological appetite suppressing signal system capable of causing adverse effects within the musculoskeletal, respiratory, and cardiovascular systems.[5] Thus, the Court of Appeals upheld the jury's ruling that morbid obesity is a legal disability.[6]

The Fourth Circuit Court of Appeals has held that a plaintiff's hypersensitivity to tobacco smoke does not constitute a handicap under the Rehabilitation Act.[7] The Court reasoned that the plaintiff had presented no evidence that her hypersensitivity would preclude her from obtaining similar employment elsewhere.[8] Once again, this ruling is probably equally applicable to the ADA.

The Courts are not uniform as to whether back injuries constitute a disability under the ADA. The Sixth Circuit Court of Appeals and a Federal District Court in New York have found that back injuries affecting employees' ability to lift were disabilities.[9] However, a Federal District Court in Oklahoma has held that an employee who suffered a work-related back injury was not an individual with a disability for purposes of the ADA.[10]

The Federal District Court for the District of Columbia has held that a firefighter, who was a carrier of the Hepatitis B virus, could not be prohibited from performing mouth-to-mouth resuscitation solely because of his disease.[11] The Court held that doing so would violate the Rehabilitation Act because, among other factors, there was medical proof that the possibility of transmission of the disease through saliva was only theoretical.[12] By implication, this ruling should also apply under the ADA.

Although alcoholism is a disability under the ADA, it does not render alcoholic employees immune from discipline or discharge. The Fourth Circuit Court of Appeals upheld the termination of an alcoholic employee who became intoxicated while on duty.[13] The case turned on the fact that the plaintiff was terminated due to his misconduct in being intoxicated while on duty, rather than because of his alcoholism.[14] The Court noted that an employer may hold a drug addict or alcoholic to the same standard of performance or behavior to which it holds other employees.[15]

A Federal District Court in Texas has ruled that an EEOC interpretive guideline stating that a diabetic who would lapse into a coma without insulin is per se disabled is inconsistent with the ADA.[16] The Court reasoned that an insulin-dependent diabetic who properly takes his medication can perform all major life activities.[17] The EEOC has issued interpretive guidance relating to the definition of "disability" under the ADA.

[44.05] REASONABLE ACCOMMODATIONS

A Federal District Court in Maryland granted summary judgment to an employer on a reasonable accommodation claim due to the fact that the employee's affidavit submitted in support of her position lacked adequate details.[18] The Court held that an employee's subjective observations as to what accommodations are needed to enable the employee to perform the job were insufficient to create a triable issue.[19]

The Ninth Circuit Court of Appeals has held that an employer may be required to transfer an employee to the same position at another location in order to meet its burden under the ADA to provide reasonable accommodation.[20] In that case, the plaintiff needed the transfer in order to obtain medical treatment.[21]

The Seventh Circuit has held that the reasonableness of accommodations under the ADA must be judged not only in relation to the employer's financial condition but also in relation to the benefit that the accommodation provides.[22] In other words, the cost of the accommodation must not be disproportionate to its benefit.

Employers need not provide an accommodation to disabled employees where doing so will cause an undue hardship on the operation of the employers' business. An undue hardship is defined as a "significant difficulty or expense incurred by a covered entity."[23]

Factors that must be considered in determining whether an accommodation would impose an undue hardship on an employer include:

- the nature and net cost of the accommodation, with due consideration for the availability of tax credits and deductions, or outside funding;
- the overall financial resources of the facility providing the accommodation, the number of persons employed there, and the effect on expenses and resources;
- the type of operation of the covered entity, including the composition, structure, and functions of its workforce, and the geographic separateness and administrative or fiscal relationship of the facility in question to the covered entity; and,

- the impact of the accommodation on the operation of the facility, including the impact on the facility's ability to conduct business.[24]

Specific inquiries: Direct inquiries about a disability are prohibited.[25] Inquiries about an applicant's ability to perform job related functions, with or without reasonable accommodation, are permissible.[26] Inquiries about impairments, which are disabilities only if they substantially limit one or more life activities, are unlawful at the pre-offer stage only if they are likely to elicit information about the applicant's disability.[27]

During the pre-offer stage, employers may not ask whether an applicant can perform a major life activity where doing so is likely to elicit information about a disability.[28] On the other hand, such inquiries are permissible if they are specifically related to the ability to perform the functions of the job.[29]

Employers may request that applicants describe or demonstrate how they would perform the job-related functions of a position since they are not likely to elicit information about a disability.[30] However, if in response to this request to demonstrate job performance, an applicant states that he or she will need a reasonable accommodation, the employer must either provide a reasonable accommodation that does not create an undue hardship or the employer must allow the applicant to simply describe how he or she would perform the job.[31]

If an employer cannot reasonably believe that an applicant's disability will interfere with the performance of the job, the employer can request that the applicant describe or demonstrate how, with or without reasonable accommodation, the applicant would perform job related functions as long as the same request is made of all applicants in the same job category.[32] On the other hand, if the employer could reasonably believe that an applicant's known disability will interfere with the performance of the job, the employer may ask the applicant to describe or demonstrate how he or she would perform the job, with or without reasonable accommodation.[33] An inquiry such as this is not a prohibited pre-offer inquiry.

An employer may inform applicants in an advertisement or on an application form that the hiring process will include a particular selection procedure such as a written test or job demonstration.[34] Further, the applicants can be asked to inform the employer of any reasonable accommodations that they will need in order to complete the selection procedure.[35]

An employer may ask an applicant whether he or she can perform a specified job function with or without reasonable accommodation.[36] However, during the pre-offer stage, employers generally may not inquire whether applicants need reasonable accommodation for the job.[37] Furthermore, where an applicant has voluntarily disclosed that a reasonable accommodation would be needed to perform the job, an employer still may not make inquiries during the pre-offer stage about the *type* of reasonable accommodation required, unless the applicant has requested reasonable accommodation as part of a required pre-offer job demonstration.[38]

Where an applicant requests an accommodation, an employer may require the applicant to document the fact that he or she has a disability and is therefore entitled to reasonable accommodation under the ADA.[39] Employers are entitled to such information because they are only obligated to provide accommodations to people who are disabled within the meaning of the ADA.[40] Furthermore, employers may require such an applicant to provide documentation concerning his or her functional limitations for which he or she is requesting a reasonable accommodation.[41]

During the pre-offer stage, employers may not ask applicants with known disabilities about the nature or severity of the disability, or whether they have other disabilities.[42]

Employers may state their attendance policy requirements and ask whether applicants can meet those requirements.[43] Furthermore, employers may ask applicants about their attendance records on their prior jobs.[44] However, employers may not inquire into the reason for an applicant's missing work during their prior job.[45] Furthermore, employers may not ask during the pre-offer stage how many days off an applicant will need from work, since this is likely to elicit information about the nature and severity of the disability.[46]

Employers are prohibited from asking applicants about their prior workers' compensation history.[47]

During the pre-offer stage, employers are permitted to ask applicants about their current illegal use of drugs since an individual who currently engages in the illegal use of drugs is not protected under the ADA.[48] However, questions about the current or prior use of lawful medication or drugs taken under the supervision of a health care provider are generally impermissible during the pre-offer stage.[49]

Employers may ask during the pre-offer stage whether an applicant has a required certification or license related to the performance of an essential or marginal job function.[50] Furthermore, an employer may ask the applicant whether he or she intends to get a necessary job related certificate or license.[51]

Employers are permitted to ask applicants questions regarding topics such as eating habits, weight, exercise habits, as long as these questions are not likely to elicit information about the existence, nature, or severity of a disability.[52] Furthermore, during the pre-offer stage, an employer may ask an applicant whether he or she drinks alcohol.[53] However, an employer may not ask the applicant whether he or she is an alcoholic since alcoholism is a protected disability under the ADA.[54]

The ADA does not prohibit employers from asking during the pre-offer stage about an applicant's arrest or conviction records.[55] However, other laws may prohibit such inquiries.

Where an employer is required by federal law to provide Affirmative Action to employees or applicants with disabilities, the employer may ask an applicant to voluntarily disclose the existence of a disability, as long as the employer actually provides Affirmative Action to such disabled individuals. Further, where federal law only permits or encourages, rather than requires, Affirmative Action, employers may invite voluntary self-identification of disabilities only if the employer uses that information to actually provide Affirmative Action for individuals with disabilities.[56]

During the pre-offer stage, an employer may not ask a third party anything that it could not ask an applicant directly.[57] On the other hand, employers may ask third parties anything that they could ask the applicant.[58]

Physical agility and physical fitness test: Physical agility tests in which applicants demonstrate their ability to perform actual or simulated job-related tasks are not medical examinations.[59] A physical fitness test in which an applicant's performance of physical criteria is measured is also not a medical examination.[60] On the other hand, tests that measure an applicant's physiological or biological responses to performance are considered medical examinations.[61]

Psychological examinations: Many tests are currently administered which can be considered psychological in nature, including IQ tests, aptitude tests, personality tests, and honesty tests.[62] Such psychological examinations are medical examinations if they provide evidence concerning whether or not an applicant has a mental disorder or impairment.[63] Further, such tests may also be considered medical examinations if they are used by an employer to determine whether an applicant has a mental impairment or to assess an applicant's general psychological health.[64] However, if the test is designed and used to measure only such factors as honesty, taste, and habits, then such tests are not normally considered medical examinations.[65]

Vision tests: Whether or not a vision test is considered a medical examination depends upon the relevant circumstances.[66] If the vision test is used to determine whether an applicant is able to read labels or distinguish objects as part of a demonstration of actual job performance, then it is not a medical examination.[67] However, if the applicant is required to submit to an ophthalmologist's or optometrist's analysis of the applicant's vision, then this is a prohibited pre-offer medical examination.[68]

Drug tests: Drug tests for the current illegal use of drugs are not considered to be medical examinations and may be administered at the pre-offer stage.[69]

However, employers may not ask information about current or prior lawful drug use if it would reveal the existence, nature, or severity of an impairment or disability.[70]

Alcohol tests: A pre-offer test for alcohol is considered a medical examination if it requires an invasive procedure such as the drawing of blood, urine, or breath.[71] Thus, those tests may not be administered during the pre-offer stage.[72]

[44.06] DEFENSES TO AN ADA ACTION

The factors that must be considered in determining whether an individual would pose a direct threat include:

- the duration of the risk;
- the nature and severity of the potential harm;
- the likelihood that the potential harm will occur; and,
- the imminence of potential harm.[73]

SUPPLEMENTAL NOTES TO CHAPTER 44

1. 29 CFR § 1630.2 (h).
2. 29 CFR § 1630.2(i).
3. *Cook v. State of Rhode Island*, U.S. Appl. Lexis 30060 (1st Cir. Nov. 22, 1993).
4. *Ibid.*
5. *Ibid.* at 11
6. *Ibid.*
7. *Gupton v. Commonwealth of Virginia*, 14 F.3d 203 (4th Cir. 1994).
8. *Ibid.*
9. *Tuck v. HCA Health Services*, 7 F.3d 465 (6th Cir. 1993); *Henchey v. Town of North Greenbush*, 831 F. Supp. 960 (N.D.N.Y. 1993).
10. *Bolton v. Schivner, Inc.*, 836 F. supp. 783 (W.D. Okla. 1993).
11. *Roe v. District of Columbia*, U.S. Dist. LEXIS 18071 (D.D.C. Dec. 21, 1993).
12. *Ibid.*
13. *Little v. Federal Bureau of Investigation*, 1993 U.S. App. LEXIS 20371 (4th Cir. 1993).
14. *Ibid.*
15. *Ibid.*
16. *Coghlan v. H.J. Heinz Co.*, 3 AD Cases 273 (DCN. Twx. 1994)
17. *Ibid.*
18. *Carrozza v. Howard County, Md.*, 1994 U.S. dist. LEXIS 4085 (D. Md. Apr. 1, 1984).
19. *Ibid.*
20. *Buckingham v. United States*, 998 F 2d 735 (9th Cir. 1993).
21. *Ibid.*
22. *Vande Zande v. Wisconsin Department of Administration*, 3 AD Cases 1636 (7th Cir. 1995).

23. 29 CFR § 1630.2 (p)

24. 29 CFR § 1630.2 (p)

25. *Ibid.*

26. *Ibid.* at N:2324.

27. *Ibid.*

28. *Ibid.*

29. *Ibid.*

30. *Ibid.* at N:2325.

31. *Ibid.*

32. *Ibid.*

33. *Ibid.*

34. *Ibid.*

35. *Ibid.*

36. *Ibid.*

37. *Ibid.* at N:2326.

38. *Ibid.*

39. *Ibid.*

40. *Ibid.*

41. *Ibid.*

42. *Ibid.*

43. *Ibid.*

44. *Ibid.*

45. *Ibid.*

46. *Ibid.* at N:2327.

47. *Ibid.*

48. *Ibid.*

49. *Ibid.*

50. *Ibid.*

51. *Ibid.*

52. *Ibid.*

53. *Ibid.* at N:2328.

54. *Ibid.*

55. *Ibid.*

56. *Ibid.*

57. *Ibid.* at N:2329.

58. *Ibid.*

59. *Ibid.*

60. *Ibid.*

61. *Ibid.*

62. *Ibid.* at N:2330.

63. *Ibid.*
64. *Ibid.*
65. *Ibid.*
66. *Ibid.* at N:2331.
67. *Ibid.*
68. *Ibid.*
69. *Ibid.*
70. *Ibid.*
71. *Ibid.*
72. *Ibid.*
73. 29 CFR § 1630.2 (r)

45

Federal Anti-Discrimination Executive Orders

[45.01]–[45.08]—NO SIGNIFICANT CHANGES SINCE MAIN VOLUME.

46

Enforcement of Executive Order 11246 and Related Laws

[46.08] NEWLY PROPOSED REGULATIONS

The Office of Federal Contract Compliance is likely to release new regulations interpreting Executive Order 11246 and is close to finalizing rules under Section 503 of the Rehabilitation Act. The enforcement of the Executive Order is expected to be expedited and enforcement mechanisms strengthened.

The proposed regulations under Section 503 of the Rehabilitation Act may increase the threshold from 50 employees and $50,000 to 150 employees and $150,000 for an affirmative action plan to be required. Further, the regulations may address whether the time limit for recordkeeping should be reduced from two years to one year, and whether contractors are obligated to affirmatively solicit from employees information regarding whether they are disabled individuals that are in need of an accommodation.

The OFCCP will also examine its enforcement procedures, including how it schedules compliance reviews, whether on-site reviews are necessary in all cases, and whether certain industries are being overlooked in compliance reviews. "Term debarment" likely will be used more often.[1]

SUPPLEMENTAL NOTES TO CHAPTER 46

1. Fair Employment Practices Newsletter, March 28, 1994, pp. 33–34.

PART THREE

FEDERAL WAGE AND HOUR LAWS

47

Introduction to the Fair Labor Standards Act

[47.01]–[47.14]—NO SIGNIFICANT CHANGES SINCE MAIN VOLUME.

48

Minimum Wage Requirements Under the FLSA

[48.04] COMPENSABLE WORKING TIME

A Court of Appeals has ruled that the appropriate test for determining whether an employee must be compensated for a meal period is whether the meal period was "predominantly-for-the-benefit-of-the-employer."[1] In so ruling, the Court rejected the test in the Department of Labor's regulations that the employee must be "completely-relieved-from-duty" in order for the meal period to be noncompensable. The predominantly-for-the-benefit-of-the-employer test is less stringent than the Department of Labor's test, allowing for consideration of different factors for different types of business. In the case-at-issue, the Court held that the meal period for police officers was not compensable because they were free to perform personal errands during their meal time.[2]

[48.09] PARTICULAR ARRANGEMENTS AS BASIS OF PAYMENT

The Ninth Circuit Court of Appeals has held that wages are "unpaid" unless they are paid on an employee's regular payday.[3] The FLSA has no explicit prompt-payment obligation. However, the liability provisions of the FLSA for unpaid minimum wages and liquidated damages would be meaningless unless there is a specified date beyond which wages can be considered unpaid.[4]

SUPPLEMENTAL NOTES TO CHAPTER 48

1. *Henson v. Pulaski County Sheriff Dept.*, 1 WH Cases 2d 1057 (8th Cir. 1993).
2. *Ibid.*
3. *Biggs v. Wilson*, 1 WH Cases 2d 897 (9th Cir. 1993).
4. *Ibid.*

49

Overtime Pay Requirements Under the FLSA

[49.13] OVERTIME FOR PUBLIC SECTOR EMPLOYEES

The United States Supreme Court has held that public employers that operate in states prohibiting collective bargaining in the public sector may provide compensatory time in lieu of cash overtime under the FLSA in accordance with individual agreements with their employees, even if the employees have designated a union representative.[1] In such a case, the employees have not designated a representative with the authority to negotiate and reach an agreement with the employer on provisions of a collective bargaining agreement authorizing the use of "comp" time.[2] Therefore, Section 7(o)(2)(A) of the FLSA allows public agencies to provide compensatory time to their employees pursuant to individual agreements with those employees.[3]

SUPPLEMENTAL NOTES TO CHAPTER 49

1. *Moreau v. Klevenhagen*, 1 WH Cases 2d 569 (1993).
2. *Ibid.*
3. *Ibid.*

50

Child Labor Laws
Under the FLSA

[50.07] LEGAL PENALTIES FOR VIOLATIONS

The Federal Court of Appeals for the District of Columbia has held that employee error is not a defense to a claim for FLSA liquidated damages.[1] In order to avoid liquidated damages, an employer must show that the act or omission giving rise to the violation was in good faith and that the employer had reasonable grounds to believe that the act or omission was not unlawful.[2]

SUPPLEMENTAL NOTES TO CHAPTER 50

1. Thomas v. Howard University Hospital, 2 WH Cases 705 (DC Cir. 1994).
2. *Ibid.*

51

FLSA Administration,
Enforcement, and Recordkeeping

[51.01]–[51.08]—NO SIGNIFICANT CHANGES SINCE MAIN VOLUME.

52

Miscellaneous Federal Wage
and Hour Laws

[52.01]–[52.07]—NO SIGNIFICANT CHANGES SINCE MAIN VOLUME.

PART FOUR

FEDERAL SAFETY
AND HEALTH LAWS

53

Introduction to the Federal Occupational Safety and Health Act

[53.01]–[53.06]—NO SIGNIFICANT CHANGES SINCE MAIN VOLUME.

54

OSHA Standards

[54.08] HAZARD COMMUNICATION

OSHA has issued a final rule regarding Hazard Communication.[1] The purpose of the final rule is to insure that the hazards of chemicals produced or imported are evaluated; and that the information concerning those hazards is transmitted to employers and employees.[2] This is done through comprehensive hazard communication programs, which must include container labeling and other forms of warnings, material safety data sheets, and employee training.[3] The evaluation of potential hazards of chemicals, and the communication of information concerning the hazards and the appropriate protective measures to employees may include provisions for:

- Developing and maintaining a written hazard communication program for the workplace, including a list of hazardous chemicals present;
- Labeling containers of chemicals in the workplace, as well as labeling containers of chemicals being shipped to other workplaces;
- Preparing and distributing material safety data sheets to employees and downstream employers; and,

- Developing and implementating employee training programs regarding hazards of chemicals and protective measures.[4]

[54.09] OSHA REFORM

Proposed legislation that would reform several of OSHA's provisions has been introduced into Congress.[5] Among other things, the proposed legislation would increase OSHA's maximum prison terms for criminal violations, expand the scope of willful violations subject to criminal actions, explicitly hold managers and supervisors subject to criminal prosecution, and institute minimum civil fines for serious violations of OSHA standards.[6]

Furthermore, the proposed legislation would expand employee involvement in matters that affect employee safety and health.[7] For example, the proposed legislation would require employers with eleven or more workers to set up labor-management committees.[8] Additionally, all employers would be required to establish written safety and health programs.[9]

The bill would also extend OSHA to state and local government workers.[10] Under the new bill, the Occupational Safety and Health Administration would play an increased role in establishing safety and health standards.[11] The Republicans have proposed their own version of the above Democratically sponsored bill.[12]

[54.09A] PERSONAL PROTECTIVE EQUIPMENT STANDARD

Osha has published a final rule governing the use of personal protective equipment.[13] The standard requires that protective equipment, including protective equipment for eyes, face, head, and extremities, protective clothing, respiratory devices, and protective shields and barriers, be provided, used, and maintained in a sanitary and reliable condition wherever they are necessary due to hazards of processes or environment, chemical hazards, radiological hazards, or mechanical irritants encountered in a manner that is capable of causing injury or impairment in the function of any part of the body through absorption, inhalation, or physical contact.[14]

If employees provide their own protective equipment, their employer is still responsible to assure that it is adequate, and that it is properly maintained.[15]

The standard also requires employers to perform a hazard assessment of the workplace to determine whether hazards are present, or likely to be present, which would necessitate the use of personal protective equipment.[16] If such hazards are present, or likely to be present, employers must select and require affected employees to use personal protective equipment that will protect them from the hazards identified in the hazard assessment; communicate the equipment selected to each affected employee; and select equipment that properly fits each affected employee.[17] Employers are further required to verify that the required hazard assessment has been performed by means of a written certification that identifies the workplace evaluated, the person certifying that the evaluation has been performed, the date of the hazard assessment, and, which identifies the document as a Certification of Hazard Assessment.[18]

Employers are also required to provide training to each employee who is required to use personal protective equipment under the requirements of the standard. The training must include information on when personal protective equipment is necessary, what protective equipment is necessary, how to properly don, doff, adjust, and wear the protective equipment, the limitations of the protective equipment, and the appropriate care, maintenance, useful life and disposal of the protective equipment.[19] Employees must demonstrate an understanding of the training and the ability to use the protective equipment properly before being allowed to perform work requiring the use of the protective equipment.[20] Furthermore, the regulations state that under certain circumstances, retraining of employees is required.[21] Finally, employers must verify that each affected employee has received and understood required training by means of a written certification that contains the name of each employee trained, the date of training, and identifies the subject of the certification.[22]

On October 20, 1994, OSHA issued a compliance memorandum stating that employers, in most cases, must provide and pay for workers' protective equipment.

[54.10] SAFETY STANDARDS FOR FALL PROTECTION IN THE CONSTRUCTION INDUSTRY

OSHA has issued a final rule pertaining to safety standards for fall protection in the construction industry.[23] However, the provisions of the final rule do not apply to circumstances when employees are making inspections, investigations, or assessments of workplace conditions prior to the actual start of construction work or after all construction work has been completed.[24] The final rule requires employers in the construction industry to install under certain circumstances personal fall arrest systems consisting of guardrail systems, safety net systems, or other personal fall arrest systems.[25]

SUPPLEMENTAL NOTES TO CHAPTER 54

1. 59 Federal Register No. 27 (February 9, 1994).

2. *Ibid.*

3. *Ibid.*

4. *Ibid.*

5. *Occupational Safety and Health Reporter,* Volume 23, Number 37 (Feb 16, 1994)

6. *Ibid.*

7. *Ibid.*

8. *Ibid.*

9. *Ibid.*

10. *Ibid.*

11. *Ibid.*

12. *Occupational Safety and Health Reporter,* Volume 23, Number 43 (March 30, 1994)

13. 29 CFR 1910, Subpart I.

14. 29 CFR §1910.132

15. *Ibid.*

16. *Ibid.*

17. *Ibid.*

18. *Ibid.*

19. *Ibid.*

20. *Ibid.*

21. *Ibid.*

22. *Ibid.*

23. 29 CFR §1910 and §1926.

24. *Ibid.*

25. *Ibid.*

55

OSHA Enforcement

[55.01]–[55.06]—NO SIGNIFICANT CHANGES SINCE MAIN VOLUME.

56

OSHA Hearings and Review

[56.01]–[56.07]—NO SIGNIFICANT CHANGES SINCE MAIN VOLUME.

57

Federal Mine
Safety and Health Act

[57.01]–[57.05]—NO SIGNIFICANT CHANGES SINCE MAIN VOLUME.

58

Federal Environment Laws

[58.01]–[58.15]—NO SIGNIFICANT CHANGES SINCE MAIN VOLUME.

PART FIVE

FEDERAL RETIREMENT, WELFARE, AND PRIVACY LAWS

59

Introduction to the Employee Retirement Income Security Act

[59.03] TYPES OF ERISA BENEFITS

The Second Circuit Court of Appeals has held that an employer's offer of 60 days of extra pay following termination that was made to induce some of its employees to remain with the company until a corporate consolidation had been completed did not create an ERISA severance plan.[1] The Court noted that ERISA was intended to apply to employee benefit plans that required ongoing administration, rather than to the payment of a benefit for which no administration was required.[2] In so ruling, the Second Circuit followed the United States Supreme Court precedence set forth in *Ft. Halifax Packing Co. v. Coyne*, in which case the Court found that ERISA does not apply to one-time lump sum severance payments that occur upon the happening of an event beyond the employer's control.[3]

[59.07] PROTECTION AGAINST ASSIGNMENTS

The United States Supreme Court has held that a transfer of unencumbered property to a defined benefit plan in order to satisfy the employer's funding obligation is a prohibited sale or exchange.[4] The Court found support for its position in Congress' concerns in enacting ERISA § 4975, that was enacted to discourage potential abuses such as the sale of property to an ERISA plan at an inflated price or satisfying a funding obligation by contributing overvalued or nonliquid property.[5] The Court felt that these concerns still existed even if the transferred property was unencumbered and not overvalued.[6] For example, one piece of property that was transferred in this case was not sold for more than three years after the pension trust put it up for sale.[7] Hence, there is an inherent risk that any property may be nonliquid for a period of time.

SUPPLEMENTAL NOTES TO CHAPTER 59

1. *James v. Fleet/Norstar Financial Group, Inc.*, 1993 U.S. App. LEXIS 10396 (2nd Cir. 1993).

2. *Ibid.*

3. 482 U.S. 1 (1987).

4. *Com v. Keystone Consolidated Industries, Inc.*, U.S. Sup. Ct., No. 91-1677 (5/24/93).

5. *Ibid.*

6. *Ibid.*

7. *Ibid.*

60

Participation, Vesting, and Funding Requirements Under ERISA

[60.01]–[60.06]—NO SIGNIFICANT CHANGES SINCE MAIN VOLUME.

61

Fiduciary Requirements of ERISA

[61.01] GENERAL FIDUCIARY RESPONSIBILITIES

The United States Supreme Court has held that ERISA does not permit a non-fiduciary to be held liable for being a knowing participant in a fiduciary's breach of its duties to an ERISA plan.[1] The Court stated that the phrase "other appropriate equitable relief" found in ERISA § 502(a) (3) does not establish grounds for awarding money damages against a person who does not stand in a fiduciary status to the plan.[2]

The United States Supreme Court has held that an insurance company which holds the assets of a pension plan in its general investment account is a fiduciary in regards to those funds.[3] In so ruling, the Court read ERISA's definition of "plan assets" in such a way that an exception for insurance contracts will apply only to those contracts that provide a fixed, guaranteed benefit.[4] The decision overrules Labor Reg § 2509, 75-2 and resolves a split on the issue among the Circuit Courts of Appeals.[5]

[61.02] SPECIFIC STANDARDS FOR PLAN FIDUCIARIES

The Seventh Circuit Court of Appeals has held that an employer that amended its pension plan twice in order to prevent an employee from participating in the plan did not violate ERISA by either interfering with protected rights or violating a fiduciary duty.[6] ERISA § 510 makes it unlawful for a person to discharge, fine, suspend, expel, discipline, or discriminate against a participant for exercising a plan right, and prohibits interfering with the attainment of any right to which a participant may become entitled.[7] The Court found no violation of § 510 in this case, because in the Seventh Circuit the party bringing a § 510 action must allege that the employer-employee relationship, rather than simply the pension plan, was changed in a discriminatory way.[8] In this case, the employer merely changed the plan's terms.[9] Therefore, no violation was found.[10]

[61.03] PROHIBITED TRANSACTIONS

An employer's amendment of its plan to deprive its employees of health benefits is not a cognizable claim under ERISA.[11]

SUPPLEMENTAL NOTES TO CHAPTER 61

1. *Meriens v. Hewitt Associates*, 1993 U.S. LEXIS 3742.
2. *Ibid.*
3. *John Hancock Mutual Life Ins. Co. v. Harris Trust and Savings Bank, trustee*, 1993 U.S. LEXIS 7940.
4. *Ibid.*
5. *Ibid.*
6. *McGath v. Auto-Body North Shore, Inc.*, 1993 U.S. App. LEXIS 27198 (7th Cir.).
7. *Ibid.*
8. *Ibid.*
9. *Ibid.*
10. *Ibid.*
11. *Schoonejongen v. Curtiss-Wright Corp.*, 115 Sup. Ct. 1223 (1995).

62

Multi-Employer
Pension Plans

[62.01]–[62.07]—NO SIGNIFICANT CHANGES SINCE MAIN VOLUME.

63

ERISA
Recordkeeping, Reporting,
and Disclosure Requirements

[63.01]–[63.08]—NO SIGNIFICANT CHANGES SINCE MAIN VOLUME.

64

ERISA Administration
and Enforcement

[64.06] LAWSUITS TO ENFORCE ERISA PROVISIONS

The Ninth Circuit Court of Appeals has held that the statute of limitations on an action against an employer for delinquent contributions to a multiemployer pension fund did not begin to run until the fund discovered the deficiency upon the completion of an audit.[1] However, the Sixth Circuit has ruled that where prior audits of monthly reports from a multiemployer fund revealed the likelihood of discrepancies, the statute of limitations would begin to run on the date of submission of the employer's monthly reports.[2]

The Sixth Circuit Court of Appeals has held that an employee whose discharge was allegedly for filing a breach of fiduciary duty suit against her employer's pension plan for losses due to embezzlement of invested funds states a retaliation claim under ERISA.[3] The Court held that an allegation of retaliation for the exercise of any rights under ERISA, not simply the right to receive pension benefits, is sufficient to state a cause of action under ERISA.[4]

[64.07] TYPES OF CIVIL ACTIONS

A Federal District Court has held that the officers and the largest shareholders of a bankrupt company can be held personally liable under ERISA for the company's unpaid pension plan contributions.[5] The court felt that the rationale behind ERISA would be violated if controlling corporate officers who had deliberately violated ERISA would be protected from liability.[6] The court based its decision on ERISA § 404(a) which requires all fiduciaries to discharge their duties under a plan solely in the interest of the plan's participants and beneficiaries, while utilizing the skill, care, prudence and diligence of a prudent person.[7]

[64.09] ERISA PREEMPTION

The Sixth Circuit Court of Appeals has held that the ERISA barred employees and unions from suing under Section 301 of the Taft Hartley Act to recover nine guaranteed pension benefits from pension-plan sponsors.[8]

SUPPLEMENTAL NOTES TO CHAPTER 64

1. *Northwest Administrators, Inc. v. Truck-A-Way*, 1993 US App Lexis 9920 (9th Cir.).
2. *Michigan United Food and Commercial Workers Unions and Drug Mercantile Employees Joint Health and Welfare Fund v. The Muir Co.*, 992 F2d 594 (6th Cir. 1993).
3. *Schwartz v. Gregori*, TN IER cases 396 (Sixth Cir. 1995).
4. *Ibid.*
5. *Ches v. Archer*, 1993 US Dist. LEXIS 9455 (WDNY).
6. *Ibid.*
7. *Ibid.*
8. *Steel Workers v. United Engineering*, 149 LRRM 2129 (Sixth Cir. 1995).

65

Federal Social Security
and Related Programs

[65.01]–[65.06]—NO SIGNIFICANT CHANGES SINCE MAIN VOLUME.

66

Federal Unemployment
and Workers' Compensation Laws

[66.01]–[66.07]—NO SIGNIFICANT CHANGES SINCE MAIN VOLUME.

67

Federal Privacy
and Related Laws

[67.01]–[67.08]—NO SIGNIFICANT CHANGES SINCE MAIN VOLUME.

68

IRCA, WARN, and Drug-Free Workplace Legislation

[68.05] THE WORKER ADJUSTMENT AND RETRAINING ACT OF 1988 (PLANT CLOSURE LAW)

Labor unions lack standing to sue for monetary damages on behalf of their members who allegedly do not receive the 60-day notice of a plant closing under WARN.[1] The individually affected members of the bargaining unit must participate in any such suit.[2]

The Third Circuit Court of Appeals has held that employers who violate WARN's 60-day notice requirement must pay damages for each calendar day of the violation, rather than only for each workday.[3]

A Federal District Court in Western Pennsylvania held that in determining whether a minimum of 50 employees have been affected by a plant closing, employees who had been recalled from layoff less than six months prior to the 60-day notice of closing must be excluded from the count as they were legally "part-time."[4]

A Federal District Court in Colorado has held that an employer's notice of plant closing to its employees that included only a veiled reference to a layoff, and made no effort to identify the affected employees or any impending layoff on any particular date, was insufficient for the employer to establish that it had acted in good faith and had reasonable grounds for believing it was not violating WARN.[5]

The Federal Courts are to apply state statutes of limitations for cases brought under the Worker Adjustment and Retraining Notification Act.[6]

SUPPLEMENTAL NOTES TO CHAPTER 68

1. *Clothing and Textile Workers v. Brown Group, Inc.*, 8 IER Cases 1423 (DC Mo. 1993).
2. *Ibid.*
3. *Steelworkers v. North Star Steel Co.*, 8 IER Cases 1281 (3rd Cir. 1993).
4. *United Mine Workers v. Florence Mining Co.*, 9 IER Cases 577 (DC W.Pa. 1994).
5. *Frymire v. Ampex Corp.*, 9 IER Cases 513 (DC Colo. 1994).
6. *Northstar Steel Co. v. Thomas*, 10 IER Cases 961 (1995).

68A

Family and
Medical Leave
Act of 1993

[68A.01] COVERAGE

The Family and Medical Leave Act (FMLA) applies to employers with 50 or more employees who work at or within a 75-mile radius of the worksite of an employee desiring to take FMLA leave.[1] The FMLA applies to employees of a covered employer provided that the employee has been working for the employer for at least 12 months prior to the leave request and has worked at least 1,250 hours during the preceding 12 month period.[2] For purposes of determining length of service, the 12 months of employment need not have been consecutive.[3]

The FMLA exempts "key" employees from its protection.[4] Key employees are those who earn a salary in the top 10% of the employer's workforce and whose return to employment following FMLA leave would result in substantial and grievous economic injury to the operations of the employer.[5] However, if a key employee requests FMLA leave, an employer who believes that the employee might be denied reinstatement based on his status as a key employee must give written notice to the employee at the time that he requests leave that he qualifies as a key employee.[6]

[68A.02] NATURE OF LEAVE

The FMLA permits eligible employees to take up to 12 weeks of unpaid leave within any 12 month period, if appropriate grounds for leave exist.[7]

Any eligible employee, male or female, is entitled to FMLA leave:

- for the birth of a son or daughter, and to care for the newborn;
- for the placement with the employee of a son or daughter for foster care or adoption;
- to care for the employee spouse, daughter, son, or parent with a serious health condition; or
- because of the employee's own serious health condition that renders the employee unable to perform his job.[8]

Pursuant to the FMLA, a "parent" is a biological parent, or one who stands or stood *in loco parentis* to the employee, but does not include a parent-in-law.[9]

A "serious health condition" is an illness, injury, impairment, or physical or mental condition that involves:

- a period of treatment or incapacity in relation to an overnight stay in a hospital or other medical care facility;
- a period of incapacity resulting in an absence of more than 3 calendar days from work or school, that also involves ongoing care by a health care provider; or,
- continuing treatment by a health care provider for a chronic or long-term health condition that is incurable or so serious that, if untreated, would likely cause a period of incapacity of more than 3 calendar days, or for prenatal care.[10]

[68A.03] SPOUSES EMPLOYED BY THE SAME EMPLOYER

Spouses who are employed by the same employer are entitled only to an aggregate of 12 weeks of FMLA leave if the purpose of the leave is:

- the birth of a child to the employees, or to care for the child after birth;
- the placement of a child for adoption or foster care with the employees; or,
- to take care of a parent with a serious health condition.[11]

If a leave is taken for a reason other than one listed above, each spouse is entitled to 12 weeks of FMLA leave, regardless of the fact that they work for the same employer.

[68A.04] INTERMITTENT AND REDUCED SCHEDULE LEAVE

Intermittent and reduced schedule leaves are available under certain circumstances.[12] "Intermittent leave" is leave that is taken in several separate blocks of time due to a single illness or injury, rather than continuously.[13] "Reduced schedule leave" is a leave that reduces an employee's usual number of working hours per workweek, or per workday.[14]

If FMLA leave is taken due to the birth or placement of a child for adoption or foster care, an employee may take intermittent or reduced schedule leave only upon consent of the employer.[15] If the leave is taken to care for a sick family member or for the employee's own serious health condition, intermittent or reduced schedule leaves are permissible when medically necessary.[16]

[68A.05] SUBSTITUTION OF PAID LEAVE

An employer may require, or an employee may elect with the consent of the employer, that accrued paid vacation, personal, or family leave be substituted for unpaid FMLA leave that relates to birth, placement of a child for foster care or adoption, or care for an ill family member.[17] Substitution of accrued paid vacation, personal or sick leave may be made for unpaid FMLA leave that is taken in order to care for a sick family member or for the employee's own serious health condition.[18] An employer may, but is not required to, allow substitution of paid sick leave for unpaid FMLA leave in any situation.[19]

[68A.06] EMPLOYEE BENEFITS DURING LEAVE

An employee's coverage under group health plans must be continued during FMLA leave under the same conditions as it would have been provided had the employee remained at work.[20] Furthermore, the employee's health benefits must be maintained in the same manner and to the same extent during FMLA leave as they were provided prior to leave.[21] If a new health plan is implemented during an employee's FMLA leave, the employee's coverage must be continued under the new plan.[22]

An employer may recover any health plan premiums that it has paid during FMLA leave from an employee who does not return to work after the expiration of the FMLA leave, unless the reason for the employee's failure to return is due to the serious health condition of the employee or his spouse, child, or parent, or other circumstances beyond the employee's control.[23]

[68A.07] EMPLOYER POSTING AND NOTICE REQUIREMENTS

Employers subject to the FMLA must post on their premises in a conspicuous location where employees are employed, a notice explaining the FMLA's provisions and explaining the procedures for filing complaints of violations of the Act with Wage and Hour.[24]

If employers have handbooks or other writings concerning employee benefits or leave rights, information concerning employee rights and obligations under the FMLA must be included.[25] If employers do not have written policies, manuals or handbooks, they must provide written guidance pertaining to an employee's rights and obligations under the FMLA at the time an employee requests leave under the FMLA.[26] When employees request FMLA leave, employers must provide specific notice pertaining to FMLA leave that includes, where appropriate:

- that the leave will be counted against their FMLA leave entitlement;
- requirements for furnishing medical certification of a serious health condition and the consequences for failing to do so;
- the employee's right to substitute paid leave and whether the employer will require the employee to do so, and the conditions related to the substitution;
- any requirement that employees present a fitness-for-duty certificate prior to restoration to employment;

- the employee's status as a "key employee" and the possibility that restoration to employment may be denied following the leave, along with an explanation of the conditions required for such denial;
- the employee's right to be restored to the same or equivalent position upon returning from leave; and,
- the employee's potential liability for health insurance premiums paid by the employer during FMLA leave if the employee fails to return to work following the leave.[27]

[68A.08]   EMPLOYEE NOTICE

Employees must provide 30 days advance notice prior to FMLA leave where the need for the leave is foreseeable based on an expected birth, placement for adoption or foster care, or planned medical treatment of the employee or family member.[28] If 30 days notice is not practicable due to a change in circumstances or other legitimate reasons, notice must be given as soon as practicable.[29] Generally, "as soon as practicable" means at least verbal notice to the employer within 1 or 2 business days of when the employee learns of the need for leave.[30] If an employee desires intermittent leave or leave on a reduced leave schedule, upon the employer's request, the employee must inform the employer of the reasons intermittent or reduced schedule leave is needed, and the schedule for treatment, if applicable.[31]

If the need for FMLA leave is not foreseeable, an employee must give his employer notice of the need for leave as soon as practicable under the circumstances.[32] Except in extraordinary situations, the notice should be given within 1 or 2 business days of learning of the need for leave.[33]

[68A.09]   MEDICAL CERTIFICATION

In response to an employee's serious health condition, or that of his spouse, son, or daughter, the employer may require that the request for leave be accompanied by medical certification.[34] Initially employers must give written notice that they will require medical certification in particular circumstances.[35] However, employers may verbally request subsequent medical certifications.[36] As a general rule, employers must give their employees at least 15 calendar days to provide the medical certification.[37] The information that may be required on the medical certification is limited.[38] The Department of Labor has developed forms that comply with the law that may be used for obtaining medical certification.[39]

If an employer doubts the validity of an employee's medical certification, the employer, at its own expense, may require the employee to go to an employer designated health care provider for a second opinion.[40] If the two opinions differ, the employer, at its own expense, may require the employee to go to a mutually agreeable health care provider, whose opinion shall be final and binding.[41]

[68A.10]   FITNESS-FOR-DUTY REPORT

If an employee takes FMLA leave due to his own serious health condition, the employer may enforce a uniformly applied policy or practice of requiring the employee to obtain a certification from his health care provider that he is able to resume work.[42] An employee may be denied job restoration until such certification is provided.[43]

[68A.11]   DENIAL OF LEAVE OR REINSTATEMENT

Employers may deny leave or reinstatement:

- In cases of foreseeable leave, if an employee fails to give 30 days notice of the need for leave, the employer may deny FMLA leave until 30 days after the date the employee provides notice;
- If medical certification is not provided in a timely manner, the employer may deny FMLA leave until the employee submits the certification;
- At the time an employee requests reinstatement, if the employer can show that the employee would not otherwise have been employed if leave had not been taken, the employer may deny restoration from leave;
- If an employee unequivocally informs his employer that he will not return to work, the employment relationship, and all accompanying FMLA obligations of the employer, cease;
- Employees who fraudulently obtain FMLA leave are not protected by its job restoration or health benefits provision;
- Uniformly applied policies governing outside employment may continue to be enforced.[44]

[68A.12]   ENFORCEMENT

Employees who feel that their FMLA rights have been violated may either:

   (1) file a complaint with the Secretary of Labor; or,

   (2) file a private lawsuit.[45]

Private lawsuits must be filed within two years after the last action that was taken in violation of the Act.[46] However, if the employer has violated the act willfully, the statute of limitations is extended to three years.[47]

[68A.13]   FINAL RULE OF THE FAMILY AND MEDICAL LEAVE ACT OF 1993

The final rule under the FMLA makes numerous significant changes from the interim rule.

Employee eligibility under the FMLA: As the interim rule stated, employees who work for employers that have fifty or more employees within a seventy-five-mile radius of the employee's work site are eligible under the FMLA.[48] However, under the final rule, the seventy-five-mile distance surrounding the worksite is no longer expressed as a radius, but rather is measured by surface miles, using surface transportation, by the shortest route from the facility where the employee needing leave is employed.[49]

Serious health condition: The final rule alters the definition of a serious health condition. A serious condition is one that requires either in-patient care in a hospital, hospice, or residential medical care facility, or that requires continuing treatment by a health care provider.[50] The final rule further states that continuing treatment by health care provider includes any one of the following:

- A period of incapacity of more than three consecutive calendar days that involves treatment two or more times by a health care provider or treatment by a health care provider on at least one occasion which results in a regimen of continuing treatment under the provider's supervision.
- A period of incapacity due to pregnancy, or for pre-natal care.
- A period of incapacity or treatment for the incapacity as a result of a chronic serious health condition.
- A period of incapacity that is either permanent or long term due to a condition for which treatment may not be effective.
- Absences to receive multiple treatments by a health care provider either for restorative surgery after an accident or other injury, or for a condition that would likely result in incapacity of more than three consecutive calendar days if medical treatment is not sought.[51]

The final rule states that substance abuse can qualify as a serious health condition if the definition of a serious health condition is otherwise met.[52] However, leave may be taken only for treatment of a substance abuse problem that is rendered by a health care provider or on referral by a health care provider.[53] Furthermore, absence due to the use of a substance, rather than for treatment, does not qualify for FMLA leave.[54]

Meaning of "unable to perform the functions of the position": In order to qualify for FMLA leave, an employee must either be unable to work at all or unable to perform any one of the essential functions of the employee's position within the meaning of the Americans with Disabilities Act.[55] Employees who are absent in order to receive medical treatment for a serious health condition are deemed to be unable to perform the essential functions of their positions during their absence for the treatment.[56]

Definition of health care provider: The final rule expands the definition of "health care provider" to include:

- Any health care provider recognized by the employer or the employer's Group Health Plan as authorized to provide certification of a serious health condition for purposes of claims; and

- Any practitioner who would otherwise qualify as health care provider within the meaning of the final rule who practices in a country other than the United States, who is authorized to practice in accordance with the law of that country, and who is performing within the scope of his practice as defined under the law.[57]

Amount of leave that can be taken: Under the new final rules, where the employer has not specified which method it will use in determining a twelve month FMLA leave period, then the method that provides the most FMLA leave entitlement to the employee will be utilized.[58] Further, the final rule prohibits an employer from counting as FMLA leave any period of time that an employee would not ordinarily have been expected to report to work if he or she was not on FMLA leave.[59]

Intermittent leave: Under the final rule, an employee may take intermittent leave *before* the birth or adoption of a child without the employer's agreement.[60] However, the employer must agree to intermittent leave taken *after* the birth or adoption of a child.[61]

Interplay between FMLA and Workers' Compensation leave: The final rule specifically permits an employer to count Workers' Compensation leave that qualifies as a serious health condition concurrently as FMLA leave.[62] However, where the employer does so, if the employee's physician states that the employee is able to return from his Workers' Compensation injury to a light duty job, but is unable to return to the same or equivalent job, the employee may decline the employer's offer of a light duty job.[63] As a result of this, the employee may lose his entitlement to Workers' Compensation payments, but is entitled to remain on unpaid FMLA leave until his twelve-week entitlement is exhausted.[64]

Designation of FMLA leave: Under the final rule the employer has the responsibility of designating leave, whether paid or unpaid, as FMLA qualifying, and to notify the employee that the leave has been designated as FMLA leave.[65] The employer's designation may only be based on information received from either the employee or the employee's spokesperson.[66] The employer's notice that leave has been designated as FMLA leave may be either oral or in writing.[67] However, if the notice is oral, it must be confirmed in writing no later than the following payday.[68]

Where the employer has the necessary knowledge to determine that leave is for an FMLA reason at the time that the leave commences, the employer must designate the leave as FMLA leave at that time.[69] On the other hand, if the employer learns that leave is taken for an FMLA purpose after the leave has begun, the employer may retroactively count the leave as FMLA leave to the extent that the leave period qualifies as FMLA leave.[70] An employer may not designate leave as FMLA leave once the employee has returned to work unless:

- The leave is short term and the employer is awaiting medical certification, and
- Where the employer did not know the reason for the leave but learns that the leave could have qualified as FMLA leave upon the employee's return to work. In such a case, the designation of the leave as FMLA leave must be made within two business days of the employee's return to work.[71]

If an employer fails to designate leave as FMLA leave, and the employee wants leave to count as FMLA leave, the employee must notify the employer of his desire within two business days of the employee's return to work.[72] If the employee does not make the notification within two business days, then the employee may not subsequently assert FMLA protections for that absence.[73]

Employee entitlement to benefits during FMLA leave: Under the final rule, an employer is not obligated to continue an employee's benefits during the leave period if those benefits are voluntarily purchased directly by the employee from an insurer, no contributions are made by the employer, the employer receives no consideration from the purchases of the benefits, and the premium for the coverage does not increase if the employment relationship terminates.[74]

Employee's failure to make premium payments: Under the final rule, before an employer may cancel an employee's health insurance coverage due to an employee's failure to pay his share of the premium payment for more than thirty days, the employer must provide written notice to the employee that payment has not been received at least fifteen days before the coverage is to cease, advising the employee that the coverage will be dropped on a specified date at least fifteen days after the date of the notice unless the payment has been received on or before that date.[75]

Employer notices to employees: Where an employee is on intermittent leave, the employer need only give notice required by 29 CFR §825.301 at the time of the employee's first absence.[76] Furthermore, this notice is not required more frequently than once every six months, and then only in conjunction with an absence, unless some of the information provided in the notice changes.[77] Even if some of the information does change, only the changed information must be provided.[78] However, the employer must always notify the employee that leave has been designated as FMLA leave.[79]

Medical certification of a serious health condition: The final rule extensively revises the employer's ability to obtain verification from the health care provider that an employee has a serious health condition under the FMLA, and the likely periods of absences of the employee.[80] Furthermore, the final rule provides a new optional medical certification form.[81]

Adequacy of a medical certification: Under the final rule, with the employee's permission, an employer's physician may contact a health care provider that it employs in order to seek clarification of information in a medical certification, but the employer may not request additional information.[82]

Where an employer requires an employee to obtain a second or third medical opinion as permitted under the regulations, the employer must reimburse the employee or the employee's family member for reasonable travel expenses.[83] Furthermore, the employee or employee's family member generally may not be required to travel outside normal commuting distances.[84]

Notice of intent to return to work: An employee is permitted to return to work earlier than originally anticipated and communicated to the employer.[85] However, the employee must provide the employer at least two business days' notice of his intent to return to work.[86]

Fitness for duty certification: Under the final rule, an employer's requirements for an employee to return to work must be job related and consistent with business necessity.[87]

SUPPLEMENTAL NOTES TO CHAPTER 68A

1. FMLA, § 101(4).
2. FMLA, § 101(2).
3. 29 CFR § 825.110(b).
4. FMLA, § 104(b).
5. *Ibid.*
6. 29 CFR § 825.219.
7. 29 CFR § 825.100.
8. FMLA, § 102(a).
9. 29 CFR § 825.113(b).
10. 29 CFR § 825.114(a).
11. 29 CFR § 825.202.
12. 29 CFR § 825.203.
13. *Ibid.*
14. *Ibid.*
15. *Ibid.*
16. *Ibid.*
17. 29 CFR § 825.207.
18. *Ibid.*
19. *Ibid.*
20. 29 CFR § 825.209.
21. *Ibid.*
22. *Ibid.*
23. 29 CFR § 825.213.
24. 29 CFR § 825.300.
25. 29 CFR § 825.301.
26. *Ibid.*
27. *Ibid.*
28. 29 CFR § 825.302.
29. *Ibid.*
30. *Ibid.*
31. *Ibid.*
32. 29 CFR § 825.303.
33. *Ibid.*

34. 29 CFR § 825.305.

35. *Ibid.*

36. *Ibid.*

37. *Ibid.*

38. 29 CFR § 825.306.

39. *Ibid.*

40. 29 CFR § 825.306.

41. *Ibid.*

42. 29 CFR § 825.310.

43. *Ibid.*

44. 29 CFR § 825.312.

45. 29 CFR § 825.400.

46. *Ibid.*

47. *Ibid.*

48. 29 CFR § 825.110.

49. 29 CFR § 825.111.

50. 29 CFR § 825.114.

51. *Ibid.*

52. *Ibid.*

53. *Ibid.*

54. *Ibid.*

55. 29 CFR § 825.115.

56. *Ibid.*

57. 29 CFR § 825.118.

58. 29 CFR § 825.200.

59. *Ibid.*

60. 29 CFR § 825.203

61. *Ibid.*

62. 29 CFR § 825.207

63. *Ibid.*

64. *Ibid.*

65. 29 CFR § 825.208.

66. *Ibid.*

67. *Ibid.*

68. *Ibid.*

69. *Ibid.*

70. *Ibid.*

71. *Ibid.*

72. *Ibid.*

73. *Ibid.*

74. 29 CFR § 825.209.

75. 29 CFR § 825.212.

76. 29 CFR § 825.301.

77. *Ibid.*

78. *Ibid.*

79. *Ibid.*

80. 29 CFR § 825.306.

81. Appendix B to 29 CFR Part 825.

82. 29 CFR § 825.307.

83. *Ibid.*

84. *Ibid.*

85. 29 CFR § 825.309.

86. *Ibid.*

87. 29 CFR § 825.310.

PART SIX

STATE LABOR LAWS

69

Introduction to State
Labor and Employment Laws

[69.01]–[69.10]—NO SIGNIFICANT CHANGES SINCE MAIN VOLUME.

70

Employment-at-Will
Developments

[70.01]–[70.09]—NO SIGNIFICANT CHANGES SINCE MAIN VOLUME.

71

Torts in the Workplace

[71.01]–[71.16]—NO SIGNIFICANT CHANGES SINCE MAIN VOLUME.

72

Alabama Labor and Employment Laws

[72.05] REGULATION AND EMPLOYMENT PRACTICES

AIDS testing and confidentiality: Alabama law provides that individuals may not be tested for HIV or AIDS without their informed consent, unless medically required, and that testing facilities must keep such tests and HIV condition confidential.[1]

[72.06A] WELFARE AND BENEFITS LAWS

Insurance coverage for alcohol abuse treatment: Alabama statutes require insurance carriers to offer an option to employers to provide for a maximum thirty-day coverage of employees undergoing in-patient or out-patient treatment for alcoholism.[2]

Insurance coverage for newborns: Alabama law requires insurance policies to include coverage of newborns.[3]

Insurer discrimination prohibited (sickle cell anemia):   Section 27-5-13 of the Alabama Code prohibits discrimination in the denial of insurance coverage because of sickle cell anemia. Alabama law also provides that insurance carriers must reimburse Optometrists, Chiropractors, Dentists, Psychologists and Podiatrists for medical services rendered if such services would be reimbursed if the same services were provided by a physician.[4]

State holidays: Alabama statutes provide that the following are state recognized holidays: New Year's Day, Martin Luther King's Birthday, Washington's Birthday, Memorial Day, July 4th, Labor Day, Veteran's Day, Thanksgiving, and Christmas Day.[5]

[72.08] UNEMPLOYMENT COMPENSATION LAWS

Aside from private sector-type employers that generally are subject to unemployment compensation coverage, Alabama statutes provide that agricultural, state government agencies, nonprofit employers, and employers employing domestic employees also are subject to Alabama Unemployment Compensation Laws.[6]

However, employees of commercial fishing vessels, railroad employees, persons self-employed, employees employed by spouse, child, or parent, minor newspaper carriers, casual employees, wholly commissioned employees, insurance and real-estate employees, hospital interns, students and spouses of students providing employee services for schools, colleges, or universities typically are excluded from coverage under the Alabama Unemployment Compensation Laws.[7]

[72.09] WORKERS' COMPENSATION LAWS

Retaliatory discharge claim dismissed: The Alabama Supreme Court upheld a decision that the termination of two employees who had filed workers' compensation claims was not wrongful in that the employees had been discharged as part of a reorganization of the employer's distribution system, rather than in retaliation because of the workers' compensation claims.[8]

Retaliatory discharge claim upheld: The Alabama Supreme Court upheld a jury award in favor of an employee who had sued her former employer on the basis that the employer had discharged her in retaliation because of her workers' compensation claim where the employer had placed limitations on medical leaves of absence without even so notifying the employee.[9]

[72.10] EMPLOYMENT-AT-WILL DEVELOPMENTS

Wrongful discharge—insurance coverage: The Alabama Supreme Court, holding that a retaliatory discharge cause of action is in the nature of a claim of tort rather than a claim arising under workers' compensation, ruled that an insurance company that provided general liability insurance to an employer must defend such employer against an employee's retaliatory discharge cause of action under Alabama's Workers' Compensation laws.[10]

[72.11] TORT ACTIONS

Sexual harassment claims: The Alabama Supreme Court, stating that whether an employer took necessary steps to cease to prevent sexual harassment of a female employee by a male co-worker is an issue of fact, reinstated a cause of action for sexual harassment even though, upon becoming aware of the harassment, the employer warned the offender about the unacceptable behavior.[11]

[72.12] TIME LIMITATIONS FOR FILING WRONGFUL DISCHARGE LAWSUITS

Time limitations for filing causes of action in Alabama for wrongful employment in violation of public policy and defamation are two years, respectively, and also two years for lawsuits based on wrongful discharge in violation of an implied contract.[12]

Punitive damages: Alabama law provides for punitive damages, in addition to backpay and compensatory damages, in wrongful discharge type cases.[13]

SUPPLEMENTAL NOTES TO CHAPTER 72

1. Code of Alabama, Section 27-20A-4.
2. Code of Alabama, Section 27-19-38.
3. Code of Alabama, Section 27-19-38.
4. Code of Alabama, Sections 27-1-10, 27-1-11, 27-1-15, 27-1-18, 27-19-39, 27-19A-4 and 27-46-1.
5. Code of Alabama, Section 1-3-8.
6. Code of Alabama, Sections 25-4-8 through 25-4-10.
7. Code of Alabama, Sections 25-4-10, 25-4-18.
8. *Graham v. Shoals Distributing, Inc.*, Nos. 1920865 and 1920866 (Ala. Sup. Ct., 1993).
9. *Gold Kist, Inc. v. Griffin*, (Ala. Sup. Ct., 11-10-94).
10. *Jackson County Hospital v. Alabama Hospital Association Trust*, No. 1911272 (Ala. Sup. Ct., 1993).
11. *Potts v. BE&K Construction Co.*, No. 1910483 (Ala. Sup. Ct., 1992).
12. Code of Alabama, Section 6-2-38.
13. *Grant v. Butler*, 590 So.2d 254 (Ala. 1991).

73

Alaska Labor and Employment Laws

[73.05] REGULATION OF EMPLOYMENT PRACTICES

Bona fide exceptions to prohibited employment practices: Alaska statutes provide that bona fide seniority systems, bona fide occupational qualifications and bona fide benefits programs are legally recognized exceptions to otherwise unfair employment practices.[1]

EEOC—certified deferral: Section 18.80.120 of the Alaska Statutes provides that the Alaska Commission for Human Rights is to serve as a certified deferral agency of the Equal Employment Opportunity Commission relative to fair employment claims filed with the EEOC.

Court review of agency decisions: Section 18.80.135 of the Alaska Statutes permits claimants and respondents to adverse decisions by the Alaska Commission for Human Rights a right of review to applicable courts within the state.

Available remedies for fair employment violations: Alaska statutes provide for punitive damages, when deemed appropriate, as well as for back pay and compensatory damages for claimants who prevail in claims before the Alaska Commission for Human Rights.[2]

Affirmative action programs (state employment):   Alaska law requires each state agency to adopt an affirmative action plan to identify persons with protected characteristics who are underutilized in their employment and establish affirmative action programs to overcome any such underutilization.[3]

Family and medical leave laws: Alaska statutes provide that employers with at least twenty-one employees must permit their employees who are employed for at least 35 hours per week or for at least six consecutive months, or for at least 17.5 hours per week for at least twelve consecutive months a leave of absence for up to twelve weeks as a result of a birth or adoption of a child or a serious medical condition of oneself or a child, spouse, or parent. Group health coverage continues but the employee may be required to pay all or part of the cost of coverage during the period he or she is on leave.[4]

Marital status discrimination (unmarried domestic partners):   The Alaska Supreme Court has held that Alaska's statute prohibiting marital status discrimination requires employers to extend spousal benefits to employees' domestic partners, even when such partners are of the same sex as that of the employee.[5]

[73.06A] WELFARE AND BENEFITS LAWS

Insurance coverage for alcohol/drug abuse treatment: Alaska laws require employers to provide mandatory coverage up to $7,000 over 24 months for combination of in-patient and out-patient treatment of employees undergoing rehabilitation for alcohol and/or drug abuse.[6]

Insurance coverage for newborns: Section 21.42.345 of Alaska Statutes mandates that employee health-related insurance policies include coverage of newborns of employees.

State holidays: Alaska statutes provide that the following are state recognized holidays: New Year's Day, Martin Luther King's Birthday, Washington's Birthday, Memorial Day, July 4th, Labor Day, Veteran's Day, Thanksgiving Day, and Christmas Day.[7]

ERISA preemption: The Alaska Supreme Court has ruled that an employee's claim that he was dismissed to prevent his giving information about possible misuse of employee benefit trust funds was preempted by the Employee Retirement Income Security Act of 1974 (ERISA).[8]

[73.08] UNEMPLOYMENT COMPENSATION LAWS

Aside from private sector employers generally subject to the coverage of Alaska's Unemployment Compensation Laws, agricultural, nonprofit, state government agencies and employers of domestic employees also are subject to the unemployment laws.[9]

Alaska law disqualifies the following individuals from collecting unemployment compensation: aliens who are unlawfully within the state, recipients of pension, retirement pay or other such annuities, and recipients of unemployment benefits from federal and other state unemployment compensation funds.[10]

Alaska's unemployment compensation law does not provide coverage to such employees as: persons self-employed; employees of commercial fishing vessels; railroad employees; wholly commissioned insurance and real estate agents; persons employed by parent, spouse, or child; casual labor; patients employed by hospitals; hospital interns; minor newspaper carriers; newspaper distributors; students and spouses of students providing employment services to schools, colleges, and universities, if under college work study program, and students at nonprofit or public education institutions who are in full-time work study programs.[11]

[73.12] TIME LIMITATIONS FOR FILING WRONGFUL DISCHARGE LAWSUITS

Alaska statutes provide that time limits for litigants to file wrongful employment lawsuits are: two years for defamation and six years for discharge in violation of implied contracts causes of action.[12]

SUPPLEMENTAL NOTES TO CHAPTER 73

1. Alaska Statutes, Section 18.80.220.
2. Alaska Statutes, Section 18.80.130.
3. Alaska Statutes, Section 44.21.503.
4. Alaska Statutes, Section 23.10.500–23.10.530.
5. *Tumes v. University of Alaska*, No. 4FA-94-43-Civ. (Alaska Sup. Ct., 1995).
6. Alaska Statutes, Section 21.42.365.
7. Alaska Statutes, Section 44.12.010–44.12.065.
8. *Andrews v. Alaska Operating Engineers—Employers Trust Fund*, Nos. 5-5615 and 4701 (Alaska Sup. Ct., 4-8-94).
9. Alaska Statutes, Sections 23.20.520, 23.20.525.
10. Alaska Statutes, Sections 23.20.360, 23.20.262, 23.20.378, 23.20.381 and 23.20.387.
11. Alaska Statutes, Section 23.20.256.
12. Alaska Statutes, Section 09.10.050 and 09.10.070.

74

Arizona Labor and Employment Laws

[74.05] REGULATION OF EMPLOYMENT PRACTICES

Disability (handicap defined):   The Arizona disability law has been modified by defining a "handicap" as any physical impairment that substantially limits one or more of an individual's major life activities, a record of such a physical impairment, or being regarded as having such a physical impairment and, further modified, to exclude an impairment caused by recent or current abuse of alcohol or drugs.[1]

Protection of perceived disability: An Arizona Court of Appeals has held that if an employer perceives an applicant or employee to have a physical disability— such as in the subject case, an ear injury causing an ear to occasionally drain fluid—and denies the applicant employment on the basis of the perceived disability, the individual may state a cause of action of discrimination under the Arizona Civil Rights Act (ACRA), the Court concluding further that the applicant was entitled to a jury trial to determine whether the applicant's condition was a handicap under ACRA and whether the employer denied employment to him because it perceived him to have a disability.[2]

Protection of "record" of disability: An Arizona Appellate Court has held that the Phoenix Fire Department violated the Arizona Civil Rights Act when it rescinded an offer of employment to an applicant after learning that the applicant had a history of cancer even though the cancer was successfully treated and in remission, the Court declining, however, to recognize a tort claim arising from the applicant's cause of action.[3]

Bona fide exceptions to prohibited employment practices: Arizona laws provide that bona fide seniority systems, bona fide occupational qualifications and bona fide benefits programs are legally recognized exceptions to otherwise unfair employment practices.[4]

EEOC—certified deferral: Arizona statutes provide that the Arizona Civil Rights Division serve as a certified deferral agency of the Equal Employment Opportunity Commission relative to the processing and investigation of fair employment practice claims filed with the EEOC.[5]

Court review of agency decisions: In the event the state deferral agency dismisses a fair employment practice charge, the charging party is permitted to bring a civil cause of action against the respondent if such action is filed within ninety days of the dismissal notification. The charging party also is permitted to bring a civil cause of action against the respondent if the state agency has not filed a civil action on behalf of the charging party within ninety days of the filing of the charge.[6]

Available remedies for fair employment violations: Arizona statutes permit a recovery of punitive damages, when deemed appropriate, as well as recovery for back pay and compensatory damages to successful litigants in fair employment practice cases.[7]

Affirmative action programs (state contracts/state employment): An Arizona Executive Order mandates state contractors to take affirmative action to ensure that applicants and employees are not discriminated in employment on the basis of race, age, color, religion, sex, or national origin. Another Arizona Executive Order requires all state agencies and state government to develop goals and timetables for the advancement in employment of underutilized minorities, females, and disabled employees.[8]

Age discrimination—failure to demonstrate constructive discharge: An employee who voluntarily resigned at age 65 under the misunderstanding that he was forced to do so, irrespective of communicated policy and correspondence to him to the contrary, was unable to sustain a constructive discharge actionable claim under Arizona's age discrimination in employment laws on the basis that he had been intentionally misled.[9]

Age discrimination—coverage extended to individuals over 70: The Arizona Civil Rights Act has been expanded to extend protection against age discrimination to individuals over 70 years of age, conforming to the protected age category under the Federal Age Discrimination in Employment Act.[10]

Drug testing protection: Arizona law protects employers from applicant and employee law suits when such employers comply with certain alcohol and drug testing procedures and requirements, as specified by the statute.[11]

AIDS testing and confidentiality: Arizona law requires an informed consent of a person prior to administering an AIDS test and forbids the disclosure of such tests unless authorized by the person tested or otherwise required to be released to certain health care providers or agencies.[12]

[74.06A] WELFARE AND BENEFITS LAWS

Insurance coverage for newborns: Arizona statutes mandate that employee health-related insurance policies include coverage of newborns, including adoptive infants less than one year old.[13]

State holidays: Arizona statutes specify the following as state recognized holidays: New Year's Day, Martin Luther King's Birthday, Washington's Birthday, Lincoln's Birthday, Memorial Day, July 4th, Labor Day, Columbus Day, Veteran's Day, Thanksgiving Day, and Christmas Day.[14]

[74.08] UNEMPLOYMENT COMPENSATION LAWS

Aside from private sector-type employers that are generally subject to unemployment compensation coverage, Arizona statutes provide that agricultural, state government agencies, nonprofit employers and employers employing domestic employees are also subject to Arizona Unemployment Compensation Laws.[15]

Arizona law disqualifies individuals from collecting unemployment compensation who are recipients of pension, retirement pay or other such annuities and recipients of unemployment benefits from federal and other state unemployment compensation funds.[16]

Arizona's unemployment compensation laws do not provide coverage of such employees as: self-employed; railroad employees; wholly commissioned insurance and real estate agents; minors employed by a parent; persons employed by a spouse or child; casual labor; student nurses and patients employed by a hospital; hospital interns; minor newspaper carriers, newspaper distributors; students and spouses of students providing employment services to schools, colleges and universities, if under college work study programs and students at non-profit or public educational institutions who are in full-time work study programs.[17]

[74.12] TIME LIMITATIONS FOR FILING WRONGFUL DISCHARGE LAWSUITS

Arizona statutes specify the following time limits to file wrongful employment lawsuits: one year for defamation; two years for discharge in violation of public policy; and three years for discharge in violation of implied contracts causes of action.[18]

SUPPLEMENTAL NOTES TO CHAPTER 74

1. Arizona Revised Statutes, Section 41-1461.4 (L. 1994, ch. 259).
2. *Boque v. Better-Bilt Aluminum Co.* (Ariz. Ct. App., 1-11-94).
3. *Burris v. City of Phoenix,* No 1 CA-CV90-0545 (Ariz. Ct. App., 1993).
4. Arizona Revised Statutes, Section 41-1463.
5. Arizona Revised Statutes, Sections 41-1402, 41-1471, 41-1481.
6. Arizona Revised Statutes, Section 41-1481.
7. Arizona Revised Statutes, Section 41-1481.
8. Executive Order 75-5; Executive Order 92-2.
9. *West v. Salt River Agricultural Improvement & Power District,* (Ariz. Ct. App., 9-8-94).
10. Arizona Revised Statutes, Section 41-1461.4 (L. 1994, ch. 258).
11. Arizona Revised Statutes, Section 23-493.
12. Arizona Revised Statutes, Sections 36-661, *et seq.*
13. Arizona Revised Statutes, Section 20-1402.
14. Arizona Revised Statutes, Sections 1-301, *et seq.*
15. Arizona Revised Statutes, Sections 23-613, 23-615, 23-615.1.
16. Arizona Revised Statutes, Sections 23-615, 23-617, 23-622.

17. Arizona Revised Statutes, Section 23-617.
18. Arizona Revised Statutes, Sections 12-541, 12-542, 12-543, 12-550 and 23-805.

75

Arkansas Labor and Employment Laws

[75.05] REGULATION OF EMPLOYMENT PRACTICES

Anti-discrimination laws: The Arkansas Civil Rights Act makes it unlawful for an employer that employs nine or more employees to discriminate in employment on the basis of race, religion, national origin or ancestry, gender, or sensory, mental or physical disability. Successful claimants under this statute may be entitled to injunctive relief, backpay up to two years from the date of filing his or her claim and compensatory and punitive damages up to certain specified monetary limits.[1]

Public Employers (age discrimination prohibited): Sections 21-2-201, *et seq.* of Arkansas statutes forbid public sector employers to discriminate in employment on the basis of ages 40 or older unless age is a bona fide occupational qualification relative to the job in question.

AIDS testing: Arkansas statutes provide that informed consent of a person prior to the administration of an AIDS test is not required where a health care provider is involved in direct contact with blood or bodily fluids in a manner that, in the judgment of a physician, is capable of transmitting the HIV virus or otherwise medically necessary.[2]

[75.06A] WELFARE AND BENEFITS LAWS

Insurance coverage for mental health treatment: Arkansas statutes provide that insurance companies must offer employers the option of covering treatment for mental health conditions of employees up to $7,500 for in-patient and out-patient services.[3]

Insurance coverage for alcohol/drug abuse treatment: Arkansas laws require insurance companies to provide an option to employers to cover up to $6,000 over 24 months for combination of in-patient and out-patient treatment of employees undergoing treatment for alcohol and/or drug abuse.[4]

Insurance coverage for newborns: Arkansas statutes mandate that employee health-related insurance policies include coverage of new births, including adoptive new births.[5]

State holidays: Arkansas statutes provide that the following are state recognized holidays: New Year's Day, Martin Luther King's Birthday, Memorial Day, July 4th, Labor Day, Veteran's Day, Thanksgiving Day, and Christmas Day.[6]

[75.08] UNEMPLOYMENT COMPENSATION LAWS

Aside from private sector employers generally subject to the coverage of Arkansas's Unemployment Compensation Laws, agricultural, nonprofit, state government agencies and employers of domestic employees also are subject to the state's unemployment laws.[7]

Arkansas law disqualifies the following individuals from collecting unemployment compensation: recipients of pension, retirement pay or other such annuities and recipients of unemployment benefits from federal and other state unemployment compensation funds.[8]

Arkansas' unemployment compensation laws do not provide coverage to such employees as: persons self-employed; employees of commercial fishing vessels; railroad employees; wholly commissioned insurance and real estate agents; persons employed by spouse or child; minors employed by parent; casual labor; patients and student nurses employed by hospitals; hospital interns; minor newspaper carriers; newspaper distributors; students and spouses of students providing employment services to schools, colleges, and universities.[9]

[75.10] EMPLOYMENT-AT-WILL DEVELOPMENTS

Implied contracts exception reaffirmed: The Eighth Circuit Court of Appeals, applying Arkansas law, acknowledging that an exception to the "at-will" rule may arise from reliance on a promise made in an employee handbook, reinstated a breach of contract claim by a former employee who had alleged that her dismissal from employment violated such a promise in an employee hand book.[10]

[75.11] TORT ACTIONS

Defamation (privilege)—The Eighth Circuit Court of Appeals, applying Arkansas law, held that an employer had a qualified privilege to disclose to local newspapers that 25 employees had been terminated for violating certain company policies, when responding to inquiries by a local small town newspaper.[12]

SUPPLEMENTAL NOTES TO CHAPTER 75

1. Ark. Laws, 1993, No. 962, 4(a).
2. Arkansas Statutes, Sections 20-15-901, *et seq.*
3. Arkansas Statutes, Section 23-86-113.
4. Arkansas Statutes, Section 23-79-139.
5. Arkansas Statutes, Sections 23-79-129, *et seq.*
6. Arkansas Statutes, Section 1-5-101, *et seq.*
7. Arkansas Statutes, Sections 11-10-208; 11-10-210; 11-10-220; 11-10-404; 11-10-507; 11-10-713.
8. Arkansas Statutes, Sections 11-10-507; 11-10-513; 11-10-517.
9. Arkansas Statutes, Section 11-10-210.
10. *Qualls v. Hickory Springs Manufacturing Co.*, No. 92-2420 (CA-8, 6-1-93).
11. Arkansas Statutes, Sections 16-56-104; 16-56-105; 16-56-115.

76

California Labor and Employment Laws

[76.05] REGULATION OF EMPLOYMENT PRACTICES

Arrest and conviction records: California employers are permitted to obtain specified arrest and convictions records, such as those that pertain to sex-related crimes, of applicants for employment, licenses, or for a volunteer position that would entail supervisory or disciplinary power over a minor, provided the prospective employer provides a copy of the applicant's or volunteer's fingerprints to the agency from which such information is sought.[1]

Sexual harassment (same sex):   The California Court of Appeals has held that same sex types of sexual harassment, whether quid pro quo or hostile environment conduct, are actionable under the California Fair Employment and Housing Act.[2]

Sexual harassment (insurance liability):   A California Appellate Court has held that a general liability insurance policy did not extend to the coverage for intentional acts of sexual harassment by the President of the employer.[3]

Bona fide exceptions to prohibited employment practices: California statutes provide that bona fide seniority systems, bona fide occupational qualifications and bona fide benefits programs are legally recognized exceptions to otherwise unfair employment practices.[4]

EEOC—certified deferral: Sections 12935 and 12960 of the California Government Code provide that the California Department of Fair Employment and Housing Commission is to serve as a certified deferral agency of the Equal Employment Opportunity Commission relative to fair employment claims filed with the EEOC.

Available remedies for fair employment violations: California statutes provide for punitive damages as well as for backpay and compensatory damages for claimants who prevail in claims before the California Department of Fair Employment and Housing Commission.[5]

Affirmative action programs (state employment):   California law requires each state agency to adopt an affirmative action plan to identify persons with protected characteristics who are underutilized in their employment and establish affirmative action programs to overcome any such underutilization.[6]

Employment references protection: California law provides that certain disclosures relative to a former employee to a prospective employer are privileged, such as nonmalicious communications concerning the job performance or qualifications of an applicant, based upon credible evidence by a former or current employer, to the prospective employer.[7]

School leave law modified: The California School Partnership Act that formerly required employers of twenty-five or more to permit employees to take four hours leave each school year per child to participate in school activities has been modified to increase the amount of leave up to forty hours per school year, although an employee is not permitted to take in excess of eight hours per calendar month.[8]

Mandatory retirement policy for tenured university faculty: A California Court of Appeals has ruled that a University of California policy requiring tenured faculty members to retire at age 70, or older, violates the California Fair Employment and Housing Act (FEHA) in that the FEHA permits faculty members to continue working on a year-to-year basis beyond age 70 if they demonstrate continuing ability and a desire to do so.[9]

AIDS testing and confidentiality: California statutes require written consent of an applicant or employee prior to the administration of an AIDS test, the result of which may not be disclosed to others without written authorization of the person so tested.[10]

[76.06A] WELFARE AND BENEFITS LAWS

Insurance coverage for alcohol treatment: California laws require insurance companies to offer employers an option to cover treatment of employees undergoing rehabilitation for alcoholism.[11]

Insurance coverage for newborns: California statutes mandate that employee health-related insurance policies include coverage of newborns of employees, including adoptive new births.[12]

State holidays: California statutes provide that the following are state recognized holidays: New Year's Day, Martin Luther King's Birthday, Washington's Birthday, Lincoln's Birthday, Memorial Day, July 4th, Labor Day, Columbus Day, Veteran's Day, Thanksgiving Day, and Christmas Day.[13]

[76.08] UNEMPLOYMENT COMPENSATION LAWS

Aside from private sector employers that generally are subject to the coverage of California's Unemployment Compensation Laws, agricultural, nonprofit, state government agencies and employers of domestic employees also are subject to the state's unemployment laws.[14]

California's unemployment compensation laws do not provide coverage to such employees as: persons self-employed; railroad employees; wholly commissioned real estate agents; persons employed by spouse or child; minors employed by parent; casual employees; patients and student nurses employed by hospitals; hospital interns; minor newspaper carriers; newspaper distributors; students and spouses of students providing employment services to schools, colleges, and universities, if under college work study program and students at nonprofit or public education institutions who are in full-time work study programs.[15]

[76.10] EMPLOYMENT-AT-WILL DEVELOPMENTS

Public policy exception extended: A California Appellate Court has ruled that the broad public policy against employment discrimination enunciated in the California Fair Employment and Housing Act may provide grounds for a wrongful discharge cause of action against an employer who, otherwise, may not have been subject to the Act's prohibitions.[16]

Public policy exception—constructive discharge: The California Supreme Court has ruled that a constructive discharge does not attach, such as to support a public policy argument, unless the employee's employer either intentionally created or knowingly permitted working conditions that were so intolerable or aggravated that such conditions would compel a reasonable person to resign his or her position.[17]

Implied employment contract—constructive discharge: The Ninth Circuit Court of Appeals, applying California law, has held that an employee who was a good worker and who had worked for the defendant company for eight years and had been given numerous salary increases, had established an implied contract as a result, and was wrongfully constructively discharged when the employee quit his job after having his annual salary decreased from $55,000 to $35,000 and reassigned from a manager's position to a night watchman and his company car taken from him.[18]

Restrictive covenants—reasonable costs attached: The Supreme Court of California has held that a law firm agreement that assessed a reasonable cost against a former partner who chose to compete against the law firm after his departure, although not a prohibition against post-employment competition, per se, was reasonable and enforceable.[19]

[76.12] TIME LIMITATIONS FOR FILING WRONGFUL DISCHARGE TYPE LAWSUITS

California statutes provide that time limits for litigants to file wrongful employment claims are: one year for defamation lawsuits and two years for discharge in violation of implied contracts causes of action.[20]

SUPPLEMENTAL NOTES TO CHAPTER 76

1. California Penal Code, Section 11105.3 (A.B. No. 3738, September 30, 1994).

2. *Mogilefsky v. Superior Court of Los Angeles*, No. B072438 (Cal. Ct. App., 12-10-93).

3. *Coit Drapery Cleaners v. Sequoia Ins. Co.*, No. A054238 (Cal. Ct. App., 5-13-93).

4. California Government Code, Sections 12940, 12941.

5. California Government Code, Section 12970.

6. California Government Code, Section 19790.

7. California Civil Code, Section 47(c) (AB No. 364, August 26, 1994).

8. California Labor Code, Section 230.8 (AB No. 2590, September 30, 1994).

9. *Dubin V. Regents of the University of California*, (Cal. Ct. App., 5-25-94).

10. California Health & Safety Code, Sections 199.20, *et seq.*

11. California Insurance Code, Section 101123.6.

12. California Insurance Code, Sections 10119, *et seq.*

13. California Government Code, Sections 6700, *et seq.*

14. California Unemployment Insurance Code, Sections 605, 629, 634–5, 639, 675, 676.

15. California Unemployment Insurance Code, Sections 601, 621, 631, 634.5, 640, 641, 642, 645, 646, 647, 649.

16. *Jennings v. Marralle*, (Cal. App. Ct., Dist. 4, 1993).

17. *Turner v. Anheuser-Busch*, (Cal. Sup. Ct., 7-25-94).

18. *Tonry v. Security Experts, Inc.*, (CA 9, 3-28-94).

19. *Howard v. Babcock*, 863 P.2d 150 (Cal. Sup. Ct., 1993).

20. California Civil Code, Sections 339 and 340.

77

Colorado Labor and Employment Laws

[77.05] REGULATION OF EMPLOYMENT PRACTICES

Bona fide exceptions to prohibited employment practices: Colorado statutes provide that bona fide seniority systems, bona fide occupational qualifications, and bona fide benefits programs are legally recognized exceptions to otherwise unfair employment practices.[1]

EEOC—certified deferral: Colorado statutes provide that the Colorado Civil Rights Commission is to serve as a certified deferral agency of the Equal Employment Opportunity Commission relative to fair employment claims filed with the EEOC.[2]

Court review of agency decisions: Colorado statutes permit claimants and respondents to adverse decisions by the Colorado Civil Rights Commission a right of review to applicable courts within the state.[3]

Affirmative action programs (state employment): Colorado law requires each state agency to adopt an affirmative action plan by which to identify persons with protected characteristics who are underutilized in their employment and establish affirmative action programs to overcome any such underutilization.[4]

Drug testing—reasonable suspicion: A Colorado Court has upheld the use of a mandatory drug test used when an employee is reasonably suspicioned of drug use in a public sector workplace.[5]

AIDS testing and confidentiality: Colorado law requires an informed consent of a person prior to the administration of an AIDS test and forbids the disclosure of such tests without the approval of such person unless otherwise required to be released to certain health care providers or agencies.[6]

[77.06A] WELFARE AND BENEFITS LAWS

"Settlement" paychecks (not severance): A Colorado Court of Appeals has ruled that employer payments made to former employees in exchange for a release of all statutory and common law claims against the employer did not constitute "severance awards" under Colorado's Unemployment Compensation Laws, such payments having no adverse affect on employees receiving unemployment compensation funds.[7]

Insurance coverage for alcohol abuse treatment: Colorado laws require insurance companies to provide employers an option to cover treatment of employees undergoing rehabilitation for alcohol abuse.[8]

Insurance coverage for newborns: Colorado statutes mandate that employee health-related insurance policies include coverage of newborns of employees.[9]

State holidays: Colorado statutes provide that the following are state recognized holidays: New Year's Day, Martin Luther King's Birthday, Washington's Birthday, Memorial Day, July 4th, Labor Day, Columbus Day, Veteran's Day, Thanksgiving Day, and Christmas Day.[10]

[77.08] UNEMPLOYMENT COMPENSATION LAWS

Aside from private sector employers generally subject to the coverage of Colorado's Unemployment Compensation Laws, agricultural, nonprofit, state government agencies, and employers of domestic employees also are subject to the unemployment laws.[11]

Colorado law disqualifies the following individuals from collecting unemployment compensation: recipients of pension, retirement pay or other such annuities, and recipients of unemployment benefits from federal and other state unemployment compensation funds.[12]

Colorado unemployment compensation laws do not provide coverage to such employees as: persons self-employed; railroad employees; wholly commissioned insurance and real estate agents; persons employed by spouse or child; minors employed by a parent; casual labor; patients and student nurses employed by hospitals; minor newspaper carriers; newspaper distributors; students and spouses of students providing employment services to schools, colleges, and universities, if under college work study program and students at nonprofit or public education institutions who are in full-time work study programs.[13]

[77.10] EMPLOYMENT-AT-WILL DEVELOPMENTS

HIV positive employee discharge: The Tenth Circuit Court of Appeals, applying Colorado law, upheld the dismissal of an HIV-positive employee's lawsuit, ruling that the termination of the employee was motivated by the employer's legitimate business decision to reorganize the employee's business division, rather than motivated by the employee's physical condition.[14]

[77.12] TIME LIMITATIONS FOR FILING WRONGFUL DISCHARGE LAWSUITS

Colorado statutes provide that time limits for litigants to file wrongful employment claims are: one year for defamation, two years for lawsuits based on discharge in violation of public policy, and two years for discharge in violation of implied contracts causes of action.[15]

SUPPLEMENTAL NOTES TO CHAPTER 77

1. Colorado Revised Statutes, Section 24-34-402.

2. Colorado Revised Statutes, Sections 24-34-305 and 24-34-306.

3. Colorado Revised Statutes, Section 24-34-306.

4. Colorado Revised Statutes, Section 24-50-141.

5. *Denver v. Casados,* 862 P. 2d 908 (Colo., 1993).

6. Colorado Revised Statutes, Sections 25-4-1401, *et seq.*

7. *Moore v. Digital Equipment Corporation,* (Colo. Ct.App., 1-27-94).

8. Colorado Revised Statutes, Section 10-16-104(9).

9. Colorado Revised Statutes, Sections 10-8-121.

10. Colorado Revised Statutes, Sections 24-11-101, 24-11-103, 24-11-109 and 24-11-111.

11. Colorado Revised Statutes, Sections 8-70-103, 8-70-109, 8-70-113, 8-70-114, 8-70-118, 8-70-120, 8-70-121 and 8-70-132.

12. Colorado Revised Statutes, Sections 8-70-131, 8-70-132.

13. Colorado Revised Statutes, Sections 8-70-103, 8-70-118, 8-70-131, 8-70-132, 8-70-135, 8-70-136 and 8-70-139.

14. *Phelps v. Field Real Estate Company,* No. 92-1029 (CA-10, 1-16-93).

15. Colorado Revised Statutes, Sections 13-80-101, 13-80-102 and 13-80-103.

78

Connecticut Labor and Employment Laws

[78.05] REGULATION OF EMPLOYMENT PRACTICES

Bona fide exceptions to prohibited employment practices: Connecticut statutes provide that bona fide seniority systems, bona fide occupational qualifications and bona fide benefits programs are legally recognized exceptions to otherwise unfair employment practices.[1]

EEOC certified deferral: Connecticut statutes provide that the Connecticut Commission on Human Rights and Opportunities is to serve as a certified deferral agency of the Equal Employment Opportunity Commission relative to fair employment claims filed with the EEOC.[2]

Court review of agency decisions: Connecticut statutes permit claimants and respondents to adverse decisions by the Connecticut Commission on Human Rights and Opportunities a right of review to applicable courts within the state.[3]

Available remedies for fair employment violations: Connecticut statutes provide for backpay and compensatory damages for claimants who prevail in claims before the Connecticut Commission for Human Rights.[4]

Affirmative action programs (state employment): Connecticut law requires each state agency to adopt an affirmative action plan to identify persons with protected characteristics who are underutilized in their employment and establish affirmative action programs to overcome any such underutilization.[5]

Family medical leave: Connecticut law requires employers of seventy-five or more employees to provide up to sixteen weeks of unpaid leave in a twenty-four-month period to those employees who have been employed for twelve months and who have worked at least 1,000 hours in the prior twelve months for: the birth or adoption of a child; to care for the serious illness of a child, spouse or parent; or for the illness of the employee. The law, however, permits the employer to require employees to exhaust all other accrued time off before being permitted such leave; provided further, that upon return from such leave, the employer must reinstate the employee to the position he or she held prior to the leave or to an equivalent position with equivalent pay and, in the event such is not available, to an equivalent position with all accrued seniority, retirement, fringe benefits, and other service credits.[6]

AIDS testing and confidentiality: Connecticut law requires an informed consent of a person prior to the administration of an AIDS test and forbids the disclosure of such test unless authorized by the person tested or otherwise required to be released to certain health care providers or agencies.[7]

[78.06] WAGE AND HOUR LAWS

Real estate commissions equate to wages: A Connecticut Court has held real estate commissions to be "wages" under Connecticut General Statutes, Section 31-72, even though real estate salespersons are exempt from coverage under Connecticut's Workers' Compensation and Unemployment Compensation laws.[8]

[78.06A] WELFARE AND BENEFITS LAWS

Insurance coverage for alcohol/drug abuse treatment: Connecticut laws require insurance policies to provide mandatory coverage of employees undergoing treatment for alcohol and/or drug abuse.[9]

Insurance coverage for newborns: Section 38a-515 of the Connecticut General Statutes mandates that employee health-related insurance policies include coverage of newborns of employees.

Insurance coverage for mental health treatment: Connecticut laws require that all employee-related insurance policies cover treatment for mental health.[10]

State holidays: Connecticut statutes provide that the following are state recognized holidays: New Year's Day, Martin Luther King's Birthday, Washington's Birthday, Lincoln's Birthday, Memorial Day, July 4th, Labor Day, Columbus Day, Veteran's Day, Thanksgiving, and Christmas Day.[11]

[78.08] UNEMPLOYMENT COMPENSATION LAWS

Aside from private sector employers generally subject to the coverage of Connecticut's Unemployment Compensation Laws, agricultural, nonprofit, state government agencies and employers of domestic employees (one or more employees in any thirteen weeks of a calendar year) also are subject to the unemployment laws.[12] Connecticut law disqualifies the following individuals from collecting unemployment compensation: recipients of pension, retirement pay or other such annuities and recipients of unemployment benefits from federal and other state unemployment compensation funds.[13]

Connecticut unemployment compensation laws do not provide coverage to such employees as: persons self-employed; railroad employees; wholly commissioned insurance and real estate agents; persons employed by spouse or child; minor employed by parent; casual labor; patients and student nurses employed by hospitals; hospital interns; minor newspaper carriers; students and spouses of students providing employment services to schools, colleges and universities, if under college work study program and students at nonprofit or public education institutions who are in full-time work study programs.[14]

[78.10] EMPLOYMENT-AT-WILL DEVELOPMENTS

Employee handbook—disclaimer upheld: A Connecticut Court of Appeals has dismissed a former employee's claim for breach of an implied contract based on disciplinary provisions in an employee handbook, the Court ruling that the handbook contained a contractual disclaimer sufficient to sustain the ongoing employment-at-will relationship between the employer and the employee.[15]

Two-year salary no employment contract: A state superior court has held that an offer letter from the defendant employer to the plaintiff guaranteeing a minimum commission of $18,000 for his first two years of employment did not constitute an employment contract for such two-year period.[16]

After acquired evidence limits front pay: A Connecticut Appellate Court has held that a jury must determine whether post-discharge discovery of the plaintiff's misconduct, in placing poison ivy on a plant manager's toilet seat which caused a severe allergic reaction to the manager, was sufficient reason to have caused the plaintiff's dismissal.[17]

Implied employment contracts—front pay inapplicable: A Connecticut Appellate Court has held that remedies for a breach of an implied employment contract, based upon language in a personnel policy manual, does not include equitable relief, such as front pay.[18]

Public policy exception—unavailable where statutory remedies exist: A Connecticut Superior Court has held that a wrongful discharge lawsuit based on a violation of public policy is permissible only if other remedies are unavailable.[19]

[78.12] TIME LIMITATIONS FOR FILING WRONGFUL DISCHARGE LAWSUITS

Connecticut statutes provide that time limits for litigants to file wrongful employment claims are: two years for defamation, three years for lawsuits based upon discharges in violation of public policy, and three years for discharge in violation of implied contracts causes of action.[20]

SUPPLEMENTAL NOTES TO CHAPTER 78

1. Connecticut General Statutes, Section 46a-60.
2. Connecticut General Statutes, Sections 46a-54, *et. seq.*
3. Connecticut General Statutes, Sections 46a-94, 46a-94a and 46a-95.
4. Connecticut General Statutes, Section 46a-86.
5. Connecticut General Statutes, Sections 4-61u; 4-61w, 4a-60 and 46a-58.
6. Connecticut General Statutes, Sections 31-51cc, *et seq.*
7. Connecticut General Statutes, Sections 19a-581, *et seq.*
8. *Tianti v. William Raveis Real Estate*, 651 A2d 1286 (Conn., 1995).
9. Connecticut General Statutes, Sections 38a-533, 38a-539.
10. Connecticut General Statutes, Section 38a-514.
11. Connecticut General Statutes, Section 1-4.
12. Connecticut General Statutes, Section 31-222.
13. Connecticut General Statutes, Sections 31-227.
14. Connecticut General Statutes, Sections 31-222, 31-235 and 31-236.
15. *Markgraff v. Hospitality Equity Inv. Inc.*, No. 30 85 01 (Conn. Supr. Ct—Judicial District of Danbury, 2-18-93).
16. *Strouch v. CDI Corporation—Northeast*, (Conn. Super, 1994).
17. *Preston v. Phelps Dodge Copper Products Company*, 35 Conn. App. 850 (Conn. App., 9-6-94).
18. *Barry v. Post-Seal International, Inc.*, 36 Conn. App. 1 (Conn. App., 9-13-94).
19. *Faulkner v. Sikorsky Aircraft*, (Conn. Super. Ct., 3-30-94).
20. Connecticut General Statutes, Sections 52-576, 52-577, 52-597.

79

Delaware Labor and Employment Laws

[79.05] REGULATION OF EMPLOYMENT PRACTICES

Bona fide exceptions to prohibited employment practices: Delaware statutes provide that bona fide seniority systems, bona fide occupational qualifications and bona fide benefits programs are legally recognized exceptions to otherwise unfair employment practices.[1]

EEOC—certified deferral: Delaware statutes provide that the Delaware Labor Department is to serve as a certified deferral agency of the Equal Employment Opportunity Commission relative to fair employment claims filed with the EEOC.[2]

Court review of agency decisions: Section 19-712 of the Delaware Code permits claimants and respondents to adverse decisions by the Delaware Commission for Human Rights a right of review to applicable courts within the state.

AIDS testing and confidentiality: Delaware law requires an informed consent of a person prior to the administration of an AIDS test and forbids the disclosure of such tests without the authorization of the person tested unless otherwise required to be released to certain health care providers or agencies.[3]

[79.06A] WELFARE AND BENEFITS LAWS

Insurance coverage for newborns: Delaware statutes mandate that employee health-related insurance policies include coverage of newborns of employees.[4]

State holidays: Delaware statutes provide that the following are state recognized holidays: New Year's Day, Martin Luther King's Birthday, Washington's Birthday, Memorial Day, July 4th, Labor Day, Columbus Day, Veteran's Day, Thanksgiving Day, and Christmas Day.[5]

[79.08] UNEMPLOYMENT COMPENSATION LAWS

Aside from private sector employers generally subject to the coverage of Delaware's Unemployment Compensation Laws, agricultural, nonprofit, state government agencies and employers of domestic employees also are subject to the unemployment laws.[6]

Delaware law disqualifies the following individuals from collecting unemployment compensation: recipients of pension, retirement pay or other such annuities and recipients of unemployment benefits from federal and other state unemployment compensation funds.[7]

Delaware's unemployment compensation laws do not provide coverage to such employees as: persons self-employed; railroad employees; wholly commissioned insurance and real estate agents; persons employed by spouse or child; minor employed by a parent; patients employed by hospitals; and students at non-profit or public education institutions that are in full-time work study programs.[8]

[79.09] WORKERS' COMPENSATION LAWS

Retaliatory discharge unlawful: A Delaware statute makes it unlawful for an employer or its agents to discharge, retaliate or discriminate against an employee because of his or her filing, or attempting to file, a claim for workers' compensation benefits, because of an employee's reporting an employer's failure to comply with the law or because of an employee's testifying in a workers' compensation hearing.[9]

[79.11] TORT ACTIONS

Fraud: A Delaware Court has ruled an employer not liable for misrepresenting that a job was permanent where the employee admitted knowing that the job was temporary and termination could occur at any time.[10]

[79.12] TIME LIMITATIONS FOR FILING WRONGFUL DISCHARGE LAWSUITS

Delaware statutes provide that time limits for litigants to file wrongful employment claims are: two years for defamation, two years for lawsuits based on wrongful discharge in violation of public policy, and three years for discharge in violation of implied contracts causes of action.[11]

SUPPLEMENTAL NOTES TO CHAPTER 79

1. Delaware Code, Section 19-711.
2. Delaware Code, Section 19-712.
3. Delaware Code, Chapter 12, 16:1201, *et seq.*
4. Delaware Code, Section 18-3511.
5. Delaware Code, Section 19-531.
6. Delaware Code, Section 19-3302.
7. Delaware Code, Sections 19-3313, 19-3314, 19-3315.
8. Delaware Code, Sections 19-3302, 19-3315.

9. Delaware Code, Section 19-2365.

10. *Merrill v. Crothall-American, Inc.*, 606 A.2d 96 (Del., 1992).

11. Delaware Code, Sections 10-8106, 10-8111 and 10-8119.

80

District of Columbia Labor and Employment Laws

[80.05] REGULATION OF EMPLOYMENT PRACTICES

Bona fide exceptions to prohibited employment practices: District of Columbia statutes provide that bona fide seniority systems, bona fide occupational qualifications and bona fide benefits programs are legally recognized exceptions to otherwise unfair employment practices.[1]

EEOC—certified deferral: District of Columbia statutes provide that the D.C. Office of Human Rights is to serve as a certified deferral agency of the Equal Employment Opportunity Commission relative to fair employment claims filed with the EEOC.[2]

Court review of agency decisions: District of Columbia statutes permit claimants and respondents to adverse decisions by the D.C. Office of Human Rights a right of review to applicable courts within the state.[3]

Available remedies for fair employment violations: District of Columbia statutes provide for backpay and compensatory damages for claimants who prevail in claims before the D.C. Office of Human Rights.[4]

Affirmative action programs (state employment):   District of Columbia law requires each D.C. agency to adopt an affirmative action plan to identify persons with protected characteristics who are underutilized in their employment and establish affirmative programs to overcome any such underutilization.[5]

Arbitration agreement enforceable: A District of Columbia Court of Appeals has held the D.C. Human Rights Act does not preclude an agreement between an employee and an employer to arbitrate employment discrimination claims and that the Civil Rights Act of 1991 did not overrule the enforceability of agreements to arbitrate discrimination claims.[6]

Family medical leave: District of Columbia law requires employers with fifty or more employees to provide up to sixteen weeks of unpaid leave during any twenty-four-month period to those employees who have worked at least 1,000 hours in the twelve months preceding the leave for the birth, adoption or placement in foster care, placement of a child for whom the employee assumes permanent parental responsibility, to care for a family member with a serious medical condition or for the illness of the employee.[7]

[80.06] WELFARE AND BENEFITS LAWS

Insurance coverage for alcohol/drug abuse treatment: District of Columbia law requires insurance policies to provide mandatory coverage for alcohol and/or drug abuse treatment.[8]

Insurance coverage for newborns: District of Columbia statutes mandate that employee health-related insurance policies include coverage of newborns of employees.[9]

Insurance coverage from mental health treatment: District of Columbia laws require insurance companies to include coverage for the treatment of mental health conditions in employer sponsored insurance policies.[10]

State holidays: District of Columbia laws provide that the following are state recognized holidays: New Year's Day, Martin Luther King's Birthday, Washington's Birthday, Memorial Day, July 4th, Labor Day, Columbus Day, Veteran's Day, Thanksgiving Day, and Christmas Day.[11]

[80.08] UNEMPLOYMENT COMPENSATION LAWS

Aside from private sector employers generally subject to the coverage of Unemployment Compensation Laws, agricultural, nonprofit, state government agencies and employers of domestic employees also are subject to the unemployment laws.[12] District of Columbia law disqualifies the following individuals from collecting unemployment compensation: recipients of pension, retirement pay or other such annuities, and recipients of unemployment benefits from federal and other state unemployment compensation funds.[13]

District of Columbia unemployment compensation laws do not provide coverage to such employees as: persons self-employed; employees of commercial fishing vessels; railroad employees; wholly commissioned insurance and real estate agents; persons employed by spouse or child; minors employed by a parent; casual labor; patients employed by hospitals; hospital interns; minor newspaper carriers; students and spouses of students providing employment services to schools, colleges, and universities, if under college work study program and students at nonprofit or public education institutions who are in full-time work study programs.[14]

[80.10] EMPLOYMENT-AT-WILL DEVELOPMENTS

Employee handbook—disclaimer upheld: The District of Columbia Court of Appeals affirmed a court below in its decision to dismiss an employee's lawsuit of wrongful discharge for failure to comply with policies and procedures in an employee handbook, the court ruling that the employee handbook contained a contractual disclaimer sufficient to sustain an ongoing employment-at-will relationship between the employer and the employee.[15]

Whistle-blower protection—court testimony not covered: A District of Columbia Court of Appeals has held that the dismissal of a nurse who contended her discharge occurred because she served as an expert witness in a medical malpractice case did not provide the basis for an actionable public policy type lawsuit.[16]

[80.12] TIME LIMITATIONS FOR FILING WRONGFUL DISCHARGE LAWSUITS

District of Columbia statutes provide that time limits for litigants to file wrongful employment claims are: one year for defamation, three years for both lawsuits based on wrongful discharge in violation of public policy, and for discharges in violation of implied contracts causes of action.[17]

SUPPLEMENTAL NOTES TO CHAPTER 80

1. D.C. Code, Section 1-2513.

2. D.C. Code, Section 1-2541.

3. D.C. Code, Section 1-2547.

4. D.C. Code, Section 1-2553.

5. D.C. Code, Sections 1-607.1, 1-1146, 1-2524.

6. *Benefits Communication Corp. v. Klieforth,* (D.C. Ct. App., 6-9-94).

7. D.C. Code, Section 36.

8. D.C. Code, Sections 35-2302, 35-2303.

9. D.C. Code, Sections 35-1101, 35-1102.

10. D.C. Code, Sections 35-2302, 35-2304, 35-2305.

11. D.C. Code, Section 28-2701.

12. D.C. Code, Section 46-101.

13. D.C. Code, Sections 46-108, 46-111.

14. D.C. Code, Section 46-101.

15. *Smith v. Union Life Insurance Co.,* No 91-CV-1239 (DC CA, 2-19-93).

16. *Carl v. Children's Hospital,* (D.C. Ct. App., 1995).

17. D.C. Code, Section 12-301; see also: *Goos v. National Ass'n of Realtors,* 715 F.Supp. 2 (D.D.C., 1989).

81

Florida Labor and Employment Laws

[81.05] REGULATION OF EMPLOYMENT PRACTICES

Bona fide exceptions to prohibited employment practices: Florida statutes provide that bona fide seniority systems, bona fide occupational qualifications, and bona fide benefits programs are legally recognized exceptions to otherwise unfair employment practices.[1]

EEOC—certified deferral: Florida statutes provide that the Florida Human Relations Commission is to serve as a certified deferral agency of the Equal Employment Opportunity Commission relative to fair employment claims filed with the EEOC.[2]

Court review of agency decisions: Florida statutes permit claimants and respondents to adverse decisions by the Florida Human Rights Commission a right of review to applicable courts within the state.[3]

Available remedies for fair employment violations: Florida statutes provide for punitive damages ($100,000 cap) when deemed appropriate, as well as for backpay and compensatory damages for claimants who prevail in claims before the Florida Human Rights Commission.[4]

Affirmative action programs (state employment): Florida law requires each state agency to adopt an affirmative action plan to identify persons with protected characteristics who are underutilized in their employment and establish affirmative action programs to overcome any such underutilization.[5]

Right of privacy protects off-duty smokers (public sector): A Florida appellate court has held that a city's interest to reduce employee insurance costs, etc., by screening-out applicants based on tobacco consumption was not sufficiently compelling to outweigh an applicant's reasonable expectation of privacy relative to details regarding his or her personal rights.[6]

Whistle-blowing statute—not retroactive: The Supreme Court of Florida, in reversing a lower court, has ruled that the Whistle-Blower's Act of 1991 that prohibits private sector employers from retaliating against employees who disclose violations of the law by their employer or refuse to participate in such violations, is not retroactive in its applicability.[7]

[81.06A] WELFARE AND BENEFITS LAWS

Insurance coverage for alcohol/drug abuse treatment: Florida laws require insurance policies to provide an option to cover alcohol and/or drug abuse treatment.[8]

Insurance coverage for newborns: Florida statutes mandate that employee health-related insurance policies include coverage of newborns of employees.[9]

State holidays: Florida statutes provide that the following are state recognized holidays: New Year's Day, Martin Luther King's Birthday, Washington's Birthday, Lincoln's Birthday, Memorial Day, July 4th, Labor Day, Veteran's Day, Thanksgiving Day, and Christmas Day.[10]

Insurance coverage for mental health treatment: Florida law requires insurance policies to provide an option to employers to include coverage for mental health treatment.[11]

[81.07] SAFETY AND HEALTH LAWS

Off-duty smoking protected (public sector):   A Florida Appellate Court has held that Florida's Constitution expressly recognizes and protects an individual's right of privacy and when there is a legitimate expectation of privacy—such as in the nature of off-duty smoking. The City of North Miami violated applicants' constitutional rights by screening applicants based on tobacco consumption.[12]

[81.08] UNEMPLOYMENT COMPENSATION LAWS

Aside from private sector employers generally subject to the coverage of Florida's Unemployment Compensation Laws, agricultural, nonprofit, the state government agencies, and employers of domestic employees also are subject to the unemployment laws.[13]

Florida law disqualifies the following individuals from collecting unemployment compensation: recipients of pension, retirement pay or other such annuities, and recipients of unemployment benefits from federal and other state unemployment compensation funds.[14]

Florida's unemployment compensation laws do not provide coverage to such employees as: persons self-employed; employees of commercial fishing vessels; railroad employees; wholly commissioned insurance and real estate agents; persons employed by spouse or child; minors employed by a parent; casual labor; student nurses employed by hospitals; hospital interns; minor newspaper carriers and students at nonprofit or public education institutions that are in full-time work study programs.[15]

[81.10] EMPLOYMENT-AT-WILL DEVELOPMENTS

Whistle-blowing—statute of limitations: A Florida Appellate Court has ruled that a 1991 Amendment to the Florida Whistle-blowing Law covering private sector employees who disclose or threaten to disclose employer violations of law, rule, or regulation or who object to or refuse to participate in any conduct that would constitute a violation of a law, rule, or regulation should be applied retroactively in that the amended law not only provided a private remedy but also was enacted to promote public good.[16]

[81.11] TORT ACTIONS

Negligent misrepresentation: A Federal District Court, applying Florida law, has held that there is no requirement to establish a preexisting duty of the employer to disclose information in a negligent misrepresentation cause of action.[17]

[81.12] TIME LIMITATIONS FOR FILING WRONGFUL DISCHARGE LAWSUITS

Florida statutes provide that time limits for litigants to file wrongful employment claims are four years for defamation and four years for discharge in violation of implied contracts causes of action.[18]

SUPPLEMENTAL NOTES TO CHAPTER 81

1. Florida Statutes, Section 760.10.
2. Florida Statutes, Sections 760.06, 760.11.
3. Florida Statutes, Section 760.11.
4. Florida Statutes, Sections 760.07, 760.11
5. Florida Statutes, Section 110.112.
6. *Kurtz v. The City of North Miami*, No. 92-2038 (Fla. Dist. Ct. of App., 11-12-93).
7. *Arrow Air, Inc. v. Walsh*, (Fla. Sup. Ct., 1994).
8. Florida Statutes, Section 627.669.
9. Florida Statutes, Sections 627-6562, 627-6575, 627-6578, 627-6579.
10. Florida Statutes, Sections 683.10–683.21.
11. Florida Statutes, Section 627.688.
12. *Kurtz v. The City of North Miami*, No. 92-2038 (Fla. Dist. Ct. App., 11-12-93).
13. Florida Statutes, Section 443.036.
14. Florida Statutes, Sections 443.036, 443.071, 443.091 and 443.101.
15. Florida Statutes, Section 443.036.
16. *Walsh v. Arror Air*, No. 90-1846 (Fla. Ct. App., 5-11-93).
17. *Golden v. Complete Holdings, Inc.*, 818 F. Supp. 1495 (M.D. Fla., 1993).
18. Florida Statutes, Section 95-11.

82

Georgia Labor and Employment Laws

[82.05] REGULATION OF EMPLOYMENT PRACTICES

Bona fide exceptions to prohibited employment practices: Georgia statutes provide that bona fide seniority systems, bona fide occupational qualifications, and bona fide benefits programs are legally recognized exceptions to otherwise unfair employment practices relative to public employment.[1]

Affirmative action programs (state employment): Georgia permits each state agency to adopt an affirmative action plan to identify persons with protected characteristics who are underutilized in their employment and establish affirmative action programs to overcome any such underutilization.[2]

[82.06A] WELFARE AND BENEFITS LAWS

Insurance coverage for mental health treatment: Georgia law requires insurance policies to provide an option to employers to include coverage for mental health treatment.[3]

Insurance coverage for newborns: Georgia statutes mandate that employee health-related insurance policies include coverage of newborns of employees.[4]

State holidays: Georgia statutes provide that the following are state recognized holidays: New Year's Day, Martin Luther King's Birthday, Washington's Birthday, Memorial Day, July 4th, Labor Day, Columbus Day, Veteran's Day, Thanksgiving Day, and Christmas Day.[5]

[82.08] UNEMPLOYMENT COMPENSATION LAWS

Aside from private sector employers generally subject to the coverage of Georgia's Unemployment Compensation Laws, agricultural, nonprofit, the state government agencies and employers of domestic employees also are subject to the unemployment laws.[6]

Georgia law disqualifies the following individuals from collecting unemployment compensation: recipients of pension, retirement pay or other such annuities and recipients of unemployment benefits from federal and other state unemployment compensation funds.[7]

Georgia's unemployment compensation laws do not provide coverage to such employees as: persons self-employed; employees of commercial fishing vessels; railroad employees; wholly commissioned insurance and real estate agents; persons employed by parent, spouse or child; casual labor; patients employed by hospitals; hospital interns; minor newspaper carriers; students and spouses of students providing employment services to schools, colleges, and universities, if under college work study program and students at nonprofit or public education institutions that are in full-time work study programs.[8]

[82.11] TORT ACTIONS

Bad faith breach of contract: A Georgia Appellate Court has ruled that, despite the employer's contention that it had discharged the plaintiff for making 271 personal long-distance telephone calls on company time, the employer had terminated the plaintiff's employment in a bad faith breach of a contract between the parties, further permitting the plaintiff a recovery of attorney's fees for bad faith performance by the employer.[9]

Negligent hiring: A Georgia Court of Appeals, in reversing a lower court and permitting the plaintiff's action against the defendant for negligent hiring to proceed, stated that a jury could find that the defendant trucking company failed to exercise the requisite duty of care in investigating the driving record of its employee who injured the plaintiff in a traffic accident, given the evidence that the employee had a record of numerous driving violations.[10]

[82.12] TIME LIMITATIONS FOR FILING WRONGFUL DISCHARGE LAWSUITS

Georgia statutes provide that time limits for litigants to file wrongful employment claims are: one year for defamation and four years for discharge in violation of implied contracts causes of action.[11]

SUPPLEMENTAL NOTES TO CHAPTER 82

1. Georgia Code Annotated, Sections 45-19-33 and 45-19-35.
2. Georgia Code Annotated, Section 45-19-35.
3. Georgia Code Annotated, Section 33-24-28.1.
4. Georgia Code Annotated, Sections 33-24-22, 33-24-24 and 33-24-28.
5. Georgia Code Annotated, Sections 1-4-1, 1-4-2, 1-4-5 and 1-4-10.
6. Georgia Code Annotated, Sections 34-8-33 and 34-8-35.
7. Georgia Code Annotated, Sections 34-8-193 and 34-8-195.
8. Georgia Code Annotated, Section 34-8-35.
9. *Building Materials Wholesale, Inc. v. Reeves*, 433 S.E.2d 346 (GA Ct. App., 1993).
10. *Smith v. Tommy Roberts Trucking Co.*, 435 S.E.2d 54 (GA Ct. App., 11-19-93).
11. Georgia Code Annotated, Sections 9-3-25 and 9-3-33; See also: *Loftin v. Brown*, 346 S.E.2d 114 (Ga. App., 1986).

83

Hawaii Labor and Employment Laws

[83.05] REGULATION OF EMPLOYMENT PRACTICES

Bona fide exceptions to prohibited employment practices: Hawaii statutes provide that bona fide seniority systems, bona fide occupational qualifications and bona fide benefits programs are legally recognized exceptions to otherwise unfair employment practices.[1]

EEOC—certified deferral: Hawaii statutes provide that the Hawaii Civil Rights Commission (Hawaii Department of Labor and Industrial Relations) is to serve as a certified deferral agency of the Equal Employment Opportunity Commission relative to fair employment claims filed with the EEOC.[2]

Court review of agency decisions: Hawaii statutes permit claimants and respondents to adverse decisions by the Hawaii Civil Rights Commission a right of review to applicable courts within the state.

Available remedies for fair employment violations: Hawaii statutes provide for punitive damages when deemed appropriate, as well as for back pay (two years only) and compensatory damages for claimants who prevail in claims before the Hawaii Civil Rights Commission.[3]

Marital status discrimination—no relative policy: The Hawaii Supreme Court has held that discharging an employee because he or she marries another employee working in the same department is marital status discrimination, even though the employee discharged had less seniority than the other, a policy the employer contended was an objective one.[4]

[83.06A] WELFARE AND BENEFITS LAWS

Insurance coverage for alcohol/drug abuse treatment: Hawaii laws require insurance policies to provide mandatory coverage for alcohol and/or drug abuse treatment.[5]

Insurance coverage for newborns: Hawaii statutes mandate that employee health-related insurance policies include coverage of newborns of employees.[6]

Insurance coverage for mental health treatment: Hawaii statutes require insurance policies to include coverage for the treatment of mental health conditions.[7]

State holidays: Hawaii statutes provide that the following are state recognized holidays: New Year's Day, Martin Luther King's Birthday, Washington's Birthday, Memorial Day, July 4th, Labor Day, Veteran's Day, Thanksgiving Day, and Christmas Day.[8]

[83.08] UNEMPLOYMENT COMPENSATION LAWS

Aside from private sector employers generally subject to the coverage of Hawaii Unemployment Compensation Laws, agricultural, nonprofit, the state government agencies and employers of domestic employees (if employer pays more than $225 to one employee in a calendar quarter) also are subject to the unemployment laws.[9]

Hawaii law disqualifies the following individuals from collecting unemployment compensation: recipients of pension, retirement pay or other such annuities, and recipients of unemployment benefits from federal and other state unemployment compensation funds.[10]

Hawaii unemployment compensation laws do not provide coverage to such employees as: persons self-employed; employees of commercial fishing vessels; railroad employees; wholly commissioned insurance and real estate agents; persons employed by spouse or child; minors employed by a parent; casual labor; hospital interns; or minor newspaper carriers.[11]

[83.12] TIME LIMITATIONS FOR FILING WRONGFUL DISCHARGE LAWSUITS

Hawaii statutes provide that time limits for litigants to file wrongful employment claims are: two years for defamation, two years for lawsuits based on discharge in violation of public policy, and six years for discharge in violation of implied contracts causes of action.[12]

SUPPLEMENTAL NOTES TO CHAPTER 83

1. Hawaii Revised Statutes, Section 378.3.
2. Hawaii Revised Statutes, Sections 368-1, *et seq.*
3. Hawaii Revised Statutes, Sections 368-17, 378-5.
4. *Ross v. Stouffer Hotel Company*, 879 P.2d 1037 (Hawaii Sup. Ct., 1994).
5. Hawaii Revised Statutes, Sections 431m-2, 431m-4.
6. Hawaii Revised Statutes, Section 431:10A-115.
7. Hawaii Revised Statutes, Sections 431m-2, 431m-4.
8. Hawaii Revised Statutes, Section 801, 8-2.
9. Hawaii Revised Statutes, Sections 383, 383-2, 383-7 and 383-9.
10. Hawaii Revised Statutes, Sections 283-23, *et seq.*
11. Hawaii Revised Statutes, Sections 383-7 and 383-29.
12. Hawaii Revised Statutes, Sections 657-1, 657-4, 657-7 and 662-4.

84

Idaho Labor and Employment Laws

[84.05] REGULATION OF EMPLOYMENT PRACTICES

Bona fide exceptions to prohibited employment practices: Idaho statutes provide that bona fide seniority systems, bona fide occupational qualifications, and bona fide benefits programs are legally recognized exceptions to otherwise unfair employment practices.[1]

EEOC—certified deferral: Idaho statutes provide that the Idaho Commission on Human Rights is to serve as a certified deferral agency of the Equal Employment Opportunity Commission relative to fair employment claims filed with the EEOC.[2]

Court review of agency decisions: Idaho statutes permit claimants and respondents to adverse decisions by the Idaho Commission on Human Rights a right of review to applicable courts within the state.[3]

Available remedies for fair employment violations: Idaho statutes provide for punitive damages ($1,500 cap), when deemed appropriate, as well as for back pay (two years only) and compensatory damages for claimants who prevail in claims before the Idaho Commission on Human Rights.[4]

[84.06A] WELFARE AND BENEFITS LAWS

State holidays: Idaho statutes provide that the following are state recognized holidays: New Year's Day, Washington's Birthday, Memorial Day, July 4th, Labor Day, Veteran's Day, Thanksgiving Day, and Christmas Day.[5]

[84.08] UNEMPLOYMENT COMPENSATION LAWS

Aside from private sector employers generally subject to the coverage of Idaho's Unemployment Compensation Laws, agricultural, nonprofit, the state government agencies and employers of domestic employees also are subject to the unemployment laws.[6]

Idaho law disqualifies the following individuals from collecting unemployment compensation: recipients of pension, retirement pay or other such annuities and recipients of unemployment benefits from federal and other state unemployment compensation funds.[7]

Idaho's unemployment compensation laws do not provide coverage to such employees as: persons self-employed; employees of commercial fishing vessels; railroad employees; wholly commissioned insurance and real estate agents;

persons employed by spouse or child; minors employed by parent; patients employed by hospitals; hospital interns; minor newspaper carriers; and students at nonprofit or public education institutions that are in full-time work study programs.[8]

[84.10] EMPLOYMENT-AT-WILL DEVELOPMENTS

Public policy exceptions—independent contractor: The Supreme Court of Idaho has held that a cause of action based on termination of employment in violation of public policy—as well as recovery of damages for breach of the covenant of good faith and fair dealing in the employment context—is not available to sales agents working as independent contractors in that wrongful discharge claims are based on the employer-employee relationship.[9]

Covenant of good faith and fair dealing: The Idaho Supreme Court held that properly drafted disclaimers in an employee handbook may bar an employee's right to successfully prosecute a wrongful discharge claim based upon an alleged breach of the implied covenant of good faith and fair dealing as well as an alleged breach of an implied employment contract.[10]

[84.12] TIME LIMITATIONS FOR FILING WRONGFUL DISCHARGE LAWSUITS

Idaho statutes provide that time limits for litigants to file wrongful employment claims are: two years for defamation, three years for lawsuits based on discharges in violation of public policy, and four years for discharge in violation of implied contracts causes of action.[11]

SUPPLEMENTAL NOTES TO CHAPTER 84

1. Idaho Code, Section 67-5910.

2. Idaho Code, Sections 67-5906, 67-5907.

3. Idaho Code, Section 67-5908.

4. Idaho Code, Section 67-5908.

5. Idaho Code, Section 73-108.

6. Idaho Code, Sections 72-1304, 72A-1315 and 72-1322C.

7. Idaho Code, Sections 72-1312 and 72-1366.

8. Idaho Code, Sections 72-1316 and 72-1316A.

9. *Ostrander v. Farm Bureau Ins. Co. of Idaho*, No. 19225 (Idaho Sup. Ct., 3-24-93).

10. *Mitchell v. Zilog, Inc.*, (Idaho Sup. Ct., 4-18-94).

11. Idaho Code, Sections 5-217, 5-219.

85

Illinois Labor and Employment Laws

[85.05] REGULATION OF EMPLOYMENT PRACTICES

Bona fide exceptions to prohibited employment practices: Illinois statutes provide that bona fide seniority systems, bona fide occupational qualifications and bona fide benefits programs are legally recognized exceptions to otherwise unfair employment practices.[1]

EEOC—certified deferral: Illinois statutes provide that the Illinois Department of Human Rights is to serve as a certified deferral agency of the Equal Employment Opportunity Commission relative to fair employment claims filed with the EEOC.[2]

Court review of agency decisions: Illinois statutes permit claimants and respondents to adverse decisions by the Illinois Department of Human Rights a right of review to applicable courts within the state.[3]

Available remedies for fair employment violations: Illinois statutes provide for backpay and compensatory damages for claimants who prevail in claims before the Illinois Department of Human Rights.[4]

Affirmative action programs (state employment): Illinois law requires each state agency to adopt an affirmative action plan to identify persons with protected characteristics who are underutilized in their employment and establish affirmative action programs to overcome any such underutilization.[5]

Anti-nepotism policy lawful: An Illinois Court of Appeals has held that an employer's policy prohibiting an employee to be under the supervision of his or her spouse does not violate the state marital status anti-discrimination law in that the policy does not differentiate on the basis of marital status, but rather differentiates between individuals married to other employees and those not married to other employees.[6]

Termination on the basis of suing former employer: An Illinois Appellate Court has held that a withdrawal of an employment offer to a new employee, in retaliation of his having sued his former employer for age and disability discrimination, violated the Illinois Human Rights Act.[7]

[85.06A] WELFARE AND BENEFITS LAWS

Insurance coverage for alcohol abuse treatment: Illinois laws require insurance policies to provide mandatory coverage for employees undergoing treatment for alcoholism.[8]

Insurance coverage for mental health treatment: Illinois law requires insurance policies to provide an option to employers to include coverage for mental health treatment.[9]

State holidays: Illinois statutes provide that the following are state recognized holidays: New Year's Day, Martin Luther King's Birthday, Washington's Birthday, Lincoln's Birthday, Memorial Day, July 4th, Labor Day, Columbus Day, Veteran's Day, Thanksgiving Day, and Christmas Day.[10]

[85.08] UNEMPLOYMENT COMPENSATION LAWS

Aside from private sector employers generally subject to the coverage of Illinois's Unemployment Compensation Laws, agricultural, nonprofit, the state government agencies and employers of domestic employees also are subject to the unemployment laws.[11]

Illinois law disqualifies the following individuals from collecting unemployment benefits: recipients of pension, retirement pay or other such annuities and recipients of unemployment benefits from federal and other state unemployment compensation funds.[12]

Illinois' unemployment compensation laws do not provide coverage to such employees as: persons self-employed; employees of commercial fishing vessels (unless operating office is located in Illinois); railroad employees; wholly commissioned insurance and real estate agents; persons employed by spouse or child; minors employed by parent; student nurses employed by hospitals; hospital interns; minor newspaper carriers; students and spouses of students providing employment services to schools, colleges, and universities, if under college work study program and students at nonprofit or public education institutions that are in full-time work study programs.[13]

[85.10] EMPLOYMENT-AT-WILL DEVELOPMENTS

Implied contract—handbook: An Illinois Appellate Court has ruled that an employee handbook may constitute an employment contract if it meets a three-prong test: (a) its language is sufficiently clear to suggest an offer has been made, (b) the handbook has been disseminated in such a manner as to ensure employee awareness of its contents, and (c) the plaintiff accepted the employer's offer by continuing to work after learning of the offer.[14]

Implied contract—oral statements: An Illinois Appellate Court has ruled that oral statements that create a reasonable belief that an employee will be entitled to specific disciplinary guidelines prior to termination may create an implied contract to follow such guidelines, thus modifying the employment-at-will relationship between the employee and his or her employer.[15]

Public policy—social relationship: A federal district court, applying Illinois law, has held that the firing of an employee because of her social relationship with a male co-worker whom she married after her termination, did not constitute a wrongful discharge in violation of public policy and, further, any claim alleging marital status discrimination was actionable only through a formal charge with the Illinois Human Rights Commission in that such Commission has exclusive jurisdiction over marital status discrimination claims.[16]

Restrictive covenants—continuing employment: An Illinois Appellate Court, although recognizing that continued employment may be sufficient consideration for a post-employment restrictive covenant not to compete if such continued employment was for a substantial period of time following execution of such covenant, held that a continuation of employment of only seven months following execution of such a restrictive covenant by an employee in the instant case was insufficient and the covenant, therefore, unenforceable.[17]

[85.11] TORT ACTIONS

Negligent retention: An Illinois Appellate Court has upheld a jury's verdict that the defendant employer was liable to the plaintiff because of its negligent retention of an employee who, during his off-duty hours caught a person urinating on the employer's premises and, while chasing the perpetrator, threw the plaintiff's 4-year-old son into the air, the court concluding that knowledge of the employee's past similar behaviors could be imputed from the employee's co-workers to the employer.[18]

[85.12] TIME LIMITATIONS FOR FILING WRONGFUL DISCHARGE LAWSUITS

Illinois statutes provide that time limits for litigants to file wrongful employment claims are: one year for defamation, two years for discharge in violation of public policy, and five years for discharge in violation of implied contracts causes of action.[19]

SUPPLEMENTAL NOTES TO CHAPTER 85

1. 775 ILCS, Sections 5/2-101, *et seq.*
2. 775 ILCS, Section 5/7-101.
3. 775 ILCS, Section 5/7-101, *et seq.*
4. 775 ILCS, Section 5/7-101, *et seq.*
5. 775 ILCS, Section 5/2-105, *et seq.*
6. *Boaden v. Dept. of Law Enforcement*, 642 NE2d 1330 (Ill. Ct. App., 1994); but see contrary ruling in *River Bend School District No. 2 v. Illinois Human Rights Commission*, 597 NE2d 842 (Ill. App., 1992).
7. *Carter Coal Co. v. Illinois Human Rights Commission*, (Ill. Ct. App., 5-2-94).
8. Illinois Revised Statutes, Chapter 215, Section 5/367(7).

9. Illinois Revised Statutes, Chapter 215, Section 5/370C.

10. Illinois Revised Statutes, Chapter 5, Sections 490/10 and 490/95.

11. 820 ILCS Sections 405/205, 405/211.1, *et seq.*

12. 820 ILCS, Sections 405/601, *et seq.*

13. 820 ILCS, Sections 405/211, *et seq.*

14. *Harden v. Playboy Enterprises*, No. 1-92-1508 (Ill. App. Ct., 11-15-93).

15. *Evans v. Gurnee Inns, Inc.*, 645 Ill. App. 556 (1994).

16. *Talley v. Washington Inventory Service*, No. 93C 1653 (ND Ill., 5-18-93).

17. *Mid-Town Petroleum, Inc. v. Gowen*, 611 NE2d 1221 (Ill. App. Ct., 1993).

18. *Bryant v. Livigni*, 619 N.E.2d 550 (Ill., 1993) See also: *Geise v. Phoenix Co. of Chicago, Inc.*, 624 NE2d 807 (Ill., 1993) for similar recovery against an employer based on negligent hiring and retention of a manager who sexually harassed an employee.

19. Illinois Revised Statutes, Chapter 735, Section 5/13-201, 5/13-202 and 5/13-205.

86

Indiana Labor and Employment Laws

[86.05] REGULATION OF EMPLOYMENT PRACTICES

Bona fide exceptions to prohibited employment practices: Indiana statutes provide that bona fide seniority systems, bona fide occupational qualifications, and bona fide benefits programs are legally recognized exceptions to otherwise unfair employment practices.[1]

EEOC—certified deferral: Indiana statutes provide that the Indiana Civil Rights Commission is to serve as a certified deferral agency of the Equal Employment Opportunity Commission relative to fair employment claims filed with the EEOC.[2]

Affirmative action programs (state employment): Indiana law requires each state agency to adopt an affirmative action plan to identify persons with protected characteristics who are underutilized in their employment and establish affirmative action programs to overcome any such underutilization.[3]

Disability—manic depressive not qualified: An Indiana Court of Appeals has ruled that a manic depressive supervisor who was subject to drastic mood swings that could possibly result in unsafe conditions for detainees, as verified by professional experts, was not qualified for the position and not unlawfully terminated because of her disability.[4]

[86.06A] WELFARE AND BENEFITS LAWS

Insurance coverage for newborns: Indiana statutes mandate that employee health-related insurance policies include coverage of newborns—including adopted children—of employees.[5]

State holidays: Indiana statutes provide that the following are state recognized holidays: New Year's Day, Martin Luther King's Birthday, Washington's Birthday, Lincoln's Birthday, Memorial Day, July 4th, Labor Day, Columbus Day, Veteran's Day, Thanksgiving Day, and Christmas Day.[6]

[86.06] UNEMPLOYMENT COMPENSATION LAWS

Aside from private sector employers generally subject to the coverage of Indiana's Unemployment Compensation Laws, agricultural, nonprofit, the state government agencies and employers of domestic employees also are subject to the unemployment laws.[7]

Indiana law disqualifies individuals from collecting unemployment compensation who are recipients of pension, retirement pay or other such annuities, and recipients of unemployment benefits from federal and other state unemployment compensation funds.[8]

Indiana's unemployment compensation laws do not provide coverage to such employees as: persons self-employed; employees of commercial fishing vessels (unless operating office is located in Indiana); railroad employees; wholly commissioned real estate agents; persons employed by spouse or child; minors employed by a parent; student nurses employed by hospitals; hospital interns; minor newspaper carriers; newspaper distributors; students and spouses of students providing employment services to schools, colleges, and universities, if under college work study program and students at nonprofit or public education institutions who are in full-time work study programs.[9]

[86.10] EMPLOYMENT-AT-WILL DEVELOPMENTS

Promissory estoppel theory upheld: An Indiana Appellate Court has held that although a former employee could not pursue a breach of oral contract claim due to the Statute of Frauds, he could nonetheless pursue his claim under the doctrine of promissory estoppel in that he contended that he had relied to his detriment on the employer's promise that he would not be terminated except for good cause.[10]

[86.11] TORT ACTIONS

Constructive fraud: A Federal District Court, applying Indiana law, permitted a former employee's lawsuit against her employer to proceed, stating that an action for constructive fraud could be established if the plaintiff could prove that she had detrimentally relied on her supervisor to account for her time, accurately, the failure of which contributed to her discharge.[11]

[86.12] TIME LIMITATIONS FOR FILING WRONGFUL DISCHARGE LAWSUITS

Indiana statutes provide that time limits for litigants to file wrongful employment lawsuits are: two years each for defamation, discharge in violation of public policy, and discharge in violation of implied contracts causes of action.[12]

SUPPLEMENTAL NOTES TO CHAPTER 86

1. Indiana Code Annotated, Sections 22-9-2-10 and 22-9-2-11.
2. Indiana Code Annotated, Sections 22-1-2, *et seq.*
3. Indiana Code Annotated, Section 4-15-12-5.
4. *Indiana Civil Rights Comm. v. Delaware County Circuit Court*, (Ind. Ct. App., 1994).
5. Indiana Code Annotated, Section 27-8-5-21.
6. Indiana Code Annotated, Section 1-1-9-1.
7. Indiana Code Annotated, Sections 22-4-2-4, 22-4-6-1, 22-4-7-1, 22-4-7-2 and 22-4-8-2.
8. Indiana Code Annotated, Sections 22-4-15-1, *et seq.*
9. Indiana Code Annotated, Sections 22-4-5-1, 22-4-1, 22-4-8-1, *et seq.*
10. *Jarbore v. Landmark Community Newspapers of Indiana*, No. 62A04-9212-CV-454 (Ind. Ct. App., 12-21-93).
11. *Williams v. Syscon Int'l., Inc.*, (N.D. Ind., 1-12-93).
12. Indiana Code Annotated, Sections 34-1-2-1.5 and 34-1-2-2.

87

Iowa Labor and Employment Laws

[87.05] REGULATION OF EMPLOYMENT PRACTICES

Bona fide exceptions to prohibited employment practices: Iowa statutes provide that bona fide occupational qualifications and bona fide benefits programs are legally recognized exceptions to otherwise unfair employment practices.[1]

EEOC—certified deferral: Iowa statutes provide that the Iowa Civil Rights Commission is to serve as a certified deferral agency of the Equal Employment Opportunity Commission relative to fair employment claims filed with the EEOC.[2]

Court review of agency decisions: Iowa statutes permit claimants and respondents to adverse decisions by the Iowa Civil Rights Commission a right of review to applicable courts within the state.[3]

Available remedies for fair employment violations: Iowa statutes provide for backpay and compensatory damages for claimants who prevail in claims before the Iowa Civil Rights Commission.[4]

Affirmative action programs (state employment): Iowa law requires each state agency to adopt an affirmative action plan to identify persons with protected characteristics who are underutilized in their employment[5] and establish affirmative action programs to overcome any such underutilization.[6]

[87.06A] WELFARE AND BENEFITS LAWS

Insurance coverage for newborns: Iowa statutes mandate that employee health-related insurance policies include coverage of newborns of employees.[7]

State holidays: Iowa statutes provide that the following are state recognized holidays: New Year's Day, Martin Luther King's Birthday, Washington's Birthday, Lincoln's Birthday, Memorial Day, July 4th, Labor Day, Veteran's Day, Thanksgiving Day, and Christmas Day.[8]

[87.08] UNEMPLOYMENT COMPENSATION LAWS

Aside from private sector employers generally subject to the coverage of Iowa's Unemployment Compensation Laws, agricultural, nonprofit, the state government agencies, and employers of domestic employees also are subject to the unemployment laws.[9]

Iowa law disqualifies individuals from collecting unemployment compensation who are recipients of pension, retirement pay, or other such annuities, recipients of unemployment benefits from federal and other state unemployment compensation funds, recipients of vacation pay, recipients of temporary disability compensation, recipients of separation or severance pay, and recipients of wages in lieu of notice.[10]

Iowa's unemployment compensation laws do not provide coverage to such employees as: persons self-employed; employees of commercial fishing vessels; railroad employees; wholly commissioned real estate agents; persons employed by spouse or child; minors employed by a parent; students and spouses of students providing employment services to schools, colleges, and universities, if under college work study program and students at nonprofit or public education institutions who are in full-time work study programs.[11]

[87.10] EMPLOYMENT-AT-WILL DEVELOPMENTS

The Iowa Supreme Court has held that an employer's discharge of an employee in retaliation for the employee's filing for partial unemployment benefits violates public policy embodied in the state's unemployment compensation laws.[12]

[87.12] TIME LIMITATIONS FOR FILING WRONGFUL DISCHARGE LAWSUITS

Iowa statutes provide that time limits for litigants to file wrongful employment lawsuits are: one year for defamation, two years for discharge in violation of public policy, and two years for discharge in violation of implied contracts causes of action.[13]

SUPPLEMENTAL NOTES TO CHAPTER 87

1. Code of Iowa, Sections 216.6 and 216.13.
2. Code of Iowa, Sections 216.5, *et seq.*
3. Code of Iowa, Sections 17A.20, *et seq.*
4. Code of Iowa, Section 216.15.
5. Code of Iowa, Sections 19B.7, *et seq.*
6. *Monson v. Iowa Civil Rights Commission,* (Iowa Sup. Ct., 1994).
7. Code of Iowa, Section 514C-1.
8. Code of Iowa, Sections 1C.1, 1C.3–1C.10.
9. Code of Iowa, Sections 96.4, 96.19.
10. Code of Iowa, Section 96.5.
11. Code of Iowa, Sections 96.3 and 96.19.
12. *Lara v. Thomas* (Iowa Sup. Ct., 1994).
13. Code of Iowa, Section 614.1.

88

Kansas Labor and Employment Laws

[88.05] REGULATION OF EMPLOYMENT PRACTICES

Bona fide exceptions to prohibited employment practices: Kansas statutes provide that bona fide seniority systems, bona fide occupational qualifications, and bona fide benefits programs are legally recognized exceptions to otherwise unfair employment practices.[1]

EEOC—certified deferral: Kansas statutes provide that the Kansas Commission on Civil Rights is to serve as a certified deferral agency of the Equal Employment Opportunity Commission relative to fair employment claims filed with the EEOC.[2]

Court review of agency decisions: Kansas statutes permit claimants and respondents to adverse decisions by the Kansas Commission on Civil Rights a right of review to applicable courts within the state.[3]

Available remedies for fair employment violations: Kansas statutes provide for punitive damages, when deemed appropriate, as well as for backpay and compensatory damages, but limited by certain enumerated limitations, for claimants who prevail in claims before the Kansas Commission on Civil Rights.[4]

Drug screens—random testing: A Federal District Court granted a preliminary injunction against the County of Leavenworth, Kansas, who sought to impose a random drug test on a secretary who merely performed clerical functions and occasionally drove her own car to deliver "meals on wheels" to the elderly, suggesting that she did not hold a "safety-sensitive" position as the County had contended.[5]

AIDS testing and confidentiality: Kansas law prohibits employment discrimination on the basis of HIV or AIDS and also regulates under what conditions AIDS test results may be disclosed.[6]

[88.06A] WELFARE AND BENEFITS LAWS

Insurance coverage for alcohol/drug abuse treatment: Kansas laws require insurance policies to provide mandatory coverage for employees undergoing treatment for alcohol and/or drug abuse.[7]

Insurance coverage for newborns: Kansas statutes mandate that employee health-related insurance policies include coverage of newborns—including adopted children—of employees.[8]

Insurance coverage for mental health treatment: Kansas law requires insurance policies to provide coverage for mental health treatment.[9]

State holidays: Kansas statutes provide that the following are state recognized holidays: New Year's Day, Washington's Birthday, Lincoln's Birthday, Memorial Day, July 4th, Labor Day, Columbus Day, Veteran's Day, Thanksgiving Day, and Christmas Day.[10]

[88.08] UNEMPLOYMENT COMPENSATION LAWS

Aside from private sector employers generally subject to the coverage of Kansas' Unemployment Compensation Laws, agricultural, nonprofit, the state government agencies and employers of domestic employees also are subject to the unemployment laws.[11]

Kansas law disqualifies individuals from collecting unemployment compensation who are recipients of pension, retirement pay, or other such annuities, recipients of unemployment benefits from federal and other state unemployment compensation funds, recipients of workers' compensation benefits, and those who voluntarily leave work to move with his/her spouse.[12]

Kansas' unemployment compensation laws do not provide coverage to such employees as: persons self-employed; employees of commercial fishing vessels, railroad employees; wholly commissioned insurance and real estate agents; persons employed by spouse or child; minors employed by a parent; casual labor; minor newspaper carriers; students providing employment services to schools, colleges, and universities, if under college work study program and students at nonprofit or public education institutions who are in full-time work study programs.[13]

[88.10] EMPLOYMENT-AT-WILL DEVELOPMENTS

Employee handbook disclaimer defeats claim: A Federal District Court, applying Kansas law, has ruled that the disclaimer language in a General Motors employment manual was sufficient to deny the plaintiff's claim that the employer had breached the provisions of such handbook.[14]

[88.12] TIME LIMITATIONS FOR FILING WRONGFUL DISCHARGE LAWSUITS

Kansas statutes provide that time limits for litigants to file wrongful employment lawsuits are: one year for defamation, two years for discharge in violation of public policy, and two years for discharge in violation of implied contracts causes of action.[15]

SUPPLEMENTAL NOTES TO CHAPTER 88

1. Kansas Statutes Annotated, Sections 44-1009, 44-1113.
2. Kansas Statutes Annotated, Section 44-1004.
3. Kansas Statutes Annotated, Section 344-240.
4. Kansas Statutes Annotated, Section 75-5011.
5. *Bannister v. Leavenworth Board of Commissioners*, 829 F.Supp. 1249 (D.Kan., 1993).
6. Kansas Statutes Annotated, Sections 65-6001, *et seq.*
7. Kansas Statutes Annotated, Section 40-2-105.
8. Kansas Statutes Annotated, Section 40-2-102.
9. Kansas Statutes Annotated, Section 40-2-105.
10. Kansas Statutes Annotated, Sections 35-107, 35-201, *et seq.*
11. Kansas Statutes Annotated, Section 44-703.

12. Kansas Statutes Annotated, Sections 44-704, 44-706.

13. Kansas Statutes Annotated, Section 44-703.

14. *Berry v. General Motors Corp.*, No. 88-2570 JWL (D. Kan., 11-30-93).

15. Kansas Statutes Annotated, Sections 60-511, *et seq.*

89

Kentucky Labor and Employment Laws

[89.05] REGULATION OF EMPLOYMENT PRACTICES

Bona fide exceptions to prohibited employment practices: Kentucky statutes provide that bona fide seniority systems, bona fide occupational qualifications, and bona fide benefits programs are legally recognized exceptions to otherwise unfair employment practices.[1]

EEOC—certified deferral: Kentucky statutes provide that the Kentucky Commission on Civil Rights is to serve as a certified deferral agency of the Equal Employment Opportunity Commission relative to fair employment claims filed with the EEOC.[2]

Court review of agency decisions: Kentucky statutes permit claimants and respondents to adverse decisions by the Kentucky Commission on Civil Rights a right of review to applicable courts within the state.[3]

Available remedies for fair employment violations: Kentucky statues provide for backpay—reduced by interim earnings—and compensatory damages for claimants who prevail in claims before the Kentucky Commission on Civil Rights.[4]

Affirmative action programs (state employment): Kentucky law requires each state agency to adopt an affirmative action plan to identify persons with protected characteristics who are underutilized in their employment and establish affirmative action programs to overcome any such underutilization.[5]

Compulsory arbitration as a condition of employment prohibited: Kentucky Statutes make it unlawful to require a job applicant or employee to sign an agreement with the employer to arbitrate all claims he or she may have against the employer in the future or waive his or her federal or state rights or benefits as a condition of initial employment or as a condition of continuing employment.[6]

Age law extended: Kentucky extended the coverage of its age discrimination law by removing the age 70 cap.[7]

[89.06A] WELFARE AND BENEFITS LAWS

Insurance coverage for alcohol abuse treatment: Kentucky laws require insurance policies to offer an option of mandatory coverage for employees undergoing treatment for alcohol abuse.[8]

Insurance coverage for newborns: Kentucky statutes mandate that employee health-related insurance policies include coverage of newborns of employees.[9]

Insurance coverage for mental health treatment: Kentucky law requires insurance policies to provide an option to employers to include coverage for mental health treatment.[10]

State holidays: Kentucky statutes provide that the following are state recognized holidays: New Year's Day, Martin Luther King's Birthday, Washington's Birthday, Lincoln's Birthday, Memorial Day, July 4th, Labor Day, Columbus Day, Veteran's Day, Thanksgiving Day, and Christmas Day.[11]

[89.08] UNEMPLOYMENT COMPENSATION LAWS

Aside from private sector employers generally subject to the coverage of Kentucky's Unemployment Compensation Laws, agricultural, nonprofit, the state government agencies, and employers of domestic employees also are subject to the unemployment laws.[12]

Kentucky law disqualifies individuals from collecting unemployment compensation who are recipients of pension, retirement pay, or other such annuities and recipients of unemployment benefits from federal and other state unemployment compensation funds.[13]

Kentucky's unemployment compensation laws do not provide coverage to such employees as: persons self-employed; employees of commercial fishing vessels (unless operating offices are located in Kentucky); railroad employees; wholly commissioned insurance and real estate agents; persons employed by parent, spouse or child; casual labor; student nurses employed by hospitals; hospital interns; minor newspaper carriers; students and spouses of students providing employment services to schools, colleges, and universities, if under college work study program and students at nonprofit or public education institutions who are in full-time work study programs.[14]

[89.10] EMPLOYMENT-AT-WILL DEVELOPMENTS

Implied fixed term: A Kentucky Court of Appeals ruled that an offer of employment stating the position will last a minimum of thirteen months creates a sufficient ambiguity by which to permit the issue to go to a jury.[15]

[89.12] TIME LIMITATIONS FOR FILING WRONGFUL DISCHARGE LAWSUITS

Kentucky statutes provide that time limits for litigants to file wrongful employment lawsuits are: one year for defamation, five years for discharge in violation of public policy, and five years for discharge in violation of implied contracts causes of action.[16]

SUPPLEMENTAL NOTES TO CHAPTER 89

1. Kentucky Revised Statutes, Section 344.100.
2. Kentucky Revised Statutes, Sections 344.180, 344.190.
3. Kentucky Revised Statutes, Section 344.240.
4. Kentucky Revised Statutes, Section 344.230.
5. Kentucky Revised Statutes, Section 18A, 140.
6. Kentucky Acts 355 (1994).
7. Kentucky Revised Statutes, Section 344.040 (effective 7-15-94).
8. Kentucky Revised Statutes, Sections 304.18-130, *et seq.*
9. Kentucky Revised Statutes, Section 304.18-039.
10. Kentucky Revised Statutes, Section 304.18-036.
11. Kentucky Revised Statutes, Sections 2.110, 2.120–2.140, 2.190.
12. Kentucky Revised Statutes, Sections 341.050, 341.055.
13. Kentucky Revised Statutes, Sections 341.360 and 341.390.
14. Kentucky Revised Statutes, Sections 341.050 and 341.055.
15. *Hunter v. Wehr Constructors, Inc.*, No. 92-CA-002104-MR (Ky. Ct. App., 11-9-93).
16. Kentucky Revised Statutes, Sections 413.120 and 413.140.

90

Louisiana Labor and Employment Laws

[90.05] REGULATION OF EMPLOYMENT PRACTICES

Bona fide exceptions to prohibited employment practices: Louisiana statutes provide that bona fide seniority systems, bona fide occupational qualifications and bona fide benefits programs are legally recognized exceptions to otherwise unfair employment practices.[1]

Court review of agency decisions: Louisiana statutes permit claimants and respondents to adverse decisions by the Louisiana Commission a right of review to applicable courts within the state.[2]

Available remedies for fair employment violations: Louisiana statutes provide for backpay—reduced by interim earnings—and compensatory damages for claimants who prevail in claims before the Louisiana Commission.[3]

AIDS testing and confidentiality: Louisiana law requires an informed consent of a person prior to the administration of an AIDS test and forbids the disclosure of such tests without the authorization of the person tested unless required to be released to certain health care providers or agencies.[4]

[90.06A] WELFARE AND BENEFITS LAWS

Insurance coverage for alcohol/drug abuse treatment: Louisiana laws require insurance policies to provide an option of mandatory coverage for employees undergoing treatment for alcohol and/or drug abuse.[5]

Insurance coverage for newborns: Louisiana statutes mandate that employee health-related insurance policies include coverage of newborns—including adopted children—of employees.[6]

Insurance coverage for mental health treatment: Louisiana law requires insurance policies to provide an option to employers to include coverage for mental health treatment.[7]

State holidays: Louisiana statutes provide that the following are state recognized holidays: New Year's Day, Martin Luther King's Birthday, Washington's Birthday, Memorial Day, July 4th, Labor Day, Columbus Day, Veteran's Day, Thanksgiving Day, and Christmas Day.[8]

[90.08] UNEMPLOYMENT COMPENSATION LAWS

Aside from private sector employers generally subject to the coverage of Louisiana's Unemployment Compensation Laws, agricultural, nonprofit, the state government agencies, and employers of domestic employees also are subject to the unemployment laws.[9]

Louisiana law disqualifies individuals from collecting unemployment compensation who are recipients of pension, retirement pay, or other such annuities, recipients of unemployment benefits from federal and other state unemployment compensation funds, recipients of wages in lieu of notice and recipients of workers' compensation funds (except certain enumerated exceptions).[10]

Louisiana's unemployment compensation laws do not provide coverage to such employees as: persons self-employed; employees of commercial fishing vessels (unless operating offices are located in Louisiana); railroad employees; wholly commissioned insurance and real estate agents; persons employed by spouse or child; minors employed by a parent; casual labor; student nurses employed by hospitals; hospital interns; minor newspaper carriers; students providing employment services to schools, colleges, and universities, if under college work study program and students at nonprofit or public education institutions who are in full-time work study programs.[11]

A Louisiana Appellate Court has ruled that the firing of an employee for misconduct because she did not exhaust her rights under the company's internal grievance procedure prior to filing an EEOC claim was not grounds to disqualify her from receiving unemployment compensation benefits.[12]

[90.10] TORT ACTIONS

Wrongful discharge and defamation claim denied: A Louisiana Appellate Court, in denying the plaintiff's claim, has reaffirmed Louisiana's employment-at-will doctrine, stating that the plaintiff's claim that she was discharged based on a false accusation of theft did not constitute wrongful discharge nor was the claim sustainable in defamation in that she failed to demonstrate that the employer published or communicated the accusation to anyone other than herself.[13]

[90.12] THE LIMITATIONS FOR FILING WRONGFUL DISCHARGE LAWSUITS

Louisiana statutes provide that the time limit for litigants to file a lawsuit based on defamation claims is one year.[14]

SUPPLEMENTAL NOTES TO CHAPTER 90

1. Louisiana Revised Statutes, Section 23:972.
2. Louisiana Revised Statutes, Section 51:2264.
3. Louisiana Revised Statutes, Section 51:2261.
4. Louisiana Revised Statutes, Sections 40:1300.11, *et seq.*
5. Louisiana Revised Statutes, Section 22:215.5.
6. Louisiana Revised Statutes, Section 22.215.1.
7. Louisiana Revised Statutes, Section 22:669.
8. Louisiana Revised Statutes, Sections 1:55, *et seq.*
9. Louisiana Revised Statutes, Sections 23:1472, *et seq.*
10. Louisiana Revised Statutes, Sections 33:1472 and 23:1601.
11. Louisiana Revised Statutes, Section 23:1472.
12. *Gobert v. Louisiana Dept. of Employment Security,* (LA. App. Ct., 3-8-95).
13. *Cormier Crooms v. Parish of Lafayette,* No. 93-526 (LA. Ct. App, 12-8-93).
14. Louisiana Civil Code Annotated, Cert. 3492.

91

Maine Labor and Employment Laws

[91.05] REGULATION OF EMPLOYMENT PRACTICES

Bona fide exceptions to prohibited employment practices: Maine statutes provide that bona fide seniority systems, bona fide occupational qualifications, and bona fide benefits programs are legally recognized exceptions to otherwise unfair employment practices.[1]

EEOC—certified deferral: Maine statutes provide that the Maine Human Rights Commission is to serve as a certified deferral agency of the Equal Employment Opportunity Commission relative to fair employment claims filed with the EEOC.[2]

Court review of agency decisions: Maine statutes permit claimants and respondents to adverse decisions by the Maine Human Rights Commission a right of review to applicable courts within the state.[3]

Available remedies for fair employment violations: Maine statutes provide for punitive damages, when deemed appropriate, as well as for backpay for claimants who prevail in claims before the Maine Human Rights Commission.[4]

Affirmative action programs (state employment): Maine law requires each state agency to adopt an affirmative action plan to identify persons with protected characteristics who are underutilized in their employment and establish affirmative action programs to overcome any such underutilization.[5]

Mental disability (compulsive sexual behavior disorders): The Maine Supreme Judicial Court has ruled that "disability," as defined by the Rehabilitation Act of 1973 and the Maine Human Rights Act, does not extend to or include "compulsive sexual behavior disorder."[6]

Religious harassment defined: The Supreme Judicial Court of Maine has held that sexually explicit taunts by one employee to another, such as sexual references to a co-worker that offended his religious beliefs, constituted religious harassment in violation of the Maine Human Rights law in that the test to determine whether a comment is of a religious nature is whether it would have occurred except for the individual's religion and that such taunts in the case at hand would not so have occurred had it not been for the plaintiff's religion.[7]

Family medical leave: Maine law requires employers with twenty-five or more employees who are employed at a permanent work site to provide up to ten weeks of unpaid leave in any two-year period to those employees with at least one year of continuous service for the birth or adoption of a child or for the illness of a child, spouse, parent or the employee; provided further, that the employer may require the employee to maintain benefits at his or her expense during such leave but must reinstate the employee to the same or equivalent position in which such employee worked prior to the leave, upon his or her return from such leave.[8]

[91.06] WAGE AND HOUR LAWS

Maine's Supreme Judicial Court has held that, although commissions are considered to be "wages" under Maine's Payment of Wages Laws, weekly sales draws paid to a salesperson as a loan, pursuant to an employment agreement between the employee and the employer, may be deducted from commissions owed the employee.[9]

[91.06A] WELFARE AND BENEFITS LAWS

Insurance coverage for alcohol/drug abuse treatment: Maine laws require insurance policies to provide mandatory coverage for employees undergoing treatment for alcohol and/or drug abuse.[10]

Insurance coverage for newborns: Maine statutes mandate that employee health-related insurance policies include coverage of newborns—including adopted children—of employees.[11]

Insurance coverage for mental health treatment: Maine law requires insurance policies to provide coverage for mental health treatment.[12]

State holidays: Maine statutes provide that the following are state recognized holidays: New Year's Day, Martin Luther King's Birthday, Washington's Birthday, Memorial Day, July 4th, Labor Day, Columbus Day, Veteran's Day, Thanksgiving Day (Judiciary), and Christmas Day.[13]

[91.08] UNEMPLOYMENT COMPENSATION LAWS

Aside from private sector employers generally subject to the coverage of Maine's Unemployment Compensation Laws, agricultural, nonprofit, the state government agencies, and employers of domestic employees are also subject to the unemployment laws.[14]

Maine law disqualifies individuals who are recipients of pension, retirement pay or other such annuities, recipients of unemployment benefits from federal and other state unemployment compensation funds, recipients of dismissal wages, recipients of wages in lieu of notice, and recipients of vacation and holiday pay[15] from collecting unemployment compensation.

Maine's unemployment compensation laws do not provide coverage to such employees as: persons self-employed; employees of commercial fishing vessels, railroad employees; wholly commissioned insurance and real estate agents; persons employed by spouse or child; minors employed by parent; patients and student nurses employed by hospitals; hospital interns; minor newspaper carriers; students and spouses of students providing employment services to schools, colleges, and universities, if under college work study program and students at nonprofit or public education institutions who are in full-time work study programs.[16]

[91.12] TIME LIMITATIONS FOR FILING WRONGFUL DISCHARGE LAWSUITS

Maine statutes provide that time limits for litigants to file wrongful employment lawsuits are: two years for defamation and six years for discharge in violation of implied contracts causes of action.[17]

SUPPLEMENTAL NOTES TO CHAPTER 91

1. Maine Revised Statutes, Title 5, Sections 4572, 4573.
2. Maine Revised Statutes, Title 5, Section 4566.
3. Maine Revised Statutes, Title 5, Section 4613.
4. Maine Revised Statutes, Title 5, Sections 4613 and 4614.
5. Maine Revised Statutes, Title 5, Section 782 and Title 23, Section 1966.
6. *Winston v. Maine Technical College System*, No. 6638 (Maine Sup. Jud. Ct., 9-1-93).
7. *Finnemore v. Bangor Hydro-Electric Co.*, (ME Sup. Jud. Ct., 1994).
8. Maine Revised Statutes Annotated, Title 26, Section 7.
9. *Community Telecommunications Corp. v. Loughran*, 651 A2d 377 (ME Sup. Jud. Ct., 1994).
10. Maine Revised Statutes, Title 24-A, Section 2842.
11. Maine Revised Statutes, Title 24-A, Section 2832.
12. Maine Revised Statutes, Title 24-A, Section 2843.
13. Maine Revised Statutes, Title 4, Section 1051.
14. Maine Revised Statutes, Title 26, Section 1043.
15. Maine Revised Statutes, Title 26, Sections 1043, 1191–1193.
16. Maine Revised Statutes, Title 26, Section 1043.
17. Maine Revised Statutes, Title 14, Sections 752, 753.

92

Maryland Labor and Employment Laws

[92.05] REGULATION OF EMPLOYMENT PRACTICES

Bona fide exceptions to prohibited employment practices: Maryland statutes provide that bona fide seniority systems, bona fide occupational qualifications, and bona fide benefits programs are legally recognized exceptions to otherwise unfair employment practices.[1]

EEOC—certified deferral: Maryland statutes provide that Maryland Commission on Human Relations is to serve as a certified deferral agency of the Equal Employment Opportunity Commission relative to fair employment claims filed with the EEOC.[2]

Court review of agency decisions: Maryland statutes permit claimants and respondents to adverse decisions by the Maryland Commission on Human Relations a right of review to applicable courts within the state.[3]

Available remedies for fair employment violations: Maryland statutes provide for backpay and compensatory damages for claimants who prevail in claims before the Maryland Commission on Human Relations.[4]

Affirmative action programs (state employment): Maryland law requires each state agency to adopt an affirmative action plan to identify persons with protected characteristics who are underutilized in their employment and establish affirmative action programs to overcome any such underutilization.[5]

AIDS testing and confidentiality: Maryland law requires an informed consent from persons prior to the administration of an AIDS test and forbids a disclosure of such test results without the authorization of the person tested unless otherwise required to be released to certain health care providers or agencies.[6]

[92.06A] WELFARE AND BENEFITS LAW

Insurance coverage for alcohol/drug abuse treatment: Maryland laws require insurance policies to provide mandatory coverage for employees undergoing treatment for alcohol and/or drug abuse.[7]

Insurance coverage for newborns: Maryland statutes mandate that employee health-related insurance policies include coverage of newborns—including adopted children—of employees.[8]

Insurance coverage for mental health treatment: Maryland law requires insurance policies to provide coverage for mental health treatment.[9]

State holidays: Maryland statutes provide that the following are state recognized holidays: New Year's Day, Martin Luther King's Birthday, Washington's Birthday, Lincoln's Birthday, Memorial Day, July 4th, Labor Day, Columbus Day, Veteran's Day, Thanksgiving Day, and Christmas Day.[10]

[92.08] UNEMPLOYMENT COMPENSATION LAWS

Aside from private sector employers generally subject to the coverage of Maryland's Unemployment Compensation Laws, agricultural, nonprofit, state government agencies, and employers of domestic employees also are subject to the unemployment laws.[11]

Maryland law disqualifies individuals from collecting unemployment compensation who are recipients of pension, retirement pay or other such annuities, recipients of unemployment benefits from federal and other state unemployment compensation funds, recipients of dismissal pay or wages in lieu of wages, recipients of vacation pay or holiday pay under certain circumstances, and those who voluntarily leave to attend school or move with their spouse.[12]

Maryland's unemployment compensation laws do not provide coverage to such employees as: persons self-employed; employees of commercial fishing vessels; railroad employees; wholly commissioned insurance and real estate agents; persons employed by spouse or child; minors employed by a parent; patients and student nurses employed by hospitals; hospital interns; minor newspaper carriers; students and spouses of students providing employment services to schools, colleges, and universities, if under college work study program, and students at nonprofit or public education institutions who are in full-time work study programs.[13]

[92.10] EMPLOYMENT-AT-WILL DEVELOPMENTS

Implied contracts—handbook modifications must be clearly communicated: A Maryland Appellate Court has ruled that a change in an employee manual that substantively modifies a previous due process right prior to termination must be clearly communicated to employees affected by the handbook in order to be effective.[14]

[92.11] TORT ACTIONS

Public-policy exception: A Maryland Appellate Court has held that an employee claiming to have been discharged in retaliation for allegedly reporting violations of applicable state law states a course of action, sufficient to go forward with the case.[15]

[92.12] TIME LIMITATIONS FOR FILING WRONGFUL DISCHARGE LAWSUITS

Maryland statutes provide that time limits for litigants to file wrongful employment lawsuits are: one year for defamation, three years for discharge in violation of public policy, and three years for discharge in violation of implied contracts causes of action.[16]

SUPPLEMENTAL NOTES TO CHAPTER 92

1. Annotated Code of Maryland, Art. 49B, Section 16.
2. Annotated Code of Maryland, Art. 49B, Sections 9A, *et seq.*
3. Annotated Code of Maryland, Art. 49B, Sections 4 and 10.
4. Annotated Code of Maryland, Art. 49B, Section 11.
5. Maryland State Personnel & Pensions Code, Sections 3-401, *et seq.*
6. Maryland General Code Annotated, Section 18-336.
7. Annotated Code of Maryland, Art. 48B, Section 490F.
8. Annotated Code of Maryland, Art. 48A, Section 438A.
9. Annotated Code of Maryland, Art. 48A, Section 477E.
10. Annotated Code of Maryland, Art. 1, Section 27.
11. Maryland Labor and Employment Code, Sections 8-101, 8-207, 8-208, 8-211, 8-212.
12. Maryland Labor and Employment Code, Sections 8-101, 8-220, 8-1001, 8-1006, 8-1008 and 8-1009.
13. Maryland Labor and Employment Code Annotated, Sections 8-208, 8-209, 8-210, 8-218, 8-219 and 8-220.
14. *Elliot v. Board of Trustees of Montgomery County Community College*, (MD App., 3-6-95).
15. *Bleich v. Florence Crittenton Services of Baltimore, Inc.*, (MD. Ct. of Spec. App., 11-2-93).
16. Maryland Courts and Judicial Proc. Code, Sections 5-101, 5-105.

93

Massachusetts Labor and Employment Laws

[93.05] REGULATION OF EMPLOYMENT PRACTICES

Bona fide exceptions to prohibited employment practices: Massachusetts statutes provide that bona fide ,seniority systems, bona fide occupational qualifications, and bona fide benefits programs are legally recognized exceptions to otherwise unfair employment practices.[1]

EEOC—certified deferral: Massachusetts statutes provide that the Massachusetts Commission Against Discrimination is to serve as a certified deferral agency of the Equal Employment Opportunity Commission relative to fair employment claims filed with the EEOC.[2]

Court review of agency decisions: Massachusetts statutes permit claimants and respondents to adverse decisions by the Massachusetts Commission Against Discrimination a right of review to applicable courts within the state.[3]

Affirmative action programs (state employment): Massachusetts law requires each state agency to adopt an affirmative action plan to identify persons with protected characteristics who are underutilized in their employment and establish affirmative action programs to overcome any such underutilization.[4]

Disability claim actionable despite prior arbitration: A Massachusetts Appellate Court had ruled that a labor arbitrator's decision that an employee was discharged for "good cause" did not foreclose the right of the employee to pursue his claim that he was terminated due to handicap in violation of the state's handicap laws.[5]

Racial harassment: A Federal District Court, applying Massachusetts law, has held that a supervisor's alleged gawking and staring at a black employee whose work station directly faced the supervisor's office window did not constitute racial harassment under the Massachusetts FEP law in that a reasonable person would expect supervisors in such a location to frequently look in the employee's direction.[6]

Disability—request for reasonable accommodation a prerequisite: Although a Massachusetts Appellate Court held that an employee recovering from a heart attack was illegally discharged for not calling in for a three day period while being hospitalized as a result of a subsequent heart attack, an employer is not obligated to make reasonable accommodations to an employee until the employee makes a request for such reasonable accommodations, even though the employer knows of the disability.[7]

[93.06A] WELFARE AND BENEFITS LAWS

Insurance coverage for alcohol abuse treatment: Massachusetts laws require insurance policies to provide mandatory coverage for employees undergoing treatment for alcohol abuse.[8]

Insurance coverage for newborns: Massachusetts statutes mandate that employee health-related insurance policies include coverage of newborns—including adopted children—of employees.[9]

Insurance coverage for mental health treatment: Massachusetts law requires insurance policies to provide coverage for mental health treatment.[10]

State holidays: Massachusetts statutes provide that the following are state recognized holidays: New Year's Day, Martin Luther King's Birthday, Washington's Birthday, Memorial Day, July 4th, Labor Day, Columbus Day, Veteran's Day, Thanksgiving Day, and Christmas Day.[11]

[93.08] UNEMPLOYMENT COMPENSATION LAWS

Aside from private sector employers generally subject to the coverage of Massachusetts' Unemployment Compensation Laws, agricultural, nonprofit, the state government agencies, and employers of domestic employees also are subject to the unemployment laws.[12]

Massachusetts law disqualifies individuals who are recipients of pension, retirement pay or other such annuities, recipients of unemployment benefits from federal and other state unemployment compensation funds, and recipients of certain workers' compensation funds from collecting unemployment compensation.[13]

Massachusetts unemployment compensation laws do not provide coverage to such employees as: persons self-employed; employees of commercial fishing vessels; railroad employees; wholly commissioned insurance and real estate agents; persons employed by spouse or child; minors employed by a parent; casual labor; patients and student nurses employed by hospitals; hospital interns; minor newspaper carriers; students and spouses of students providing employment services to schools, colleges, and universities, if under college work study program and students at nonprofit or public education institutions who are in full-time work study programs.[14]

[93.10] EMPLOYMENT-AT-WILL DEVELOPMENTS

The Massachusetts Supreme Judicial Court has held that in order for the public policy exception to the employment-at-will doctrine to apply, the statutory right in question must relate to or arise out of the employee's employment status and, therefore, the termination of an employee for engaging in a shareholders' derivative cause of action against his employer did not meet such criteria, even though the employee had a statutory right in Massachusetts to so participate in the lawsuit.[15]

[93.12] TIME LIMITATIONS FOR FILING WRONGFUL DISCHARGE LAWSUITS

Massachusetts statutes provide that time limits for litigants to file wrongful employment lawsuits are: three years for defamation, three years for discharge in violation of public policy, and six years for discharge in violation of implied contract causes of action.[16]

SUPPLEMENTAL NOTES TO CHAPTER 93

1. Massachusetts General Laws, Chapter 151B, Section 4.
2. Massachusetts General Laws, Chapter 151B, Section 5.
3. Massachusetts General Laws, Chapter 30A, Section 14.
4. Massachusetts General Laws, Chapter 35, Section 53A.
5. *Carr v. Transgas, Inc.*, 623 NE2d 505 (Mass. App., 12-6-93).
6. *Lewis v. The Gillette Co.*, No. 90-12257-WF (DC Mass., 7-21-93).
7. *Talbert Trading Co. v. Massachusetts Commission Against Discrimination*, (Mass. App. Ct., 1994).

8. Massachusetts General Laws, Chapter 175, Section 110(4).

9. Massachusetts General Laws, Chapter 175, Section 47C.

10. Massachusetts General Laws, Chapter 175, Section 47B.

11. Massachusetts General Laws, Chapter 4, Section 7.

12. Massachusetts General Laws, Chapter 151A, Sections 4A, 6, 8-8B.

13. Massachusetts General Laws, Chapter 151A, Sections 1, 4A, 6, 25, 26 and 47.

14. Massachusetts General Laws, Chapter 151A, Sections 1, 2, 4, 4A and 6.

15. *King v. Driscoll*, 63S NE2d 488 (Mass. Sup. Jud. Ct., 1994).

16. Massachusetts General Laws, Chapter 260, Sections 2, 2A, 4.

94

Michigan Labor and Employment Laws

[94.05] REGULATION OF EMPLOYMENT PRACTICES

Bona fide exceptions to prohibited employment practices: Michigan statutes provide that bona fide seniority systems and bona fide occupational qualifications are legally recognized exceptions to otherwise unfair employment practices.[1]

EEOC—certified deferral: Michigan statutes provide that the Michigan Civil Rights Commission is to serve as a certified deferral agency of the Equal Employment Opportunity Commission relative to fair employment claims filed with the EEOC.[2]

Court review of agency decisions: Michigan statutes permit claimants and respondents to adverse decisions by the Michigan Civil Rights Commission a right of review to applicable courts within the state.[3]

Available remedies for fair employment violations: Michigan statutes provide for punitive damages, when deemed appropriate, as well as for backpay and compensatory damages for claimants who prevail in claims before the Michigan Civil Rights Commission.[4]

Affirmative action programs (state employment): Michigan law requires each state agency to adopt an affirmative action plan to identify persons with protected characteristics who are underutilized in their employment and establish affirmative action programs to overcome any such underutilization.[5]

Whistle-blowing act: The Michigan Supreme Court, interpreting the Michigan Law, held that it was in violation of the Michigan Whistle-blowing Act to discharge an employee for filing criminal assault and battery charges against a fellow employee relative to a work-related confrontation that occurred at their workplace during work hours.[6]

Age—reverse discrimination unsupported: A Michigan Court of Appeals has ruled that denying a 49-year old early retirement because of his relatively young age was not a violation of Michigan's Age Discrimination Laws.[7]

Sexual harassment—supervisor's rape of employee did not violate state statute: A Michigan Appellate Court, in narrowly construing Michigan's law on sexual harassment, has ruled that a supervisor's rape of an employee did not constitute quid pro quo sexual harassment for which the employer could be liable in that no employment decision was based upon whether the employee submitted to the rape or not.[8]

Sexual orientation harassment: A Michigan Appellate Court has ruled that although harassment or discrimination on the basis of a person's sexual orientation is not covered by the Michigan Elliott-Larsen Civil Rights Act, a male employee subjected to homosexual advances by his supervisor had an actionable claim of unlawful harassment in that such actions were directly related to his status as a male, as distinguished from his sexual orientation, and thus, fell within the statute.[9]

AIDS testing and confidentiality: Michigan law requires informed consent of a person prior to the administration of an AIDS test and forbids a disclosure of such results unless authorized by the person tested, unless otherwise required to be released to certain health care providers or agencies.[10]

[94.06A] WELFARE AND BENEFITS LAWS

Insurance coverage for alcohol/drug abuse treatment: Michigan laws require insurance policies to provide mandatory coverage for employees undergoing treatment for alcohol and/or drug abuse.[11]

Insurance coverage for newborns: Michigan statutes mandate that employee health-related insurance policies include coverage of newborns of employees.[12]

State holidays: Michigan statutes provide that the following are state recognized holidays: New Year's Day, Martin Luther King's Birthday, Washington's Birthday, Lincoln's Birthday, Memorial Day, July 4th, Labor Day, Columbus Day, Veteran's Day, Thanksgiving Day, and Christmas Day.[13]

[94.08] UNEMPLOYMENT COMPENSATION LAWS

Aside from private sector employers generally subject to the coverage of Michigan's Unemployment Compensation Laws, agricultural, nonprofit, state government agencies and employers of domestic employees also are subject to the unemployment laws.[14]

Michigan law disqualifies individuals from collecting unemployment compensation who are recipients of pension, retirement pay or other such annuities, recipients of unemployment benefits from federal and other state unemployment compensation funds, and participants in wildcat strikes in violation of labor agreements.[15]

Michigan's unemployment compensation laws do not provide coverage to such employees as: persons self-employed; railroad employees; wholly commissioned insurance and real estate agents; persons employed by a spouse or child; minors employed by a parent; minor newspaper carriers; students and spouses of students providing employment services to schools, colleges, and universities, if under college work study program, and students at nonprofit or public education institutions who are in full-time work study programs.[16]

[94.09] WORKERS' COMPENSATION LAWS

A Michigan Court of Appeals has ruled that a psychiatrist's restriction of a workers' compensation claimant to work in areas other than those worked by a coworker with whom he had a previous altercation, and the failure of the employer to find another such job, entitled the employee to workers' compensation benefits under Michigan law.[17]

[94.10] EMPLOYMENT-AT-WILL DEVELOPMENTS

Promissory estoppel unsubstantiated: A Michigan Appellate Court has held that an employee's resignation of his previous employment to take a position with a new employer and the expenses and costs associated with the relocation of his family to such new location do not provide sufficient consideration to support a promissory estoppel cause of action in that such inconvenience and costs associated with such a move merely are customary and necessary incidents with changing jobs, the court relying upon *Marrero v. McDonnell Douglas Capital Corp.*, 505 NW2d 275 (Mich. App., 1993).[18]

Public policy exception—refusal to engage in illegal conduct for employer—notice required: A Michigan Court of Appeals has ruled that, in order for an alleged constructively discharged employee to sustain a public policy violation lawsuit, based upon her resignation in refusing to continue performing certain job functions for her employer that she believed constituted fraud, she must first have brought the matter to the attention of her employer. She must have provided her employer an opportunity to properly respond to her complaint, which she failed to do.[19]

[94.11] TORT ACTIONS

Retaliatory discharge for filing workers' compensation claim—tort: A Michigan Appellate Court has ruled that a lawsuit alleging retaliatory discharge for filing a workers' compensation claim is grounded in tort rather than in contract law.[20]

[94.12] TIME LIMITATIONS FOR FILING WRONGFUL DISCHARGE LAWSUITS

Michigan statutes provide that time limits for litigants to file wrongful employment lawsuits are: one year for defamation, three years for discharge in violation of public policy, and six years for discharge in violation of implied contracts causes of action.[21]

SUPPLEMENTAL NOTES TO CHAPTER 94

1. Michigan Compiled Laws, Sections 37.2208 and 37.2211.
2. Michigan Compiled Laws, Sections 37.2601, *et seq.*
3. Michigan Compiled Laws, Section 37.2606.
4. Michigan Compiled Laws, Section 37.2605.
5. Michigan Compiled Laws, Sections 125.1221, *et seq.*
6. *Dudewicz v. Norris-Schmid,* 443 Mich. 68 (Mich. S. Ct., 7-27-93).
7. *Zoppi v. Chrysler Corporation,* (Mich. App. Ct., 7-6-94).
8. *Champion v. Nationwide Security, Inc.,* (Mich. Ct. App., 5-16-94).
9. *Barbour v. Department of Social Services,* 497 NW2d 216 (Mich. Ct. App., 1993).
10. Michigan Statutes, Sections 14.15, 1501, *et seq.*
11. Michigan Compiled Statutes, Section 500.3425.
12. Michigan Compiled Statutes, Section 500.3611.
13. Michigan Compiled Statutes, Sections 18.856, 18.861, 18.862, 18.881 and 18.891.
14. Michigan Compiled Laws, Sections 421.41, 421.42.
15. Michigan Compiled Laws, Sections 421.27–421.29.
16. Michigan Compiled Laws, Sections 421.23, 421.42, *et seq.*
17. *Wilkins v. General Motors Corporation,* (Mich. Ct. App., 5-2-94).
18. *Meerman v. Murco,* (Mich. App., 6-7-94).
19. *Vagts v. Perry Drug Stores, Inc.,* (Mich. Ct. App., 4-5-94).
20. *Phillips v. Butterball Farms Company, Inc.,* No. 165049 (Mich. Ct. App., 10-4-93).
21. Michigan Compiled Laws, Sections 600.5805 and 600.5807.

95

Minnesota Labor and Employment Laws

[95.05] REGULATION OF EMPLOYMENT PRACTICES

Bona fide exceptions to prohibited employment practices: Minnesota statutes provide that bona fide seniority systems and bona fide occupational qualifications are legally recognized exceptions to otherwise unfair employment practices.[1]

EEOC—certified deferral: Minnesota statutes provide that the Minnesota Commission of the Department of Human Rights is to serve as a certified deferral agency of the Equal Employment Opportunity Commission relative to fair employment claims filed with the EEOC.[2]

Available remedies for fair employment violations: Minnesota statutes provide for back-pay and compensatory damages for claimants who prevail in claims before the Minnesota Commission of the Department of Human Rights.[3]

Affirmative action programs (state employment): Minnesota law requires each state agency to adopt an affirmative action plan to identify persons with protected characteristics who are underutilized in their employment and establish affirmative action programs to overcome any such underutilization.[4]

Age discrimination claim—discharged for dating a client: A Minnesota Appellate Court has held that an employer's dismissal of a 48-year-old secretary was not on the basis of her age, particularly in light of the fact that she was hired at age 47, holding further that the dismissed employee had failed to counter the employer's rebuttal of a presumption of age discrimination by the fact that it had dismissed her for just cause: dating a client against company policy.[5]

Compulsory arbitration agreement enforced: A Minnesota Court of Appeals, deferring to the U.S. Supreme Court Case of *Gilmer v. Interstate/Johnson Lake Corp.*, granted an order requiring an employee to arbitrate her employment discrimination claims—the decision of which precluded her sex and age discrimination cause of action under the Minnesota Human Rights Act—pursuant to an agreement she signed required for securities industry registration, agreeing to "arbitrate any dispute, claim or controversy that may arise between me and my firm . . .," language similar to the arbitration agreement in the *Gilmer* case.[6]

AIDS testing and confidentiality: Minnesota law provides that information about HIV test results of private and public sector employees must be kept private and confidential.[7]

[95.06A] WELFARE AND BENEFITS LAW

Insurance coverage for alcohol/drug abuse treatment: Minnesota laws require insurance policies to provide coverage for treatment of employees undergoing rehabilitation for alcohol and/or drug abuse.[8]

Insurance coverage for newborns: Minnesota statutes mandate that employee health-related insurance policies include coverage of newborns—including adopted children—of employees.[9]

Insurance coverage for mental health treatment: Minnesota law requires insurance policies to provide mandatory coverage for out-patient treatment of mental health conditions if in-patient treatment is so covered.[10]

State holidays: Minnesota statutes provide that the following are state recognized holidays: New Year's Day, Martin Luther King's Birthday, Washington's Birthday, Lincoln's Birthday, Memorial Day, July 4th, Labor Day, Columbus Day, Veteran's Day, Thanksgiving Day, and Christmas Day.[11]

[95.08] UNEMPLOYMENT COMPENSATION LAWS

Aside from private sector employers generally subject to the coverage of Minnesota's Unemployment Compensation Laws, agricultural, nonprofit, state government agencies, and employers of domestic employees also are subject to the unemployment laws.[12]

Minnesota law disqualifies individuals who are recipients of pension, retirement pay or other such annuities, recipients of unemployment benefits from federal and other state unemployment compensation funds, recipients of termination, severance or wages in lieu of notice, recipients of vacation allowance, and recipients of workers' compensation funds[13] from collecting unemployment compensation.

Minnesota's unemployment compensation laws do not provide coverage to such employees as: persons self-employed; railroad employees; wholly commissioned insurance and real estate agents; persons employed by spouse or child; minors employed by a parent; casual labor; patients and student nurses employed by hospitals; hospital interns; minor newspaper carriers; students providing employment services to schools, colleges, and universities, if under college work study program and students at nonprofit or public education institutions who are in full-time work study programs.[14]

A Minnesota Court of Appeals has held that a gay hair stylist who quit his employment as a result of harassment over his sexual orientation, after his managers failed to address his complaints about such harassment, was entitled to unemployment benefits under Minnesota's Unemployment Compensation Laws.[15]

[95.10] EMPLOYMENT-AT-WILL DEVELOPMENTS

Fixed term agreement: Reversing a trial court's decision, a Minnesota Appellate Court has held that a one-year written employment agreement applied despite the employer's characterization that the employee's separation was a layoff rather than a discharge.[16]

Covenant of good faith and fair dealing: The Eighth Circuit Court of Appeals, applying Minnesota law, reconfirmed that the employment-at-will relationship is not impaired unless the employer and employee make specific and definite provisions to the contrary; and, moreover, Minnesota does not recognize an implied covenant of good faith and fair dealing in the employment context.[17]

[95.11] TORT ACTIONS

Whistle-blower claim denied: A Minnesota Appellate Court has denied an employee's cause of action under the Minnesota Whistle-blower Act, concluding that the employee failed to show that he knew or even suspected the Company was violating the law, that the Company had not engaged in the practices contended and, even if the employer had engaged in such behavior, it would not have involved matters of public importance.[18]

Intentional infliction of emotional distress unsubstantiated: A Minnesota Appellate Court has held that a supervisor's legitimate discussion with an employee about her demeanor and dress, even suggesting that her apparel may have given some fellow workers the impression she was a "slut," was insufficient to establish an "intentional infliction of emotional distress" cause of action.[19]

Defamation—manner of escorting terminated employee: A Minnesota Appellate Court has held actionable a terminated employee's defamation and emotional distress lawsuit against his employer on the basis of the manner in which the employee was escorted out of the workplace. The court concluded that the fact his superior accompanied him to his office, remained in the office while he packed his belongings and thereafter escorted him out of the building in full view of other employees could be construed by a jury that the employee was dishonest and could not be trusted to leave the building on his own.[20]

Negligent retention: A Minnesota Appellate Court, in reversing a lower court's summary judgment, ruled that a murdered co-worker's estate could proceed with its action against the defendant employer on the grounds that it had retained an employee who had a history of violence and abuse and who had repeatedly threatened the employee, subsequently murdered, while at work, despite the fact that the employee murdered the co-worker a week after his resignation and off the company premises.[21]

[95.12] TIME LIMITATIONS FOR FILING WRONGFUL DISCHARGE LAWSUITS

Minnesota statutes provide that time limits for litigants to file wrongful employment lawsuits are: two years each for defamation, discharge in violation of public policy, and discharge in violation of implied contracts causes of action.[22]

SUPPLEMENTAL NOTES TO CHAPTER 95

1. Minnesota Statutes, Sections 363.02 and 363.03.
2. Minnesota Statutes, Sections 363.05, 363.06 and 363.071.
3. Minnesota Statutes, Section 363.071.
4. Minnesota Statutes, Sections 43A.19 and 43A.191.
5. *Ward v. Employee Development Corporation*, (Minn. Ct. of App., 5-17-94).
6. *Johnson v. Piper Jaffray, Inc.*, (Minn. Ct. of App., 5-10-94).
7. Minnesota Statutes, Section 144.768.
8. Minnesota Statutes, Section 62A.149.
9. Minnesota Statutes, Sections 62A.042, *et seq.*
10. Minnesota Statutes, Section 62A.152.
11. Minnesota Statutes, Section 645.44.
12. Minnesota Statutes, Section 268.04.
13. Minnesota Statutes, Sections 268.04, 268.08 and 268.09.

14. Minnesota Statutes, Sections 268.04 268.06, 268.09.

15. *Hanke v. Safari Hair Adventure*, (Minn. Ct. of App., 3-1-94).

16. *Helborg v. Community Work & Development Industries, Inc.*, (Minn. Ct. App., 1-4-94).

17. *Poff v. Western National Mutual Insurance*, (CA-8, 1-7-94).

18. *Wheeler v. The St. Paul Companies*, No. C1-93-1495 (Minn. Ct. App., 1-18-94).

19. *Heiling v. State of Minnesota*, (Minn. App., 8-2-94).

20. *Bolton v. Department of Human Services*, (Minn. App., 1995).

21. *Yunkers v. Honeywell, Inc.*, 409 N.W.2d 419 (Minn. App. Ct., 1993).

22. Minnesota Statutes, Section 541.07.

96

Mississippi Labor and Employment Laws

[96.05] REGULATION OF EMPLOYMENT PRACTICES

Affirmative action programs (state employment):   Mississippi law requires some designated state agencies to adopt an affirmative action plan to identify persons with protected characteristics who are underutilized in their employment and establish affirmative action programs to overcome any such underutilization.[1]

Racial discrimination—supervisor's use of epithets: The Fifth Circuit Court of Appeals has held that a supervisor's use of racial epithets when referring to African-American employees could be grounds by which to substantiate discriminatory animus with respect to discharge of the plaintiff, particularly absent employer evidence establishing that the plaintiff would have been terminated regardless of the supervisor's racism.[2]

Drug test statute extended: Mississippi has extended its Drug Testing Law, formerly lapsed in 1993, by imposing conditions to which employers must comply, such as specimen collection procedures, notice and confidentiality requirements, etc., but also providing some protection against lawsuits if such conditions and requirements are met.[3]

[96.06A] WELFARE AND BENEFITS LAWS

Insurance coverage for alcohol/drug abuse treatment: Mississippi laws require insurance policies to provide mandatory coverage for treatment of employees undergoing rehabilitation for alcohol abuse.[4]

Insurance coverage for newborns: Mississippi statutes mandate that employee health-related insurance policies include coverage of newborns of employees.[5]

State holidays: Mississippi statutes provide the following as state recognized holidays: New Year's Day, Martin Luther King's Birthday, Washington's Birthday, Memorial Day, July 4th, Labor Day, Veteran's Day, Thanksgiving Day, and Christmas Day.[6]

[96.08] UNEMPLOYMENT COMPENSATION LAWS

Aside from private sector employers generally subject to the coverage of Mississippi's Unemployment Compensation Laws, agricultural, nonprofit, the state government agencies, and employers of domestic employees also are subject to the unemployment laws.[7]

Mississippi law disqualifies individuals who are recipients of pension, retirement pay, or other such annuities, recipients of unemployment benefits from federal and other state unemployment compensation funds, recipients of backpay or other compensation allocable to a week and persons voluntarily leaving work to marry, to move with a spouse or to meet domestic obligations[8] from collecting unemployment compensation.

Mississippi's unemployment compensation laws do not provide coverage to such employees as: persons self-employed; employees of commercial fishing vessels (unless operating offices are located in Mississippi); railroad employees; wholly commissioned insurance and real estate agents; persons employed by spouse or child; minor children employed by a parent; casual labor; patients and student nurses employed by hospitals; hospital interns; minor newspaper carriers; students and spouses of students providing employment services to schools, colleges, and universities, if under college work study program and students at nonprofit or public education institutions who are in full-time work study programs.[9]

[96.11] TORT ACTIONS

Whistle-blowing—tort: The Mississippi Supreme Court has ruled that an at-will employee has an actionable cause in tort when discharged for reporting illegal acts on the part of the employer or refusing to participate in an illegal act at work.[10]

Defamation—qualified privilege: The Fifth Circuit Court of Appeals, interpreting Mississippi law, upheld a lower court's summary judgment against an employee's defamation claim against his employer. The lower court ruled that the employer's alleged defamatory statements were qualifiedly privileged and that the employee had failed to establish such statements to be excessively published or made with such malice as to remove the privilege, where the statements related to a personnel matter and the supervisor to whom they were made had a legitimate and direct interest in the reasons surrounding the employer's personnel decision.[11]

[96.12] TIME LIMITATIONS FOR FILING WRONGFUL DISCHARGE LAWSUITS

Mississippi statutes provide that time limits for litigants to file wrongful employment lawsuits are: one year for defamation, six years for discharge in violation of public policy, and three years for discharge in violation of implied contracts causes of action.[12]

SUPPLEMENTAL NOTES TO CHAPTER 96

1. Mississippi Code, Sections 57-67-37, 57-69-1, *et seq.*
2. *Brown v. East Mississippi Electric Power Assn.*, No. 91-7245 (CA-5, 5-4-93).
3. Mississippi Code, Section 71-7-1, *et seq.*
4. Mississippi Code, Sections 83-9-27, 83-9-31.
5. Mississippi Code, Section 82-9-33, *et seq.*
6. Mississippi Code, Section 3-3-7.
7. Mississippi Code, Sections 71-5-11, 71-5-357.
8. Mississippi Code, Sections 71-5-11, 71-5-13 and 71-5-513.
9. Mississippi Code, Sections 71-5-11, 71-5-513.
10. *McArn v. Allied Bruce-Terminix Co.*, No. 90-CA-939 (Miss. S. Ct., 8-19-93).
11. *Esmark Apparel, Inc. v. James*, 10 F3d 1156 (CA-5, 1994).
12. Mississippi Code, Sections 15-1-29, 15-1-35 and 15-1-49.

97

Missouri Labor and Employment Laws

[97.05] REGULATION OF EMPLOYMENT PRACTICES

Bona fide exceptions to prohibited employment practices: Missouri statutes provide that bona fide seniority systems, bona fide occupational qualifications and bona fide benefits programs are legally recognized exceptions to otherwise unfair employment practices.[1]

EEOC—certified deferral: Missouri statutes provide that the Missouri Commission on Human Rights is to serve as a certified deferral agency of the Equal Employment Opportunity Commission relative to fair employment claims filed with the EEOC.[2]

Available remedies for fair employment violations: Missouri statutes provide for punitive damages, when deemed appropriate, as well as for backpay and compensatory damages for claimants who prevail in claims before the Missouri Commission on Human Rights.[3]

Affirmative action programs (state employment): Missouri law requires state agencies to adopt an affirmative action plan to identify persons with protected characteristics who are underutilized in their employment and establish affirmative action programs to overcome any such underutilization.[4]

Disability-memory deficit: A Missouri Appellate Court has held that an employee suffering from a loss of memory and related mental deficiencies after a cerebral aneurysm failed to show disability bias in that he could not perform essential functions of the job in question, even with reasonable accommodations.[5]

Pregnancy discrimination unsubstantiated: A Missouri Appellate Court has held an employer justified in terminating a pregnant employee who had left work unfinished, called in to report that she was not motivated to come to work and, upon her return to work, refused to meet with her manager about her performance deficiencies. The Court held such refusal to constitute insubordination rather than pregnancy discrimination.[6]

AIDS testing and confidentiality: Missouri law provides that employers must maintain records concerning an applicant or employee's HIV test results or HIV infection status in a confidential manner.[7]

[97.06] WAGE AND HOUR LAWS

A Missouri Appellate Court has ruled that WARN payments are wages under Missouri's Payment of Wages Law and, therefore, are deductible from unemployment compensation benefits.[8]

[97.06A] WELFARE AND BENEFITS LAW

Insurance coverage for alcohol/drug abuse treatment: Missouri laws require insurance policies to provide mandatory coverage for treatment of employees undergoing rehabilitation for alcohol abuse and a required option to cover treatment for drug abuse.[9]

Insurance coverage for newborns: Missouri statutes mandate that employee health-related insurance policies include coverage of newborns—including adopted children—of employees.[10]

Insurance coverage for mental health treatment: Missouri law requires insurance policies to provide an option to cover treatment for mental health conditions.[11]

State holidays: Missouri statutes provide the following as state recognized holidays: New Year's Day, Martin Luther King's Birthday, Washington's Birthday, Lincoln's Birthday, Memorial Day, July 4th, Labor Day, Columbus Day, Veteran's Day, Thanksgiving Day, and Christmas Day.[12]

[97.08] UNEMPLOYMENT COMPENSATION LAWS

Aside from private sector employers generally subject to the coverage of Missouri's Unemployment Compensation Laws, agricultural, nonprofit, state government agencies, and employers of domestic employees also are subject to the unemployment laws.[13]

Missouri law disqualifies individuals from collecting unemployment compensation who are recipients of pension, retirement pay, or other such annuities, recipients of unemployment benefits from federal and other state unemployment compensation funds, and recipients of workers' compensation funds for temporary disability.[14]

Missouri's unemployment compensation laws do not provide coverage to such employees as: persons self-employed; railroad employees; wholly commissioned insurance and real estate agents; persons employed by spouse or child; minor children employed by a parent; minor newspaper carriers; students and spouses of students providing employment services to schools, colleges, and universities, if under college work study program and students at nonprofit or public education institutions who are in full-time work study programs.[15]

[97.10] EMPLOYMENT-AT-WILL DEVELOPMENTS

Employment contract not breached: A Missouri Appellate Court has ruled an employer did not breach a written employment agreement where it continued to pay the employee the last three months of the agreement but ordered the employee to perform no more for the company and to refrain from contacting or talking to customers during such three month period.[16]

[97.11] TORT ACTIONS

Fraudulent misrepresentation: A Missouri Appellate Court upheld a jury award to an employer as a result of a former salesperson's fraudulently misrepresenting that he did not have a covenant not to compete with his former employer, the Court holding that all the elements to support fraudulent misrepresentation claim were shown.[17]

[97.12] TIME LIMITATIONS FOR FILING WRONGFUL DISCHARGE LAWSUITS

Missouri statutes provide that time limits for litigants to file wrongful employment lawsuits are: two years for defamation, five years for discharge in violation of public policy, and five years for discharge in violation of implied contracts causes of action.[18]

SUPPLEMENTAL NOTES TO CHAPTER 97

1. Missouri Revised Statutes, Section 213.055.
2. Missouri Revised Statutes, Sections 213.030, 213.070 and 213.075.
3. Missouri Revised Statutes, Sections 213.075, 213.111.
4. Missouri Revised Statutes, Sections 33.750, *et seq.*, 37.020.
5. *Welshans v. Boatmen's Bancshares*, No. 62511 (Mo. Ct. App., 1-18-94).
6. *McMullen v. McRaven*, (Mo. Ct. App., 9-6-94).
7. Missouri Revised Statutes, Sections 191.650, *et seq.*
8. *Division of Employment Security v. Labor Industrial Relations Commission*, (Mo. Ct. App., 1994).
9. Missouri Revised Statutes, Section 376.779.
10. Missouri Revised Statutes, Section 376.406.
11. Missouri Revised Statutes, Section 376.381.
12. Missouri Revised Statutes, Sections 9.010–9.100.
13. Missouri Revised Statutes, Sections 288.032, 288.034.
14. Missouri Revised Statutes, Sections 288.034, 288.040.
15. Missouri Revised Statutes, Section 288.030, 288.034.
16. *Simpson v. Maxon Systems, Inc.*, 886 SW2d 92 (Mo. Ct. App., 1994).
17. *Refrigeration Industries v. Nemmers*, (Mo. Ct. App., 7-26-94).
18. Missouri Revised Statutes, Sections 516.120, 516.140.

98

Montana Labor and Employment Laws

[98.05] REGULATION OF EMPLOYMENT PRACTICES

Bona fide exceptions to prohibited employment practices: Montana statutes provide that bona fide seniority systems, bona fide occupational qualifications, and bona fide benefits programs are legally recognized exceptions to otherwise unfair employment practices.[1]

EEOC—certified deferral: Montana statutes provide that the Montana Commission for Human Rights is to serve as a certified deferral agency of the Equal Employment Opportunity Commission relative to fair employment claims filed with the EEOC.[2]

Available remedies for fair employment violations: Montana statutes provide for back pay and compensatory damages for claimants who prevail in claims before the Montana Commission for Human Rights.[3]

Affirmative action programs (state employment):   Montana law requires state agencies to adopt an affirmative action plan to identify persons with protected characteristics who are underutilized in their employment and establish affirmative action programs to overcome any such underutilization.[4]

AIDS testing and confidentiality: Montana law requires informed consent of a person prior to the administration of an AIDS test and forbids the disclosure of such test results without the authorization of the person tested unless otherwise required to be released to certain health care providers or agencies.[5]

[98.06A] WELFARE AND BENEFITS LAW

Insurance coverage for alcohol/drug abuse treatment: Montana laws require insurance policies to provide mandatory coverage for treatment of employees undergoing rehabilitation for alcohol and/or drug abuse.[6]

Insurance coverage for newborns: Montana statutes mandate that employee health-related insurance policies include coverage of newborns—including adopted children—of employees.[7]

Insurance coverage for mental health treatment: Montana law requires insurance policies to provide mandatory coverage for mental health treatment.[8]

State holidays: Montana statutes provide that the following are state recognized holidays: New Year's Day, Martin Luther King's Birthday, Washington's Birthday, Lincoln's Birthday, Memorial Day, July 4th, Labor Day, Columbus Day, Veteran's Day, Thanksgiving Day, and Christmas Day.[9]

[98.08] UNEMPLOYMENT COMPENSATION LAWS

Aside from private sector employers generally subject to the coverage of Montana's Unemployment Compensation Laws, agricultural, nonprofit, state government agencies, and employers of domestic employees also are subject to the unemployment laws.[10]

Montana law disqualifies individuals who are recipients of pension, retirement pay or other such annuities, recipients of unemployment benefits from federal and other state unemployment compensation funds, recipients of wages in lieu of notice and recipients of workers' compensation or social security disability payments from collecting unemployment compensation.[11]

Montana's unemployment compensation laws do not provide coverage to such employees as: persons self-employed; railroad employees; wholly commissioned insurance and real estate agents; persons employed by spouse or child; minor children employed by a parent; patients employed by hospitals; minor newspaper carriers; students and spouses of students providing employment services to schools, colleges, and universities, if under college work study program and students at nonprofit or public education institutions who are in full-time work study programs.[12]

[98.10] EMPLOYMENT-AT-WILL DEVELOPMENTS

The Montana Supreme Court has held that whether the discharge of an employee for working for a competitor during vacation was a sufficient "good cause" ground to discharge the employee under the Montana's Wrongful Discharge from Employment Act was a question of fact.[13]

The Montana Supreme Court has held that an employer had sufficient cause to terminate an employee under Montana's Wrongful Discharge from Employment Act on the basis that the employee had threatened his supervisors.[14]

[98.12] TIME LIMITATIONS FOR FILING WRONGFUL DISCHARGE LAWSUITS

Montana statutes provide time limits for litigants to file wrongful employment lawsuits to be one year relative to at-will employees' lawsuits based on discharge without cause, retaliatory discharges for refusing to violate a public policy or for reporting a public policy violation and discharges in violation of employee handbook rules.[15]

SUPPLEMENTAL NOTES TO CHAPTER 98

1. Montana Code Annotated, Sections 49-2-303, 49-2-402 through 49-2-405, 49-3-103.
2. Montana Code Annotated, Sections 49-2-501, 49-2-505, 49-3-601 and 49-3-304.
3. Montana Code Annotated, Sections 49-2-505, *et seq.*
4. Montana Code Annotated, Sections 39-29-102, 39-20-201.
5. Montana Code Annotated, Sections 50-16-1001, *et seq.*
6. Montana Code Annotated, Section 33-22-703.
7. Montana Code Annotated, Section 33-22-130.
8. Montana Code Annotated, Section 33-22-703.
9. Montana Code Annotated, Sections 1-1-216, 1-1-225.
10. Montana Code Annotated, Sections 39-51-202, 39-51-204 and 39-51-206.
11. Montana Code Annotated, Sections 39-51-504, 39-51-2203, 30-51-2302, *et seq.*
12. Montana Code Annotated, Sections 39-51-204, 39-51-205, 39-51-2203.
13. *Morton v. M-W M, Inc.*, No. 93-433, (Montana Sup. Ct., 1994).
14. *Koepplin v. Zortman Mining, Inc.*, 881 P.2d 1306 (Mont. Sup. Ct., 1994).
15. Montana Code Annotated, Sections 39-2-901, *et seq.*

99

Nebraska Labor and Employment Laws

[99.05] REGULATION OF EMPLOYMENT PRACTICES

Bona fide exceptions to prohibited employment practices: Nebraska statutes provide that bona fide seniority systems, bona fide occupational qualifications, and bona fide benefits programs are legally recognized exceptions to otherwise unfair employment practices.[1]

EEOC—certified deferral: Nebraska statutes provides that the State FEP Commission is to serve as a certified deferral agency of the Equal Employment Opportunity Commission relative to fair employment claims filed with the EEOC.[2]

Court review of agency decisions: Nebraska statutes permit claimants and respondents to adverse decisions by the State FEP Commission a right of review to applicable courts within the state.[3]

Affirmative action programs (state employment): Nebraska law requires state agencies to adopt an affirmative action plan to identify persons with protected characteristics who are underutilized in their employment and establish affirmative action programs to overcome any such underutilization.[4]

Disability statute: The Nebraska Legislature has expanded the Nebraska Fair Employment Practices statute to mirror the substantial provisions of the Americans with Disabilities Act of 1990 and the Rehabilitation Act of 1973, defining such terms as "qualified individual with a disability," "reasonable accommodations," and so forth.[5]

[99.06A] WELFARE AND BENEFITS LAWS

Insurance coverage for alcohol/drug abuse treatment: Nebraska laws require insurance policies to provide an option to cover treatment of employees undergoing rehabilitation for alcohol abuse.[6]

Insurance coverage for newborns: Nebraska statutes mandate that employee health-related insurance policies include coverage of newborns of employees.[7]

State holidays: Nebraska statutes provide that the following are state recognized holidays: New Year's Day, Martin Luther King's Birthday, Washington's Birthday, Memorial Day, July 4th, Labor Day, Columbus Day, Veteran's Day, Thanksgiving Day, and Christmas Day.[8]

[99.08] UNEMPLOYMENT COMPENSATION LAWS

Aside from private sector employers generally subject to the coverage of Nebraska's Unemployment Compensation Laws, agricultural, nonprofit, the state government agencies, and employers of domestic employees also are subject to the unemployment laws.[9]

Nebraska law disqualifies individuals from collecting unemployment compensation who are recipients of pension, retirement pay, or other such annuities, recipients of unemployment benefits from federal and other state unemployment compensation funds and recipients of wages in lieu of notice, severance pay and/or workers' compensation funds for partial disability.[10]

Nebraska's unemployment compensation laws do not provide coverage to such employees as: persons self-employed; railroad employees; wholly commissioned insurance and real estate agents; persons employed by spouse or child; minor children employed by a parent; patients employed by hospitals; hospital interns; minor newspaper carriers; newspaper distributors; students and spouses of students providing employment services to schools, colleges, and universities, if under college work study program and students at nonprofit or public education institutions who are in full-time work study programs.[11]

[99.10] EMPLOYMENT-AT-WILL DEVELOPMENTS

Implied employment contract—"until retirement" does not constitute: The Nebraska Supreme Court has ruled that a manager's oral statement to a salesperson that he would have an inside sales position "until his retirement" did not provide sufficient specificity to remove the employee's "at-will" relationship with the employer.[12]

Implied contract—handbook discretionary: The Nebraska Supreme Court, in upholding a decision by a lower Court, ruled that an employee handbook that had discretionary language within it as to the manner and method of enforcing disciplinary action did not provide an employee a sufficient basis for a wrongful discharge claim, the employee having been discharged for leaving her work area and climbing into a loft to lie down.[13]

[99.12] TIME LIMITATIONS FOR FILING WRONGFUL DISCHARGE LAWSUITS

Nebraska statutes provide that time limits for litigants to file wrongful employment lawsuits are: one year for defamation, four years for discharge in violation of public policy, and four years for discharge in violation of implied contracts causes of action.[14]

SUPPLEMENTAL NOTES TO CHAPTER 99

1. Revised Statutes of Nebraska, Section 48-1108.
2. Revised Statutes of Nebraska, Sections 48-117–48-1124.
3. Revised Statutes of Nebraska, Section 48-1120.
4. Revised Statutes of Nebraska, Section 48-1122.
5. L. 1993, Legislative Bill 124.
6. Revised Statutes of Nebraska, Sections 44-769, 44-778, *et seq.*
7. Revised Statutes of Nebraska, Sections 44-769, 44-778, *et seq.*
8. Revised Statutes of Nebraska, Section 62-301.
9. Revised Statutes of Nebraska, Sections 48-602, 48-603, 48-604.
10. Revised Statutes of Nebraska, Sections 48-602, *et seq.*
11. Revised Statutes of Nebraska, Sections 48-602, 48-604, 48-628.
12. *Hamersky v. Nicholson Supply Co.*, 246 Neb. 156 (1994).
13. *Rains v. Bocton, Dickinson & Company*, (Neb. Sup. Ct., 1994).
14. Revised Statutes of Nebraska, Sections 25-206, 25-207, 25-208, 25-212.

100

Nevada Labor and Employment Laws

[100.05] REGULATION OF EMPLOYMENT PRACTICES

Bona fide exceptions to prohibited employment practices: Nevada statutes provide that bona fide seniority systems and bona fide benefits programs are legally recognized exceptions to otherwise unfair employment practices.[1]

EEOC—certified deferral: Nevada statutes provide that the State FEP Commission is to serve as a certified deferral agency of the Equal Employment Opportunity Commission relative to fair employment claims filed with the EEOC.[2]

Court review of agency decisions: Nevada statutes permit claimants and respondents to adverse decisions by the State FEP Commission a right of review to applicable courts within the state.[3]

Available remedies for fair employment violations: Nevada statutes provide for backpay and compensatory damages for claimants who prevail in claims before the State Commission.[4]

AIDS—confidentiality: Nevada law forbids disclosure of confidential medical information about employees or other persons having or suspected of having communicable diseases including AIDS.[5]

[100.06A] WELFARE AND BENEFITS LAWS

Insurance coverage for alcohol/drug abuse treatment: Nevada laws require insurance policies to provide mandatory coverage for treatment of employees undergoing rehabilitation for alcohol and/or drug abuse.[6]

Insurance coverage for newborns: Nevada statutes mandate that employee health-related insurance policies include coverage of newborns—including adopted children—of employees.[7]

State holidays: Nevada statutes provide that the following are state recognized holidays: New Year's Day, Martin Luther King's Birthday, Washington's Birthday, Memorial Day, July 4th, Labor Day, Veteran's Day, Thanksgiving Day, and Christmas Day.[8]

[100.08] UNEMPLOYMENT COMPENSATION LAWS

Aside from private sector employers generally subject to the coverage of Nevada's Unemployment Compensation Laws, agricultural, nonprofit, state government agencies, and employers of domestic employees also are subject to the unemployment laws.[9]

Nevada law disqualifies individuals from collecting unemployment compensation who are recipients of pension, retirement pay or other such annuities, recipients of unemployment benefits from federal and other state unemployment compensation funds, and recipients of wages in lieu of notice, severance pay, vacation pay, and backpay due to unlawful discharge.[10]

Nevada's unemployment compensation laws do not provide coverage to such employees as: persons self-employed; railroad employees; persons employed by spouse or child; minor children employed by a parent; patients and student nurses employed by hospitals; minor newspaper carriers; students and spouses of students providing employment services to schools, colleges, and universities, if under college work study program and students at nonprofit or public education institutions who are in full-time work study programs.[11]

[100.12] TIME LIMITATIONS FOR FILING WRONGFUL DISCHARGE LAWSUITS

Nevada statutes provide that time limits for litigants to file wrongful employment lawsuits are: two years for defamation, three years for discharge in violation of public policy, and four years for discharge in violation of implied contracts causes of action.[12]

SUPPLEMENTAL NOTES TO CHAPTER 100

1. Nevada Revised Statutes, Sections 613.350 and 613.380.
2. Nevada Revised Statutes, Sections 233.150, 233.160, *et seq.*
3. Nevada Revised Statutes, Section 613.420.
4. Nevada Revised Statutes, Sections 233.170, 213.180.
5. Nevada Revised Statues, Section 441A.220.
6. Nevada Revised Statutes, Section 689B.030.
7. Nevada Revised Statutes, Section 689B.033.
8. Nevada Revised Statutes, Sections 236.015, 236.040.
9. Nevada Revised Statutes, Sections 612.055, 612.090, 612.095, 612.110, 612.120, 612.121.
10. Nevada Revised Statutes, Sections 612.375, 612.380, *et seq.*
11. Nevada Revised Statutes, Sections 612.070, 612.105, 612.117, 612.118, *et seq.*
12. Nevada Revised Statutes, Section 11-190.

101

New Hampshire Labor and Employment Laws

[101.05] REGULATION OF EMPLOYMENT PRACTICES

Bona fide exceptions to prohibited employment practices: New Hampshire statutes provide that bona fide seniority systems, bona fide occupational qualifications, and bona fide benefits programs are legally recognized exceptions to otherwise unfair employment practices.[1]

EEOC—certified deferral: New Hampshire statutes provide that the State Commission for Human Rights is to serve as a certified deferral agency of the Equal Employment Opportunity Commission relative to fair employment claims filed with the EEOC.[2]

Court review of agency decisions: New Hampshire statutes permit claimants and respondents to adverse decisions by the State Commission for Human Rights a right of review to applicable courts within the state.[3]

Available remedies for fair employment violations: New Hampshire statutes provide for administrative fines, when deemed appropriate, as well as for backpay and compensatory damages for claimants who prevail in claims before the New Hampshire State Commission for Human Rights.[4]

Affirmative action programs (state employment): A New Hampshire Executive Order encourages state agencies to adopt an affirmative action plan to identify persons with protected characteristics who are underutilized in their employment and establish affirmative action programs to overcome any such underutilization.[5]

AIDS testing and confidentiality: New Hampshire law requires the informed consent of a person prior to the administration of an AIDS test and forbids the disclosure of the results of an AIDS test without the authorized approval by the person or unless otherwise required to be released to certain health care providers or agencies.[6]

[101.06A] WELFARE AND BENEFITS LAWS

Insurance coverage for newborns: New Hampshire statutes mandate that employee health-related insurance policies include coverage of newborns—including adopted children—of employees.[7]

Insurance coverage for mental health treatment: New Hampshire law requires insurance policies to provide mandatory coverage for mental health treatment.[8]

State holidays: New Hampshire statutes provide that the following are state recognized holidays: New Year's Day, Washington's Birthday, Memorial Day, July 4th, Labor Day, Columbus Day, Veteran's Day, Thanksgiving Day, and Christmas Day.[9]

[101.08] UNEMPLOYMENT COMPENSATION LAWS

Aside from private sector employers generally subject to the coverage of New Hampshire's Unemployment Compensation Laws, agricultural, nonprofit, and state government agencies also are subject to the unemployment laws.[10]

New Hampshire law disqualifies individuals who are recipients of pension, retirement pay, or other such annuities and recipients of unemployment benefits from federal and other state unemployment compensation funds from collecting unemployment compensation.[11]

New Hampshire's unemployment compensation laws do not provide coverage to such employees as: persons self-employed; railroad employees; wholly commissioned insurance and real estate agents; persons employed by parent, spouse or child; casual labor; patients and student nurses employed by hospitals; hospital interns; minor newspaper carriers; students and spouses of students providing employment services to schools, colleges, and universities, if under college work study programs and students at nonprofit or public education institutions who are in full-time work study programs.[12]

[101.10] EMPLOYMENT-AT-WILL DEVELOPMENTS

Handbook disclaimer sufficient defense: The New Hampshire Supreme Court has ruled that a disclaimer in an employee handbook advising employees that such handbook was merely a guidebook, rather than a contract of employment, was an adequate defense to a breach of contract claim by plaintiff.[13]

[101.12] TIME LIMITATIONS FOR FILING WRONGFUL DISCHARGE LAWSUITS

New Hampshire statutes provide that time limits for litigants to file wrongful employment lawsuits are: three years each for defamation, discharge in violation of public policy, and discharge in violation of implied contracts causes of action.[14]

SUPPLEMENTAL NOTES TO CHAPTER 101

1. New Hampshire Revised Statutes, Chapter 354-A:7.
2. New Hampshire Revised Statutes, Chapters 354-A:3, *et seq.*
3. New Hampshire Revised Statutes, Chapter 354-A:22.
4. New Hampshire Revised Statutes, Chapter 354-A:21.
5. New Hampshire Executive Order 18-3.
6. New Hampshire Revised Statutes, Chapters 141-F:1, *et seq.*
7. New Hampshire Revised Statutes, Chapter 415.18.
8. New Hampshire Revised Statutes, Chapter 415.18-a.
9. New Hampshire Revised Statutes, Chapters 288.1, 288.2.
10. New Hampshire Revised Statutes, Chapters 282-A:8, 282-A:9, 282-A:19.
11. New Hampshire Revised Statutes, Chapters 282-A:9, 282-A:14, *et seq.*
12. New Hampshire Revised Statutes, Chapter 282-A:9, *et seq.*
13. *Butler v. Walker Power, Inc.*, No. 91-141 (N.H. Sup. Ct., 7-19-93).
14. New Hampshire Revised Statutes, Chapter 508.4.

102

New Jersey Labor and Employment Laws

[102.05] REGULATION OF EMPLOYMENT PRACTICES

Bona fide exceptions to prohibited employment practices: New Jersey statutes provide that bona fide seniority systems, bona fide occupational qualifications, and bona fide benefits programs are legally recognized exceptions to otherwise unfair employment practices.[1]

EEOC—certified deferral: New Jersey statutes provide that the Division of Civil Rights is to serve as a certified deferral agency of the Equal Employment Opportunity Commission relative to fair employment claims filed with the EEOC.[2]

Court review of agency decisions: New Jersey statutes permit claimants and respondents to adverse decisions by the Division of Civil Rights a right of review to applicable courts within the state.[3]

Available remedies for fair employment violations: New Jersey statutes provide for punitive damages, when deemed appropriate, as well as for backpay and compensatory damages for claimants who prevail in claims before the Division of Civil Rights.[4]

Affirmative action programs (state employment):   New Jersey law requires state agencies to adopt an affirmative action plan to identify persons with protected characteristics who are underutilized in their employment and establish affirmative action programs to overcome any such underutilization.[5]

Sexual harassment—hostile work environment defined: The New Jersey Supreme Court, in establishing a standard by which to define hostile work environment types of sexual harassment, set forth the following criteria: (1) such conduct or behavior would not have occurred but for the employee's sex, and (2) such conduct was so severe or pervasive as to have made a reasonable person of the same sex and in the same position believe that the conditions of employment had been altered to such an extent that the working environment had become intimidating, hostile or abusive.[6]

Whistle-blowing claim unsupported: A New Jersey Appellate Division Court has ruled that the discharge of a researcher who protested conducting controversial, albeit lawful, drug research, was not a violation of New Jersey's Conscientious Employee Protection Act, the Court holding that the statute was not intended to provide a remedy for the dismissal of an employee who merely disagreed with an employer's lawful decision.[7]

Family medical leave: New Jersey law requires employers of fifty employees or more to provide up to twelve weeks of unpaid leave in a twenty-four-month period to those employees who have worked at least 1000 hours for the year prior to the commencement of the leave for the birth or adoption of a child or the serious health condition of a family member, pursuant to other conditions and restrictions as specified in the statute.[8]

[102.06A] WELFARE AND BENEFITS LAWS

Insurance coverage for alcohol/drug abuse treatment: New Jersey laws require insurance policies to provide mandatory coverage for treatment of employees undergoing rehabilitation for alcohol abuse.[9]

Insurance coverage for newborns: New Jersey statutes mandate that employee health-related insurance policies include coverage of newborns of employees.[10]

State holidays: New Jersey statutes provide the following as state recognized holidays: New Year's Day, Martin Luther King's Birthday, Washington's Birthday, Lincoln's Birthday, Memorial Day, July 4th, Labor Day, Columbus Day, Veteran's Day, Thanksgiving Day, and Christmas Day.[11]

[102.08] UNEMPLOYMENT COMPENSATION LAWS

Aside from private sector employers generally subject to the coverage of New Jersey's Unemployment Compensation Laws, agricultural, nonprofit, state government agencies, and employers of domestic employees also are subject to the unemployment laws.[12]

New Jersey law disqualifies individuals who are recipients of pension, retirement pay, or other such annuities, recipients of unemployment benefits from federal and other state unemployment compensation funds, and recipients of wages in lieu of notice and disability pay under temporary benefits law from collecting unemployment compensation.[13]

New Jersey's unemployment compensation laws do not provide coverage to such employees as: persons self-employed; railroad employees; wholly commissioned insurance and real estate agents; persons employed by spouse or child; minor children employed by a parent; patients employed by hospitals; hospital interns; students and spouses of students providing employment services to schools, colleges, and universities, if under college work study program and students at nonprofit or public education institutions who are in full-time work study programs.[14]

[102.10] EMPLOYMENT-AT-WILL DEVELOPMENTS

Implied contracts—handbook disclaimers: The New Jersey Supreme Court has held that, to be effective, a "just cause" disclaimer in an employee handbook must be prominently displayed so as to highlight it from other text and must be written in language so clear that no employee could reasonably think that the employer publishing the handbook is assuming legally binding obligations relative to the provisions contained in the handbook, such as to state (1) that the employment relationship is terminable at the will of either party, (2) that it is terminable with or without cause, and (3) that is terminable without prior notice.[15]

[102.12] TIME LIMITATIONS FOR FILING WRONGFUL DISCHARGE LAWSUITS

New Jersey statutes provide that time limits for litigants to file wrongful employment lawsuits are: one year for defamation, six years for discharge in violation of public policy, and six years for discharge in violation of implied contracts causes of action.[16]

SUPPLEMENTAL NOTES TO CHAPTER 102

1. New Jersey Statutes Annotated, Sections 10:5-2, 10:5-12.
2. New Jersey Statutes Annotated, Sections 10:5-13, 10:05-14, *et seq.*
3. New Jersey Statutes Annotated, Section 10:5-21.
4. New Jersey Statutes Annotated, Sections 10:5-17, 10:5-27.
5. New Jersey Statutes Annotated, Sections 11A:7-3, *et seq.*
6. *Lehman v. Toys 'R' Us, Inc.*, (NJ Sup. Ct., 7-14-93).
7. *Young v. Schering Corp.*, (NJ App. Div., 1994).
8. New Jersey Statutes Annotated, Section 11B.
9. New Jersey Statutes Annotated, Sections 17B:27-46.1.
10. New Jersey Statutes Annotated, Sections 17B:27-30.
11. New Jersey Statutes Annotated, Sections 36:2-2, *et seq.*
12. New Jersey Statutes Annotated, Sections 43:21-4, 43:21-8, 43:21-19.
13. New Jersey Statutes Annotated, Sections 43:21-4, *et seq.*
14. New Jersey Statutes Annotated, Sections 43:21-19.
15. *Nicosia v. Wakefern Food Corp.*, (NJ Sup. Ct., 6-30-94); See also *Witkowski v. Thomas J. Lipton, Inc.*, (NJ Sup. Ct., 6-30-94).
16. New Jersey Statutes Annotated, Sections 2A:14-1, *et seq.*

103

New Mexico Labor and Employment Laws

[103.05] REGULATION OF EMPLOYMENT PRACTICES

Bona fide exceptions to prohibited employment practices: New Mexico statutes provide that bona fide seniority systems and bona fide occupational qualifications are legally recognized exceptions to otherwise unfair employment practices.[1]

EEOC—certified deferral: New Mexico statutes provide that the New Mexico Human Rights Commission is to serve as a certified deferral agency of the Equal Employment Opportunity Commission relative to fair employment claims filed with the EEOC.[2]

Affirmative action programs (state employment):   A New Mexico Executive Order requires state agencies to adopt an affirmative action plan to identify persons with protected characteristics who are underutilized in their employment and establish affirmative action programs to overcome any such underutilization.[3]

[103.06A] WELFARE AND BENEFITS LAWS

Insurance coverage for alcohol/drug abuse treatment: New Mexico laws require insurance policies to provide an option to cover treatment of employees undergoing rehabilitation for alcohol abuse.[4]

Insurance coverage for newborns: New Mexico statutes mandate that employee health-related insurance policies include coverage of newborns—including adopted children—of employees.[5]

State holidays: New Mexico statutes provide the following as state recognized holidays: New Year's Day, Martin Luther King's Birthday, Washington's Birthday, Memorial Day, July 4th, Labor Day, Columbus Day, Veteran's Day, Thanksgiving Day, and Christmas Day.[6]

[103.08] UNEMPLOYMENT COMPENSATION LAWS

Aside from private sector employers generally subject to the coverage of New Mexico's Unemployment Compensation Laws, agricultural, nonprofit, state government agencies, and employers of domestic employees also are subject to the unemployment laws.[7]

New Mexico law disqualifies individuals who are recipients of pension, retirement pay, or other such annuities and recipients of unemployment benefits from federal and other state unemployment compensation funds from collecting unemployment compensation.[8]

New Mexico's unemployment compensation laws do not provide coverage to such employees as: persons self-employed; railroad employees; wholly commissioned insurance and real estate agents; persons employed by spouse or child; minor children employed by a parent; patients employed by hospitals; minor newspaper carriers; students providing employment services to schools, colleges, and universities, if under college work study program and students at nonprofit or public education institutions who are in full-time work study programs.[9]

[103.10] EMPLOYMENT-AT-WILL DEVELOPMENTS

Implied contract not sustainable: The New Mexico Supreme Court held that discipline and discharge provisions in an employee handbook were not sufficiently explicit to create a "just cause" standard for discharge and did not limit the employer's right to terminate an employee absent just cause.[10]

[103.11] TORT ACTIONS

Negligent retention: The New Mexico Court of Appeals, in granting judgment in the dismissal of the plaintiff's claim that the defendant employer had failed to exercise the requisite standard of care in hiring an employee who the plaintiff contended had embezzled funds from it, refused to dismiss the plaintiff's claims that the employer had failed to exercise its requisite duty of care in retaining such employee, the court concluding that the latter contention involved a different set of facts regarding the employer's continuing duties.[11]

[103.12] TIME LIMITATIONS FOR FILING WRONGFUL DISCHARGE LAWSUITS

New Mexico statutes provide that time limits for litigants to file wrongful employment lawsuits are: three years for defamation, four years for discharge in violation of public policy, and four years for discharge in violation of implied contracts causes of action.[12]

SUPPLEMENTAL NOTES TO CHAPTER 103

1. New Mexico Statutes, Section 28-1-7.
2. New Mexico Statutes, Section 28-1-10.
3. New Mexico Executive Order 85-15.
4. New Mexico Statutes, Section 59A-23-6.
5. New Mexico Statutes, Section 59A-22-33.
6. New Mexico Statutes, Sections 12-5-2, 12-5-5, 12-5-7, 12-5-9.
7. New Mexico Statutes, Sections 51-1-42, 51-1-43.
8. New Mexico Statutes, Sections 51-1-4, 51-1-7, 51-1-42.
9. New Mexico Statutes, Sections 51-1-7, 51-1-42.
10. *Hartbarger v. Frank Paxton Co.*, No. 19-913 (N.M.S. Ct., 7-21-93).
11. *Los Ranchitos v. Tierre Grande, Inc.*, 861 P.2d 263 (N.M. Ct. App., 1993).
12. New Mexico Statutes, Sections 37-1-4, 37-1-8.

104

New York Labor and Employment Laws

[104.05] REGULATION OF EMPLOYMENT PRACTICES

Bona fide exceptions to prohibited employment practices: New York statutes provide that bona fide occupational qualifications and bona fide benefits programs are legally recognized exceptions to otherwise unfair employment practices.[1]

EEOC—certified deferral: New York statutes provide that the Commission of Human Rights is to serve as a certified deferral agency of the Equal Employment Opportunity Commission relative to fair employment claims filed with the EEOC.[2]

Court review of agency decisions: New York statutes permit claimants and respondents to adverse decisions by the Commission of Human Rights a right of review to applicable courts within the state.[3]

Available remedies for fair employment violations: New York statutes provide for backpay and compensatory damages for claimants who prevail in claims before the Commission of Human Rights.[4]

Affirmative action programs (state employment):   New York law requires each state agency to adopt an affirmative action plan to identify persons with protected characteristics who are underutilized in their employment and establish affirmative action programs to overcome any such underutilization.[5]

Sex based discharge requires affirmative evidence: A federal district court in New York held that a female employee failed to demonstrate affirmative evidence that her discharge was based on sex, despite her allegations that her discharge was occasioned by a negative reaction by male superiors who were displeased with her decision to discharge a male subordinate.[6]

Arbitration clause unenforceable: New York's Appellate Division refused to uphold a lower court's injunction that enjoined a broker-employer from commencing an action in any other judicial forum, as provided in an agreement with a former employee, the Court ruling that the lower Court had no jurisdiction to grant such injunction.[7]

Off-duty activities—discharge for dating no violation: A New York Appeals Court has held that the New York statute that makes it unlawful for an employer to discriminate against, discipline or discharge an employee for off-duty leisure time does not extend to the protection of a married employee who is discharged for dating an employee other than his or her spouse, a behavior in violation of a company policy on the subject, inasmuch as such dating activities do not meet the "recreational" test of the statute.[8]

Breastfeeding protection: New York law provides a right of mothers to breastfeed in any public or private place where they are authorized to be.[9]

AIDS testing and confidentiality: New York law requires informed consent of individuals prior to the administration of an AIDS test and forbids the disclosure of the results of such tests unless authorized by the person so tested or otherwise required to be released to certain health care providers or agencies.[10]

Jury and witness duty: Employers who employ more than ten employees may not withhold the first fifteen dollars of the daily wages of any employee serving on jury duty during the first three days of jury service.[11]

[104.06] PAYMENT OF MANUAL WORKERS

A New York statute requires employers to pay manual workers weekly, and not later than seven calendar days after the end of the week in which wages are earned.[12]

[104.06A] WELFARE AND BENEFITS LAWS

Insurance coverage for alcohol/drug abuse treatment: New York laws require insurance policies to provide an option to cover treatment of employees undergoing rehabilitation for alcohol and/or drug abuse.[13]

Insurance coverage for newborns: New York statutes mandate that employee health-related insurance policies include coverage of newborns—including adopted children—of employees.[14]

Insurance coverage for mental health treatment: New York law requires insurance policies to provide an option for coverage of mental health treatment.[15]

State holidays: New York statutes provide the following as state recognized holidays: New Year's Day, Martin Luther King's Birthday, Washington's Birthday, Lincoln's Birthday, Memorial Day, July 4th, Labor Day, Columbus Day, Veteran's Day, Thanksgiving Day, and Christmas Day.[16]

[104.08] UNEMPLOYMENT COMPENSATION LAWS

Aside from private sector employers generally subject to the coverage of New York's Unemployment Compensation Laws, agricultural, nonprofit, state government agencies and employers of domestic employees also are subject to the unemployment laws.[17]

New York law disqualifies individuals from collecting unemployment compensation who are recipients of pension, retirement pay, or other such annuities, recipients of unemployment benefits from federal and other state unemployment compensation funds, and recipients of benefits under another law.[18]

New York's unemployment compensation laws do not provide coverage to such employees as: persons self-employed; railroad employees; wholly commissioned real estate agents; persons employed by spouse or child; minor children employed by a parent; casual labor; students and spouses of students providing employment services to schools, colleges, and universities, if under college work study program and students at nonprofit or public education institutions who are in full-time work study programs.[19]

[104.09] WORKERS' COMPENSATION LAWS

A New York Appellate Division affirmed the State's Workers' Compensation Board who had held that an employee who had been terminated for absenteeism was discharged for reasonable cause, rather than discharged in retaliation for filing a workers' compensation claim, based in part upon the failure of the employee to establish a causal relationship between his activities in obtaining workers' compensation and his employer's reason for termination.[20]

[104.10] EMPLOYMENT-AT-WILL DEVELOPMENTS

Implied contract requirements: A New York Appellate Court has held that in order to overcome the presumption of an employment-at-will relationship, an employee must show that: (a) he or she was induced to leave former employment by assurances that the employer only dismisses employees "for cause," (b) the "for cause" assurances were embodied in the document, (c) the employee relied upon such assurances to his or her detriment, and (d) the employment was subject to said "for cause" assurances.[21]

[104.12] TIME LIMITATIONS FOR FILING WRONGFUL DISCHARGE LAWSUITS

New York statutes provide that time limits for litigants to file wrongful employment lawsuits are: one year for defamation, and six years for discharge in violation of implied contracts causes of action.[22]

SUPPLEMENTAL NOTES TO CHAPTER 104

1. Consolidated Laws of New York, Executive Laws, Section 296.
2. Consolidated Laws of New York, Executive Laws, Sections 293, 294, *et seq.*
3. Consolidated Laws of New York, Executive Laws, Section 298.
4. Consolidated Laws of New York, Executive Laws, Section 297.
5. New York Executive Order, Section 1-1-1.3.
6. *Flynn v. Goldman, Sachs & Co.*, No. 91 Cir. 0035 (SD, NY, 11-8-93).
7. *In re Application of Todd Leake*, (NY App. Div., 3-2-95).
8. *State of New York v. Wal-Mart Stores*, (NY App. Div., 1995).
9. NY CLS Civil Rights Law, Section 79-e, 79-i (effective June 15, 1994).
10. Consolidated Laws of New York, Public Health Laws, Section 2780, *et seq.*
11. Judiciary Law, § 519.
12. New York Labor Law, § 6.25.
13. Consolidated Laws of New York, Insurance Laws, Sections 3221(1)(6)(A), *et seq.*
14. Consolidated Laws of New York, Insurance Laws, Section 3221(k)(5)(A).
15. Consolidated Laws of New York, Insurance Laws, Section 3221(l)(5)(A).
16. New York General Constitution, Section 24.
17. Consolidated Laws of New York, Labor Laws, Sections 560, *et seq.*
18. Consolidated Laws of New York, Labor Laws, Sections 511, 592, 593, 600.
19. Consolidated Laws of New York, Labor Laws, Section 511; Mental Hygiene Law, Section 33.09.
20. *Conklin v. City of Newburgh*, (NY App. Div., 6-9-94).
21. *O'Reilly v. Citibank, N.A.*, No. 91-07744 (NY Sup. Ct., 11-8-93).
22. Consolidated Laws of New York, Civil Practice, Sections 213, 215 *et seq.*

105

North Carolina Labor and Employment Laws

[105.05] REGULATION OF EMPLOYMENT PRACTICES

Bona fide exceptions to prohibited employment practices: North Carolina statutes provide that bona fide seniority systems and bona fide occupational qualifications are legally recognized exceptions to otherwise unfair employment practices.[1]

EEOC—certified deferral: North Carolina statutes provide that the State Human Relations Commission is to serve as a certified deferral agency of the Equal Employment Opportunity Commission relative to public employees' fair employment claims filed with the EEOC.[2]

Affirmative action programs (state employment): North Carolina law requires state agencies to adopt an affirmative action plan to identify persons with protected characteristics who are underutilized in their employment and establish affirmative action programs to overcome any such underutilization.[3]

Drug screens—random testing: A North Carolina Appellate Court held that the Raleigh-Durham Airport Authority did not violate an airport mechanic's rights under the North Carolina Constitution and public policy when it required the mechanic to submit to a random drug test.[4]

[105.06A] WELFARE AND BENEFITS LAWS

Insurance coverage for alcohol/drug abuse treatment: North Carolina laws require insurance policies to provide an option to cover treatment of employees undergoing rehabilitation for alcohol and/or drug abuse.[5]

Insurance coverage for newborns: North Carolina statutes mandate that employee health-related insurance policies include coverage of newborns—including adopted children—of employees.[6]

State holidays: North Carolina statutes provide that the following are state recognized holidays: New Year's Day, Martin Luther King's Birthday, Washington's Birthday, Memorial Day, July 4th, Labor Day, Columbus Day, Veteran's Day, Thanksgiving Day, and Christmas Day.[7]

[105.08] UNEMPLOYMENT COMPENSATION LAWS

Aside from private sector employers generally subject to the coverage of North Carolina's Unemployment Compensation Laws, agricultural, nonprofit, state government agencies and employers of domestic employees also are subject to the unemployment laws.[8]

North Carolina law disqualifies individuals from collecting unemployment compensation who are recipients of pension, retirement pay, or other such annuities, recipients of unemployment benefits from federal and other state unemployment compensation funds, and recipients of backpay awards.[9]

North Carolina's unemployment compensation laws do not provide coverage to such employees as: persons self-employed; employees of commercial fishing vessels; railroad employees; wholly commissioned insurance and real estate agents; persons employed by spouse or child; minor children employed by a parent; casual labor; patients employed by hospitals; hospital interns; minor newspaper carriers; newspaper distributors; students and spouses of students providing employment services to schools, colleges, and universities, if under college work study program and students at nonprofit or public education institutions who are in full-time work study programs.[10]

[105.09] WORKERS' COMPENSATION LAWS

Retaliatory discharge claim: The North Carolina Supreme Court ruled it was reversible error for a lower court to deny the employer the right to introduce evidence to show there was no disparate treatment of the plaintiff in its defense of a workers' compensation retaliatory discharge claim since it was critical to the employer's position to demonstrate its treatment of similarly situated employees.[11]

[105.10] EMPLOYMENT-AT-WILL DEVELOPMENTS

Public policy exception: A North Carolina Appellate Court has held that an employee who was discharged for failure to submit to a drug test in a "safety-sensitive" position was not discharged in violation of public policy in that public safety concerns substantially outweighed such privacy rights under state and federal constitutional provisions.[12]

Public policy exception—retaliation: A North Carolina Appellate Court has ruled that the termination of an employee after she informed her superiors of her intention to testify truthfully, if called to testify pursuant to a subpoena, violated public policy.[13]

[105.12] TIME LIMITATIONS FOR FILING WRONGFUL DISCHARGE LAWSUITS

North Carolina statutes provide that time limits for litigants to file wrongful employment lawsuits are: one year for defamation, and three years for discharge in violation of public policy.[14]

SUPPLEMENTAL NOTES TO CHAPTER 105

1. General Statutes of North Carolina, Sections 126-16, 126-36, 168A-9.
2. General Statutes of North Carolina, Sections 143.422.2, *et seq.*
3. General Statutes of North Carolina, Sections 143-128(d), 168A-11.
4. *Boescke v. Raleigh-Durham Airport Authority*, 432 S.E.2d 137 (N.C. Ct. App., 1993).
5. General Statutes of North Carolina, Section 58-51-50.
6. General Statutes of North Carolina, Section 58-51-25.
7. General Statutes of North Carolina, Sections 103-4, 103-7, 103-9, 103-10.
8. General Statutes of North Carolina, Sections 96-8, *et seq.*
9. General Statutes of North Carolina, Sections 96-4, 96-8, 19-12, *et seq.*
10. General Statutes of North Carolina, Sections 96-8, *et seq.*
11. *Abels v. Renfro Corporation*, 436 SE 2d 822 (N.C.S.Ct., 12-3-93).
12. *Boesche v. Raleigh-Durham Airport*, No. 9215SC23 (N.C. Ct. of App., 7-20-93).
13. *Daniel v. Carolina Sunrock Corp.*, No. 929 SC 479 (N.C. Ct. of App., 6-1-93).
14. General Statutes of North Carolina, Sections 1-52, 1-54.

106

North Dakota Labor and Employment Laws

[106.05] REGULATION OF EMPLOYMENT PRACTICES

Bona fide exceptions to prohibited employment practices: North Dakota statutes provide that bona fide seniority systems, bona fide occupational qualifications, and bona fide benefits programs are legally recognized exceptions to otherwise unfair employment practices.[1]

EEOC—certified deferral: North Dakota statutes provide that the State Department of Labor is to serve as a certified deferral agency of the Equal Employment Opportunity Commission relative to fair employment claims filed with the EEOC.[2]

Available remedies for fair employment violations: North Dakota statutes provide for backpay and compensatory damages for claimants who prevail in claims before the State Department of Labor.[3]

AIDS testing and confidentiality: North Dakota law requires an informed consent of an individual prior to the administration of an AIDS test and prohibits the disclosure of the results of an AIDS test without the person's approval unless required to be released to certain health care providers or other agencies.[4]

[106.06A] WELFARE AND BENEFITS LAWS

Insurance coverage for alcohol/drug abuse treatment: North Dakota laws require insurance policies to provide mandatory coverage for treatment of employees undergoing rehabilitation for alcohol and/or drug abuse where 25 or more employees are employed.[5]

Insurance coverage for newborns: North Dakota statutes mandate that employee health-related insurance policies include coverage of newborns—including adopted children—of employees.[6]

Insurance coverage for mental health treatment: North Dakota law requires insurance policies to provide mandatory coverage for mental health treatment.[7]

State holidays: North Dakota's statutes provide the following as state recognized holidays: New Year's Day, Martin Luther King's Birthday, Washington's Birthday, Memorial Day, July 4th, Labor Day, Veteran's Day, Thanksgiving Day, and Christmas Day.[8]

[106.08] UNEMPLOYMENT COMPENSATION LAWS

Aside from private sector employers generally subject to the coverage of North Dakota's Unemployment Compensation Laws, agricultural, nonprofit, state government agencies, and employers of domestic employees also are subject to the unemployment laws.[9]

North Dakota law disqualifies individuals who are recipients of pension, retirement pay, or other such annuities and recipients of unemployment benefits from federal and other state unemployment compensation funds from collecting unemployment compensation.[10]

North Dakota's unemployment compensation laws do not provide coverage to such employees as: persons self-employed; railroad employees; wholly commissioned insurance and real estate agents; persons employed by spouse or child; minor children employed by a parent; casual labor; patients and student nurses employed by hospitals; minor newspaper carriers; students and spouses of students providing employment services to schools, colleges, and universities, if under college work study program and students at nonprofit or public education institutions who are in full-time work study programs.[11]

[106.11] TORT ACTIONS

Defamation—privilege: The Supreme Court of North Dakota affirmed a lower court's summary judgment in a defamation claim by a school superintendent against his employer, a school board, the court ruling that statements made at school board meetings that the superintendent had cost the school district money, ran a sloppy program, etc., were pertinent to school board matters and, thus, absolutely privileged.[12]

[106.12] TIME LIMITATIONS FOR FILING WRONGFUL DISCHARGE LAWSUITS

North Dakota statutes provide that time limits for litigants to file wrongful employment lawsuits are: two years for defamation, and six years for discharge in violation of public policy and discharge in violation of implied contracts causes of action.

SUPPLEMENTAL NOTES TO CHAPTER 106

1. North Dakota Century Code, Sections 14-02.4-02, 14-02.4-05, 14-02.4-06, 14-02.4-08, 14-02.09 and 14-02.18.
2. North Dakota Century Code, Sections 14-02.4-19, 14-02.4-21.
3. North Dakota Century Code, Sections 14-02.4-20, *et seq.*
4. North Dakota Century Code, Sections 23-07.5-01, *et seq.*
5. North Dakota Century Code, Section 26.1-36-08.
6. North Dakota Century Code, Section 26.1-36-07.
7. North Dakota Century Code, Section 26.1-36-09.
8. North Dakota Century Code, Sections 1-03-01, *et seq.*
9. North Dakota Century Code, Section 52-01-01.
10. North Dakota Century Code, Sections 52-01-01, *et seq.*
11. North Dakota Century Code, Sections 52-01-01, *et seq.*
12. *Rykowsky v. Dickinson Public School District #1*, 508 NW2d 348 (N.D. Sup. Ct., 1993).

107

Ohio Labor and Employment Laws

[107.05] REGULATION OF EMPLOYMENT PRACTICES

Bona fide exceptions to prohibited employment practices: Ohio statutes provide that bona fide seniority systems, bona fide occupational qualifications, and bona fide benefits programs are legally recognized exceptions to otherwise unfair employment practices.[1]

EEOC—certified deferral: Ohio statutes provide that the Ohio Civil Rights Commission is to serve as a certified deferral agency of the Equal Employment Opportunity Commission relative to fair employment claims filed with the EEOC.[2]

Court review of agency decisions: Ohio statutes permit claimants and respondents to adverse decisions by the Ohio Civil Rights Commission a right of review to applicable courts within the state.[3]

Affirmative action programs (state employment):   Ohio law requires state agencies to adopt an affirmative action plan to identify persons with protected characteristics who are underutilized in their employment and establish affirmative action programs to overcome any such underutilization.[4]

Pregnancy discrimination—leave policy flawed: An Ohio Appellate Court, in affirming a lower court decision has ruled that a leave of absence policy for pregnancy and childbirth was actually one that effectively provided that the pregnant employee would be permanently replaced by another individual and did not meet the statutory requirements that a pregnant employee who takes a leave for childbirthing purposes must be returned to her regular or similar position upon her return from leave without any decrease in pay.[5]

[107.06A] WELFARE AND BENEFITS LAWS

Insurance coverage for alcohol abuse treatment: Ohio laws require insurance policies to provide mandatory coverage for a combination of in-patient and out-patient treatment of employees undergoing rehabilitation for alcohol abuse.[6]

Insurance coverage for newborns: Ohio statutes mandate that employee health-related insurance policies include coverage of newborns—including adopted children—of employees.[7]

State holidays: Ohio statutes specify the following as state recognized holidays: New Year's Day, Martin Luther King's Birthday, Washington's Birthday, Memorial Day, July 4th, Labor Day, Columbus Day, Veteran's Day, Thanksgiving Day, and Christmas Day.[8]

[107.08] UNEMPLOYMENT COMPENSATION LAWS

Aside from private sector employers generally subject to the coverage of Ohio's Unemployment Compensation Laws, agricultural, nonprofit, state government agencies, and employers of domestic employees also are subject to the unemployment laws.[9]

Ohio law disqualifies individuals who are recipients of pension, retirement pay, or other such annuities, recipients of unemployment benefits from federal and other state unemployment compensation funds, recipients of wages in lieu of notice, dismissal or separation allowance, recipients of temporary partial disability payments under workers compensation laws and recipients of Social Security benefits from collecting unemployment compensation.[10]

Ohio's unemployment compensation laws do not provide coverage to such employees as: persons self-employed; railroad employees; wholly commissioned insurance agents; persons employed by spouse or child; minors employed by a parent; casual labor; patients and student nurses employed by hospitals; hospital interns; minor newspaper carriers; students and spouses of students providing employment services to schools, colleges, and universities, if under college work study program and students at nonprofit or public education institutions who are in full-time work study programs.[11]

[107.10] EMPLOYMENT-AT-WILL DEVELOPMENTS

Public policy exception: An Ohio Appellate Court has held that a person's termination because of handicap constitutes a violation of public policy in that the state's FEP statute did provide the exclusive remedy for handicap discrimination.[12]

Promissory estoppel: An Ohio Court of Appeals has held actionable a promissory estoppel lawsuit based on allegations that the plaintiff relied upon promises by her superiors that she could take another week off from work following her husband's suicide, only to be called and discharged by her superior while off during said week.[13]

[107.11] TORT ACTIONS

Defamation—privileged communications: An Ohio Appellate Court has ruled that supervisory statements, made pursuant to an attempted resolution of an employee grievance arising out of a collective bargaining agreement, are privileged statements, which privilege serves as an absolute defense to plaintiff's allegation in the lawsuit in question.[14]

Intentional infliction of emotional distress: An Ohio Appellate Court has held that the fact that a manager threw his note pad across the room and screamed at the plaintiff during her discharge was insufficient to support an emotional distress cause of action in that such conduct was not so outrageous in character, and so extreme in degree, as to go beyond all possible bounds of decency as to be regarded as atrocious and utterly intolerable in a civilized community.[15]

[107.12] TIME LIMITATIONS FOR FILING WRONGFUL DISCHARGE LAWSUITS

Ohio statutes provide time limits for litigants to file wrongful employment lawsuits that are: one year for defamation, four years for discharge in violation of public policy, and six years for discharge in violation of implied contracts causes of action.[16]

SUPPLEMENTAL NOTES TO CHAPTER 107

1. Ohio Statutes, Section 4112.02.
2. Ohio Statutes, Sections 4112.03, *et seq.*
3. Ohio Statutes, Sections 4112.06, 4112.061.
4. Ohio Statutes, Sections 9.47, 125.11.1, 5525.03.
5. *Morse v. Sudan, Inc. d/b/a Nutri-System*, (Ohio App. Ct., 8-11-94).
6. Ohio Statutes, Section 3923.29.
7. Ohio Statutes Annotated, Section 2923.24.
8. Ohio Statutes, Sections 1.14, 5.20–5.225.
9. Ohio Statutes, Section 4141.01.
10. Ohio Statutes, Sections 4141.01, 4141.29 and 4141.31.
11. Ohio Statutes, Sections 4141.01, 4141.29, 4141.31.
12. *Clipson v. Schlessman*, No. E-92-27 (Ohio Ct. of App., 6-18-93).
13. *Cox v. Commercial Parts and Service*, (Ohio App. Ct., 8-11-94).
14. *Stiles v. Chrysler Motors Corp.*, No. L-92-196 (Ohio Ct. of App.—6th District, 6-30-93).
15. *Juergens v. Strang, Klabnik & Assoc.*, (Ohio Ct. App., 7-14-94).
16. Ohio Statutes, Sections 2305.7, 2305.9, 2305.11.

108

Oklahoma Labor and Employment Laws

[108.05] REGULATION OF EMPLOYMENT PRACTICES

Bona fide exceptions to prohibited employment practices: Oklahoma statutes provide that bona fide seniority systems, bona fide occupational qualifications, and bona fide benefits programs are legally recognized exceptions to otherwise unfair employment practices.[1]

EEOC—certified deferral: Oklahoma statutes provide that the Oklahoma Human Rights Commission is to serve as a certified deferral agency of the Equal Employment Opportunity Commission relative to fair employment claims filed with the EEOC.[2]

Court review of agency decisions: Oklahoma statutes permit claimants and respondents to adverse decisions by the Oklahoma Human Rights Commission a right of review to applicable courts within the state.[3]

Affirmative action programs (state employment):   Oklahoma law requires state agencies to adopt an affirmative action plan to identify persons with protected characteristics who are underutilized in their employment and establish affirmative action programs to overcome any such underutilization.[4]

Disability law—contributing factor sufficient to establish violation: The Tenth Circuit Court of Appeals, interpreting and applying Oklahoma law, has ruled that if a disability plays a part in an adverse employment decision, such as a layoff in this case, a violation of the Oklahoma Anti-Discrimination Act occurs. The court held also, that had the Oklahoma legislature intended that a disability be the "sole" reason for an adverse employment decision in order to substantiate a violation, the legislature should have used such language in the statute.[5]

AIDS testing and confidentiality: Oklahoma law requires an informed consent of an individual prior to the administration of an AIDS test and forbids the disclosure of the results of such test unless authorized by the person so tested otherwise required to be released to certain health care providers or agencies.[6]

Drug testing statute: Oklahoma has enacted a statute entitled the *Standards for Workplace Drug and Alcohol Testing Act* that permits employers to require drug and alcohol testing in five specific circumstances: applicant screening, reasonable suspicion, post-accident, random under certain specified situations, and no-notice testing as a part of a post-rehabilitation program for up to two years; it provided further that any employer so testing applicants and employees must state its policy, identify substances it will be testing, describe its testing procedures, outline consequences of refusal to submit to such testing or of a positive test, provide appropriate postings and confidentiality associated with such testing and provide an employee assistance program as part of its policy.[7]

[108.06A] WELFARE AND BENEFITS LAWS

Insurance coverage for newborns: Oklahoma statutes mandate that employee health-related insurance policies include coverage of newborns—including adopted children—of employees.[8]

State holidays: Oklahoma statutes specify the following as state recognized holidays: New Year's Day, Martin Luther King's Birthday, Washington's Birthday, Memorial Day, July 4th, Labor Day, Veteran's Day, Thanksgiving Day, and Christmas Day.[9]

[108.08] UNEMPLOYMENT COMPENSATION LAWS

Aside from private sector employers generally subject to the coverage of Oklahoma's Unemployment Compensation Laws, agricultural, nonprofit, the state government agencies, and employers of domestic employees also are subject to the unemployment laws.[10]

Oklahoma law disqualifies individuals who are recipients of pension, retirement pay, or other such annuities and recipients of unemployment benefits from federal and other state unemployment compensation funds from collecting unemployment compensation.[11]

Oklahoma's unemployment compensation laws do not provide coverage to such employees as: persons self-employed; railroad employees; wholly commissioned insurance and real estate agents; persons employed by spouse or child; minors employed by a parent; patients and student nurses employed by hospitals; hospital interns; minor newspaper carriers; students and spouses of students providing employment services to schools, colleges, and universities, if under college work study program and students at nonprofit or public education institutions who are in full-time work study programs.[12]

[108.12] TIME LIMITATIONS FOR FILING WRONGFUL DISCHARGE LAWSUITS

Oklahoma statutes provide time limits for litigants to file wrongful employment lawsuits that are: one year for defamation, two years for discharge in violation of public policy, and three years for discharge in violation of implied contracts causes of action.[13]

SUPPLEMENTAL NOTES TO CHAPTER 108

1. Oklahoma Statutes Annotated, Sections 25:1302, *et seq.*
2. Oklahoma Statutes Annotated, Sections 25:1501–1503.
3. Oklahoma Statutes Annotated, Sections 25:1502, *et seq.*
4. Oklahoma Statutes Annotated, Sections 40:195.1, 74.840.2.
5. *Bentley v. Cleveland County Board of County Commissioners,* 41 F3d 600 (CA-10, 1994).
6. Oklahoma Statutes Annotated, Section 63:1-502.2 *et seq.*
7. *Oklahoma Standards for Workplace Drug and Alcohol Testing Act,* 1993.
8. Oklahoma Statutes Annotated, Section 36:6058.
9. Oklahoma Statutes Annotated, Sections 25:282.1, 82.2, 87, 90.3.
10. Oklahoma Statutes Annotated, Sections 40:1–208, *et seq.*
11. Oklahoma Statutes Annotated, Sections 40:1–210, *et seq.*
12. Oklahoma Statutes Annotated, Section 40:1–210.
13. Oklahoma Statutes Annotated, Section 12:95.

109

Oregon Labor and Employment Laws

[109.05] REGULATION OF EMPLOYMENT PRACTICES

Bona fide exceptions to prohibited employment practices: Oregon statutes provide that bona fide seniority systems, bona fide occupational qualifications, and bona fide benefits programs are legally recognized exceptions to otherwise unfair employment practices.[1]

EEOC—certified deferral: Oregon statutes provide that the Oregon Bureau of Labor and Industries is to serve as a certified deferral agency of the Equal Employment Opportunity Commission relative to fair employment claims filed with the EEOC.[2]

Court review of agency decisions: Oregon statutes permit claimants and respondents to adverse decisions by the Oregon Bureau of Labor and Industries a right of review to applicable courts within the state.[3]

Available remedies for fair employment violations: Oregon statutes provide for punitive damages (of no more than $3,500), when deemed appropriate, as well as for backpay and compensatory damages (of no more than $250) for claimants who prevail in claims before the Oregon Bureau of Labor and Industries.[4]

Affirmative action programs (state employment): Oregon law requires each state agency to adopt an affirmative action plan to identify persons with protected characteristics who are underutilized in their employment and establish affirmative action programs to overcome any such underutilization.[5]

Sexual harassment claim actionable: An Oregon Court of Appeals has held actionable a sexual harassment lawsuit in which the claimant alleged that while she was employed by the defendant, her supervisor—who had been cited for previous sexual harassment of another employee—had sexually harassed her, referring to her as a "Sex-atary," and "a snippy bitch," and had failed to take action against a co-worker who had intentionally touched her breast, despite the fact that her supervisor was terminated by management after it had learned of the supervisor's behavior. The court concluded that a jury could find, from the supervisor's history, that the employer knew or should have known of the supervisor's behavior and failed to take appropriate remedial action against the supervisor.[6]

Drug testing—active alcoholism: An Oregon Court has ruled that the Oregon Handicapped Persons Civil Rights Act protects active alcoholics.[7]

AIDS testing and confidentiality: Oregon law requires an informed consent of an individual prior to the administration of an AIDS test and forbids unauthorized disclosure of such tests unless required to be released to certain health care providers or agencies.[8]

AIDS accommodation: An Oregon statute provides that an employer is not required to reasonably accommodate an employee who is physically impaired by the HIV infection unless such employee provides his or her employer with HIV test information.[9]

[109.06A] WELFARE AND BENEFITS LAWS

Insurance coverage for alcohol/drug abuse treatment: Oregon laws require insurance policies to provide mandatory coverage for treatment of employees undergoing rehabilitation for alcohol and/or drug abuse.[10]

Insurance coverage for newborns: Oregon statutes mandate that employee health-related insurance policies include coverage of newborns of employees.[11]

Insurance coverage for mental health treatment: Oregon statutes require insurance policies provide mandatory coverage for mental health treatment.[12]

State holidays: Oregon statutes provide the following as state recognized holidays: New Year's Day, Martin Luther King's Birthday, Washington's Birthday, Memorial Day, July 4th, Labor Day, Veteran's Day, Thanksgiving Day, and Christmas Day.[13]

[109.08] UNEMPLOYMENT COMPENSATION LAWS

Aside from private sector employers generally subject to the coverage of Oregon's Unemployment Compensation Laws, agricultural, nonprofit, state government agencies, and employers of domestic employees also are subject to the unemployment laws.[14]

Oregon law disqualifies individuals who are recipients of pension, retirement pay or other such annuities, recipients of unemployment benefits from federal and other state unemployment compensation funds and recipients of vacation pay from collecting unemployment compensation.[15]

Oregon's unemployment compensation laws do not provide coverage to such employees as: persons self-employed; railroad employees; wholly commissioned insurance and real estate agents; persons employed by parent, spouse or child; casual labor; patients and student nurses employed by hospitals; hospital interns; minor newspaper carriers; students and spouses of students providing employment services to schools, colleges, and universities, if under college work study program and students at nonprofit or public education institutions who are in full-time work study programs.[16]

[109.10] EMPLOYMENT-AT-WILL DEVELOPMENTS

Public policy exception—retaliatory discharge for protesting gender discrimination: An Oregon Court of Appeals has held that a discharge in retaliation of an employee's resistance to discrimination, such as gender discrimination in the subject case, aimed at vindicating a statutory right, as distinguished from a discharge in violation of a statutory right, provides a basis for an actionable public policy type lawsuit.[17]

[109.11] TORT ACTIONS

Constructive discharge—fulfilling statutory requirements: An Oregon Appellate Court has ruled that an employee who claimed that she was constructively discharged because she repeatedly brought inventory inaccuracies to her employer's attention in compliance with state law requirements, could pursue her wrongful discharge lawsuit.[18]

Intentional infliction of emotional distress—sexual harassment/constructive discharge: An Oregon Appellate Court, in reinstating a former employee's claims for intentional infliction of emotional distress and constructive discharge, ruled that a supervisor's uninvitingly rubbing his hands and body on the employee's shoulders, back, and buttocks permitted an inference of the element of intent, sufficient to establish a cause of action.[19]

[109.12] TIME LIMITATIONS FOR FILING WRONGFUL DISCHARGE LAWSUITS

Oregon statutes provide time limits for litigants to file wrongful employment lawsuits that are: two years for defamation, two years for discharge in violation of public policy, and three years for discharge in violation of implied contracts causes of action.[20]

SUPPLEMENTAL NOTES TO CHAPTER 109

1. Oregon Revised Statutes, Sections 659.028, 659.030.
2. Oregon Revised Statutes, Sections 659.035, 659.060.
3. Oregon Revised Statutes, Sections 183.310, 183.550, *et seq.*
4. Oregon Revised Statutes, Sections 20.107, 240.560, 659.035, *et seq.*
5. Oregon Revised Statutes, Sections 182.100, 240.015.
6. *Mains v. II Morrow, Inc.* (Ore. Ct. App., 6-22-94).
7. *Braun v. American Int'l Health & Rehabilitation Services, Inc.*, 846 A2d 1151 (Or., 1993).
8. Oregon Revised Statutes, Section 433.045.
9. Oregon Revised Statutes, Section 433.045.
10. Oregon Revised Statutes, Section 743.556.
11. Oregon Revised Statutes, Section 743.707.
12. Oregon Revised Statutes, Section 743.556.
13. Oregon Revised Statutes, Section s 187.010–187.020.
14. Oregon Revised Statutes, Sections 657.025, 657.045, 657.050, 657.072, 657.092.

15. Oregon Revised Statutes, Sections 657.030, 657.176, 657.205, 657.210, 657.221.

16. Oregon Revised Statutes, Sections 657.025, 657.030, 657.050, 657.056, 657.060, 657.075, 657.080, 657.085.

17. *Goodette v. LTM, Inc.* (Ore. Ct. App., 5-25-94).

18. *Dolby v. Sisters of Providence in Oregon,* No. CA A7675 (Oregon Ct. App., 12-8-93).

19. *McGanty v. Staudenrous,* No. CA A75978 (Oregon Ct. App., 1993).

20. Oregon Revised Statutes, Sections 12.080, 12.110.

110

Pennsylvania Labor and Employment Laws

[110.05] REGULATION OF EMPLOYMENT PRACTICES

Bona fide exceptions to prohibited employment practices: Pennsylvania statutes provide that bona fide seniority systems, bona fide occupational qualifications, and bona fide benefits programs are legally recognized exceptions to otherwise unfair employment practices.[1]

EEOC—certified deferral: Pennsylvania statutes provide that the Pennsylvania Human Relations Commission is to serve as a certified deferral agency of the Equal Employment Opportunity Commission relative to fair employment claims filed with the EEOC.[2]

Court review of agency decisions: Pennsylvania statutes permit claimants and respondents to adverse decisions by the Pennsylvania Human Relations Commission a right of review to applicable courts within the state.[3]

Available remedies for fair employment violations: Pennsylvania statutes provide for backpay and compensatory damages for claimants who prevail in claims before the Pennsylvania Human Relations Commission.[4]

Affirmative action programs (state employment): Pennsylvania law requires state agencies to adopt an affirmative action plan to identify persons with protected characteristics who are underutilized in their employment and establish affirmative action programs to overcome any such underutilization.[5]

AIDS testing and discrimination (state employees): A Pennsylvania Executive Order forbids testing of state employees for AIDS or the HIV infection as a condition of employment and also forbids employment discrimination against state employees on the basis of AIDS or HIV infection as long as such employees are able to perform their duties.[6]

[110.06A] WELFARE AND BENEFITS LAWS

Insurance coverage for alcohol/drug abuse treatment: Pennsylvania laws require insurance policies to provide mandatory coverage for treatment of employees undergoing rehabilitation for alcohol and/or drug abuse.[7]

Insurance coverage for newborns: Pennsylvania statutes mandate that employee health-related insurance policies include coverage of newborns of employees.[8]

State holidays: Pennsylvania statutes specify the following as state recognized holidays: New Year's Day, Martin Luther King's Birthday, Washington's Birthday, Memorial Day, July 4th, Labor Day, Columbus Day, Veteran's Day, Thanksgiving Day, and Christmas Day.[9]

[110.08] UNEMPLOYMENT COMPENSATION LAWS

Aside from private sector employers generally subject to the coverage of Pennsylvania's Unemployment Compensation Laws, agricultural, nonprofit, state government agencies, and employers of domestic employees also are subject to the unemployment laws.[10]

Pennsylvania law disqualifies individuals who are recipients of pension, retirement pay or other such annuities, recipients of unemployment benefits from federal and other state unemployment compensation funds and recipients of vacation pay from collecting unemployment compensation.[11]

Pennsylvania's unemployment compensation laws do not provide coverage to such employees as: persons self-employed; railroad employees; wholly commissioned insurance and real estate agents; persons employed by parent, spouse or child; casual labor; patients and student nurses employed by hospitals; hospital interns; minor newspaper carriers; students and spouses of students providing employment services to schools, colleges, and universities, if under college work study program and students at nonprofit or public education institutions who are in full-time work study programs.[12]

A Commonwealth Court has ruled that an employee who quit her job as a result of being subjected to sexual harassment by a regional manager who had made sexually suggestive remarks to her in the presence of her immediate supervisor who took no corrective actions as to such suggestive remark, could not be denied unemployment compensation benefits on the basis that she had not formally complained to management in that her supervisor did nothing to correct the blatant sexual suggestion when such was made in his presence.[13]

[110.10] EMPLOYMENT-AT-WILL DEVELOPMENTS

Validity of disclaimer—a jury question: Despite a disclaimer in an employee handbook, a federal district court, applying Pennsylvania law, ruled that since the disclaimer in a salary administration plan did not contain express language that the document was not intended to create a contract of employment, the plaintiff would be permitted to pursue his lawsuit.[14]

Leave of absence approval—implied contract: The Pennsylvania Superior Court has held that despite the containment of an at-will disclaimer in an employee handbook, the employer's approval of a leave of absence pursuant to the handbook provisions gave rise to an enforceable contract that the employee would be reinstated to his former job upon expiration of the leave.[15]

Whistle-blower claim denied: The Superior Court of Pennsylvania has held that a managerial employee, who claimed she was discharged because she complained about her employer's decision to appoint a doctor, whose abilities she questioned, to the position of Chief of Pediatric Neurosurgery, did not provide a basis for a whistle-blowing cause of action under the theory that she was discharged in violation of public policy.[16]

Public policy exception—no statutory duty to protect: The Third Circuit Court of Appeals, applying Pennsylvania law, refused to extend the public policy exception to the "at-will" rule to a plaintiff in which the plaintiff, as a former employee, reasonably believed the employer had directed an employee to perform an unlawful act, even though the plaintiff was mistaken regarding the alleged "unlawful act."[17]

[110.11] TORT ACTIONS

Bad faith discharge: A Federal District Court, applying Pennsylvania law, has ruled actionable a sales representative's allegations that he was wrongfully discharged with specific intent to harm by his employer in that, *inter alia*, the employer maliciously and purposely took from him the most lucrative portions of his sales territory and commenced to review his sales record on a monthly, rather than a quarterly or yearly basis, as was the case previously.[18]

[110.12] TIME LIMITATIONS FOR FILING WRONGFUL DISCHARGE LAWSUITS

Pennsylvania statutes provide time limits for litigants to file wrongful employment lawsuits to be: one year for defamation, two years for discharge in violation of public policy, and four years for discharge in violation of implied contracts causes of action.[19]

SUPPLEMENTAL NOTES TO CHAPTER 110

1. Pennsylvania Statutes, Title 43, Sections 953, 954, 955.
2. Pennsylvania Statutes, Title 43, Sections 952, *et seq.*

3. Pennsylvania Statutes, Title 43, Sections 336.5, 960, 962.

4. Pennsylvania Statutes, Title 43, Sections 959, 961.2, 962.

5. Pennsylvania Statutes, Title 43, Section 1101.201, Title 72, Section 4752.1.

6. Pennsylvania Executive Order 1989-5.

7. Pennsylvania Statutes, Title 40, Sections 908-2, *et seq.*

8. Pennsylvania Statutes, Title 40, Sections 752, *et seq.*

9. Pennsylvania Statutes, Title 44, Sections 11, 16, 19.2, 22, 26–34, 38, 46.6.

10. Pennsylvania Statutes, Title 43, Sections 753.902, *et seq.*

11. Pennsylvania Statutes, Title 43, Sections 753, 792, 802, 804, *et seq.*

12. Pennsylvania Statutes, Title 43, Sections 753, 801, 802, 802.4, 892.

13. *Peddicord v. Unemployment Board of Review*, (Penn. Commw., 8-18-94).

14. *Smith v. Never, Tiseo and Hindo, Ltd.*, No. 92-6799 (ED Penn., 10-22-93).

15. *Neihaus v. Delaware Valley Medical Center*, No. 4063 (PA Super, 1993).

16. *Holervinski v. Children's Hospital of Pittsburgh*, 648 A2d 712 (1994).

17. *Clark v. Modern Group, Ltd.*, No. 92-2048 (CA-3, 11-18-93).

18. *Altopiedi v. Memorex Telex Corp.*, 834 F.Supp 800 (E.D. Pa., 1993).

19. Pennsylvania Statutes, Title 42, Sections 5523, *et seq.*

111

Rhode Island Labor and Employment Laws

[111.05] REGULATION OF EMPLOYMENT PRACTICES

Bona fide exceptions to prohibited employment practices: Rhode Island statutes provide that bona fide occupational qualifications are legally recognized exceptions to otherwise unfair employment practices.[1]

EEOC—certified deferral: Rhode Island statutes provide that the state FEP Commission is to serve as a certified deferral agency of the Equal Employment Opportunity Commission relative to fair employment claims filed with the EEOC.[2]

Court review of agency decisions: Rhode Island statutes permit claimants and respondents to adverse decisions by the state FEP Commission a right of review to applicable courts within the state.[3]

Available remedies for fair employment violations: Rhode Island statutes provide for punitive damages, in cases of malice or ill will, as well as for backpay and compensatory damages for claimants who prevail in claims (for intentional discrimination) before the state FEP Commission.[4]

Affirmative action programs (state employment): Rhode Island law requires each state agency to adopt an affirmative action plan to identify persons with protected characteristics who are underutilized in their employment and establish affirmative action programs to overcome any such underutilization.[5]

Family medical leave: Rhode Island law requires employers with at least fifty employees to provide up to thirteen weeks of leave during a two-year period to those employees who have worked an average of at least thirty hours per week during the twelve-month period preceding the leave for the birth or adoption of a child, to care for a sick spouse, child, or parent, or for the illness of the employee. The law also provides that the employee must be returned to his or her regular or comparable position at the same level of pay, benefits, seniority, and that the employee is to be reimbursed at such time by the employer for the costs he or she has paid to retain benefits during such leave.[6]

AIDS testing: Rhode Island law prohibits AIDS testing as a condition of employment, or continuing employment, unless a competent medical authority determines there is a clear and present danger of transmitting the AIDS virus from an infected employee to others.[7]

[111.06A] WELFARE AND BENEFITS LAWS

Insurance coverage for alcohol/drug abuse treatment: Rhode Island laws require insurance policies to provide mandatory coverage for treatment of employees undergoing rehabilitation for alcohol and/or drug abuse.[8]

Insurance coverage for newborns: Rhode Island statutes mandate that employee health-related insurance policies include coverage of newborns—including adopted children—of employees.[9]

State holidays: Rhode Island statutes specify the following as state recognized holidays: New Year's Day, Martin Luther King's Birthday, Washington's Birthday, Memorial Day, July 4th, Labor Day, Columbus Day, Veteran's Day, Thanksgiving Day, and Christmas Day.[10]

[111.08] UNEMPLOYMENT COMPENSATION LAWS

Aside from private sector employers generally subject to the coverage of Rhode Island's Unemployment Compensation Laws, agricultural, nonprofit, state government agencies, and employers of domestic employees also are subject to the unemployment laws.[11]

Rhode Island law disqualifies individuals who are recipients of pension, retirement pay, or other such annuities, recipients of unemployment benefits from federal and other state unemployment compensation funds, and recipients of vacation pay from collecting unemployment compensation.

Rhode Island's unemployment compensation laws do not provide coverage to such employees as: persons self-employed; employees of commercial fishing vessels; railroad employees; wholly commissioned insurance and real estate agents; persons employed by parent, spouse or child; casual labor; patients employed by hospitals; students providing employment services to schools, colleges, and universities, if under college work study program and students at nonprofit or public education institutions who are in full-time work study programs.[12]

[111.10] EMPLOYMENT-AT-WILL DEVELOPMENTS

Promise to provide references breach denied: The Rhode Island Supreme Court, in reversing a lower court decision, has held that a former employer's failure to fulfill a promise to provide the plaintiff with a positive reference was not sustainable in that the plaintiff had failed to show that the employer's negative references were a substantial or primary cause in his failure to secure employment.[13]

[111.11] TORT ACTIONS

Corporate negligence: A Rhode Island Court has held that although a hospital may be liable for its negligent renewal of a physician's staff privileges, there was no evidence in the instant case to demonstrate that the hospital's renewal procedures should have uncovered the physician's reluctance to perform the medical procedures in question.[14]

SUPPLEMENTAL NOTES TO CHAPTER 111

1. Rhode Island General Laws, Section 28-5-7.

2. Rhode Island General Laws, Sections 28-5-13, 28-5-16, 28-5-18.

3. Rhode Island General Laws, Sections 28-5-24.1, 28-5-29.

4. Rhode Island General Laws, Sections 28-5-24, 28-5-29.1.

5. Rhode Island General Laws, Sections 28-5-40, 28-5-1-1.

6. Rhode Island General Laws, Section 28-48-1, *et seq.*

7. Rhode Island General Laws, Section 23-6-22.

8. Rhode Island General Laws, Section 27-38-1.

9. Rhode Island General Laws, Sections 23-24-6-9, *et seq.*

10. Rhode Island General Laws, Sections 25-1-1, 25-2-30, *et seq.*

11. Rhode Island General Laws, Sections 28-42-3, 28-42-13.

12. Rhode Island General Laws, Sections 28-42-3, 28-42-8, 28-42-10.

13. *Wells v. Urex Winter Optical*, (R.I. Sup. Ct., 1-19-94).

14. *Rodrigues v. Mariam Hospital*, 623 A.2d 456 (R.I., 1993).

112

South Carolina Labor and Employment Laws

[112.05] REGULATION OF EMPLOYMENT PRACTICES

Bona fide exceptions to prohibited employment practices: South Carolina statutes provide that bona fide seniority systems, bona fide occupational qualifications, and bona fide benefits programs are legally recognized exceptions to otherwise unfair employment practices.[1]

EEOC—certified deferral: South Carolina statutes provide that the South Carolina Commission on Human Rights is to serve as a certified deferral agency of the Equal Employment Opportunity Commission relative to fair employment claims filed with the EEOC.[2]

Court review of agency decisions: South Carolina statutes permit claimants and respondents to adverse decisions by the South Carolina Commission on Human Rights a right of review to applicable courts within the state.[3]

Affirmative action programs (state employment): South Carolina law requires each state agency to adopt an affirmative action plan to identify persons with protected characteristics who are underutilized in their employment and establish affirmative programs to overcome any such underutilization.[4]

[112.06A] WELFARE AND BENEFITS LAWS

Insurance coverage for newborns: South Carolina statutes mandate that employee health-related insurance policies include coverage of newborns—including adopted children—of employees.[5]

State holidays: South Carolina statutes specify the following as state recognized holidays: New Year's Day, Martin Luther King's Birthday, Washington's

Birthday, Memorial Day, July 4th, Labor Day, Columbus Day, Veteran's Day, Thanksgiving Day, and Christmas Day.[6]

[112.08] UNEMPLOYMENT COMPENSATION LAWS

Aside from private sector employers generally subject to the coverage of South Carolina's Unemployment Compensation Laws, agricultural, nonprofit, state government agencies, and employers of domestic employees also are subject to the unemployment laws.[7]

South Carolina law disqualifies individuals who are recipients of pension, retirement pay or other such annuities, recipients of unemployment benefits from federal and other state unemployment compensation funds and recipients of benefits to which the person is not entitled from collecting unemployment compensation.[8]

South Carolina's unemployment compensation laws do not provide coverage to such employees as: persons self-employed; employees of commercial fishing vessels; railroad employees; wholly commissioned insurance and real estate agents; persons employed by parent, spouse or child; casual labor; patients and student nurses employed by hospitals; hospital interns; minor newspaper carriers; students and spouses of students providing employment services to schools, colleges, and universities, if under college work study program and students at nonprofit or public education institutions who are in full-time work study programs.[9]

[112.10] EMPLOYMENT-AT-WILL DEVELOPMENTS

Restrictive covenants—liquidated damages: A South Carolina Appellate Court has held that a partnership agreement specifying that a partner pay liquidated damages in the event of post-employment competition was not a noncompetition agreement, per se, and therefore was not subject to the "reasonableness" test associated with covenants not to compete type agreements.[10]

[112.11] TORT ACTIONS

Negligent supervision: A South Carolina Appellate Court, in reversing a jury verdict, held that the employer could not be liable for failing to exercise a requisite duty of care in supervising an employee who had sexually assaulted one of its clients, the plaintiff. The court ruled that there was no evidence in the employee's work activities or personnel history sufficient to alert the employer that the employee would engage in such behavior.[11]

[112.12] TIME LIMITATIONS FOR FILING WRONGFUL DISCHARGE LAWSUITS

South Carolina statutes provide time limits for litigants to file wrongful employment lawsuits to be: two years for defamation, three years for discharge in violation of public policy, and three years for discharge in violation of implied contracts causes of action.[12]

SUPPLEMENTAL NOTES TO CHAPTER 112

1. Code of Laws of South Carolina, Section 1-13-80.
2. Code of Laws of South Carolina, Sections 1-13-70, 1-13-90.
3. Code of Laws of South Carolina, Sections 1-13-90, *et seq.*
4. Code of Laws of South Carolina, Section 1-13-110.
5. Code of Laws of South Carolina, Section 38-71-140.
6. Code of Laws of South Carolina, Sections 53-5-10, 53-5-80.
7. Code of Laws of South Carolina, Sections 41-27-120, 41-27-210, 41-27-230.
8. Code of Laws of South Carolina, Sections 41-27-260, 41-27-370, 41-35-120.
9. Code of Laws of South Carolina, Sections 41-27-120, 41-27-260.
10. *Hunt and Co. v. Davis*, 437 SE2d 557 (S.C. Ct. App., 1993).
11. *Brockingham v. Pee Dee Health Center*, 433 S.E.2d 16 (S.C. Ct. App., 1993).
12. Code of Laws of South Carolina, Sections 15-3-530, 15-3-550.

113

South Dakota Labor and Employment Laws

[113.05] REGULATION OF EMPLOYMENT PRACTICES

Bona fide exceptions to prohibited employment practices: South Dakota statutes provide that bona fide seniority systems, bona fide occupational qualifications, and bona fide benefits programs are legally recognized exceptions to otherwise unfair employment practices.[1]

EEOC—certified deferral: South Dakota statutes provide that the South Dakota Division of Human Rights is to serve as a certified deferral agency of the Equal Employment Opportunity Commission relative to fair employment claims filed with the EEOC.[2]

Court review of agency decisions: South Dakota statutes permit claimants and respondents to adverse decisions by the South Dakota Division of Human Rights a right of review to applicable courts within the state.[3]

Available remedies for fair employment violations: South Dakota statutes provide for back pay and compensatory damages for claimants who prevail in claims before the South Dakota Division of Human Rights.[4]

Affirmative action programs (state employment): South Dakota law requires state agencies to adopt an affirmative action plan to identify persons with protected characteristics who are underutilized in competitive exams and establish affirmative action programs to overcome any such underutilization.[5]

[113.06A] WELFARE AND BENEFITS LAWS

Insurance coverage for alcohol treatment: South Dakota laws require insurance policies to provide an option to cover treatment of employees undergoing rehabilitation for alcohol abuse.[6]

Insurance coverage for newborns: South Dakota statutes mandate that employee health-related insurance policies include coverage of newborns—including adopted children—of employees.[7]

State holidays: South Dakota statutes specify the following as state recognized holidays: New Year's Day, Martin Luther King's Birthday, Washington's Birthday, Memorial Day, July 4th, Labor Day, Columbus Day, Veteran's Day, Thanksgiving Day, and Christmas Day.[8]

[113.08] UNEMPLOYMENT COMPENSATION LAWS

Aside from private sector employers generally subject to the coverage of South Dakota's Unemployment Compensation Laws, agricultural, nonprofit, state government agencies, and employers of domestic employees also are subject to the unemployment laws.[9]

South Dakota law disqualifies individuals who are recipients of pension, retirement pay or other such annuities, recipients of unemployment benefits from federal and other state unemployment compensation funds, recipients of vacation pay and wages in lieu of notice, recipients of workers' compensation funds, recipients of disability payments, recipients of termination, severance, or dismissal pay, and recipients of holiday pay from collecting unemployment compensation.[10]

South Dakota's unemployment compensation laws do not provide coverage to such employees as: persons self-employed; railroad employees; wholly commissioned insurance agents; persons employed by parent, spouse or child; patients and student nurses employed by hospitals; hospital interns; minor newspaper carriers; students and spouses of students providing employment services to schools, colleges, and universities, if under college work study program and students at non-profit or public education institutions who are in full-time work study programs.[11]

[113.10] EMPLOYMENT-AT-WILL DEVELOPMENTS

Implied contract—letter promises: The Fourth Circuit Court of Appeals, applying South Dakota Law, has held that an employer's letter to employees which promised that employees would not be discharged except for good cause constitutes an enforceable contract, the Court concluding that the letter's content intended to surrender the Company's statutory at-will powers to discharge.[12]

[113.11] TORT ACTIONS

Retaliatory discharge for filing a workers' compensation claim: The South Dakota Supreme Court has ruled that a retaliatory discharge for filing a workers' compensation claim type lawsuit is actionable and falls outside the employment-at-will rule.[13]

[113.12] TIME LIMITATIONS FOR FILING WRONGFUL DISCHARGE LAWSUITS

South Dakota statutes provide time limits for litigants to file wrongful employment lawsuits to be: two years for defamation, three years for discharge in violation of public policy, and six years for discharge in violation of implied contracts causes of action.[14]

SUPPLEMENTAL NOTES TO CHAPTER 113

1. South Dakota Compiled Laws, Sections 20-13-10, 20-13-16, 20-13-18.
2. South Dakota Compiled Laws, Sections 20-13-27, 20-13-31, 20-13-35, 20-13-45.
3. South Dakota Compiled Laws, Sections 1-26-1, 20-13-47, *et seq.*
4. South Dakota Compiled Laws, Sections 20-12-6, 20-13-35.1.
5. South Dakota Admin. Reg., Sections 55:01:02204, 55.01:06:12.
6. South Dakota Compiled Laws, Sections 58-18-7.1, 58-18-7.2.
7. South Dakota Compiled Laws, Section 58-18-13.
8. South Dakota Compiled Laws, Sections 1-5-1, 1-5-1.2.
9. South Dakota Compiled Laws, Sections 61-1-4, 61-1-10.2, 61-1-10.3, 61-1-24, 61-1-25, 61-1-27.
10. South Dakota Compiled Laws, Sections 61-6-15, 61-6-20, 61-6-21.
11. South Dakota Compiled Laws, Sections 61-1-10.9, 61-1-11-18, 61-1-22, 61-1-23, 61-1-26, 61-1-28, 61-1-30.
12. *Lesmeister v. American Celloid Co.*, No. 92-35865D (CA-4, 9-9-93).
13. *Niesent v. Homestake Mining Company of California*, No. 17933 (S.D. Sup. Ct., 1993).
14. South Dakota Compiled Laws, Sections 15-2-13, *et seq.*

114

Tennessee Labor and Employment Laws

[114.05] REGULATION OF EMPLOYMENT PRACTICES

Bona fide exceptions to prohibited employment practices: Tennessee statutes provide that bona fide seniority systems, bona fide occupational qualifications (religion, sex, and age), and bona fide benefits programs are legally recognized exceptions to otherwise unfair employment practices.[1]

EEOC—certified deferral: Tennessee statutes provide that the Tennessee Human Rights Commission is to serve as a certified deferral agency of the Equal Employment Opportunity Commission relative to fair employment claims filed with the EEOC.[2]

Court review of agency decisions: Tennessee statutes permit claimants and respondents to adverse decisions by the Tennessee Human Rights Commission a right of review to applicable courts within the state.[3]

Available remedies for fair employment violations: Tennessee statutes provide for back-pay and compensatory damages for claimants who prevail in claims before the Tennessee Human Rights Commission.[4]

Disability—monocular vision not a handicap: A Tennessee Appellate Court has held that a condition of monocular vision, although a visual impairment, does not substantially limit one or more major life activities within the meaning of the state discrimination laws against handicapped persons.[5]

Whistle-blower claim unsupported: The Sixth Circuit Court of Appeals, interpreting Tennessee law, affirmed a decision below in which the district court dismissed an employee's claim under the Tennessee Public Protection Act, finding her discharge was not over her filing a sexual harassment complaint but rather over her breaching confidential information.[6]

[114.06A] WELFARE AND BENEFITS LAWS

Insurance coverage for alcohol/drug abuse treatment: Tennessee laws require insurance policies to provide an option to cover treatment of employees undergoing rehabilitation for alcohol and/or drug abuse.[7]

Insurance coverage for newborns: Tennessee statutes mandate that employee health-related insurance policies include coverage of newborns of employees.[8]

Insurance coverage for mental health treatment: Tennessee statutes require insurance policies to provide mandatory coverage for mental health treatment unless specifically excluded or rejected by the employer.[9]

State holidays: Tennessee statutes specify the following as state recognized holidays: New Year's Day, Martin Luther King's Birthday, Washington's Birthday, Memorial Day, July 4th, Labor Day, Columbus Day, Veteran's Day, Thanksgiving Day, and Christmas Day.[10]

[114.08] UNEMPLOYMENT COMPENSATION LAWS

Aside from private sector employers generally subject to the coverage of Tennessee's Unemployment Compensation Laws, agricultural, non-profit, state government agencies, and employers of domestic employees also are subject to the unemployment laws.[11]

Tennessee law disqualifies individuals who are recipients of pension, retirement pay, or other such annuities, recipients of unemployment benefits from federal and other state unemployment compensation funds and recipients of wages in lieu of notice, and certain workers' compensation payments from collecting unemployment compensation.[12]

Tennessee's unemployment compensation laws do not provide coverage to such employees as: persons self-employed; employees of commercial fishing vessels of less than 10 years; railroad employees; wholly commissioned insurance and real estate agents; persons employed by parent, spouse or child; patients employed by hospitals; students and spouses of students providing employment services to schools, colleges, and universities, if under college work study program and students at nonprofit or public education institutions who are in full-time work study programs.[13]

[114.12] TIME LIMITATIONS FOR FILING WRONGFUL DISCHARGE LAWSUITS

Tennessee statutes provide time limits for litigants to file wrongful employment lawsuits that are: one year for defamation and one year for discharge in violation of implied contracts causes of action.[14]

SUPPLEMENTAL NOTES TO CHAPTER 114

1. Tennessee Code Annotated, Sections 4-21-406, 4-21-407.

2. Tennessee Code Annotated, Sections 4-21-202, 4-21-302, 4-21-304.

3. Tennessee Code Annotated, Section 4-21-307.

4. Tennessee Code Annotated, Sections 4-21-306, 4-21-311.

5. *Hallums v. Coca-Cola Bottling Co.*, No. 01-A-01-9302-CH-00047 (Tenn. Ct. of App., 10-13-93).

6. *Davis v. Sports & Recreation, Inc.*, No. 93-6132 (CA 6, 11-24-94).

7. Tennessee Code Annotated, Section 56-7-1009.

8. Tennessee Code Annotated, Section 56-7-1001.

9. Tennessee Code Annotated, Section 56-7-1003.

10. Tennessee Code Annotated, Sections 25-1-101, 15-2-101, *et seq.*

11. Tennessee Code Annotated, Sections 50-7-206, 50-7-207.

12. Tennessee Code Annotated, Sections 50-7-207, 50-7-213, 50-7-303.

13. Tennessee Code Annotated, Section 50-7-207.

14. Tennessee Code Annotated, Sections 28-3-103, 28-3-104, *et seq.*

115

Texas Labor and Employment Laws

[115.05] REGULATION OF EMPLOYMENT PRACTICES

Bona fide exceptions to prohibited employment practices: Texas statutes provide that bona fide seniority systems, bona fide occupational qualifications, and bona fide benefits programs are legally recognized exceptions to otherwise unfair employment practices.[1]

EEOC—certified deferral: Texas statutes provide that the Texas Human Rights Commission is to serve as a certified deferral agency of the Equal Employment Opportunity Commission relative to fair employment claims filed with the EEOC.[2]

Court review of agency decisions: Texas statutes permit claimants and respondents to adverse decisions by the Texas Human Rights Commission a right of review to applicable courts within the state.[3]

Affirmative action programs (state employment): Texas law requires state agencies to adopt an affirmative action plan to identify persons with protected characteristics who are underutilized in their employment and establish affirmative action programs to overcome any such underutilization.[4]

Disability—skin condition not a handicap: A Texas Appellate Court has held that an employees' eczema was not a handicap under the state's handicap discrimination laws. The Court concluded that the skin condition did not qualify as a "health impairment that requires special ambulatory devices or services," as defined in the statute.[5]

Disability definitions: The Texas Human Rights Act has been amended to mandate reasonable accommodations, to specify burden of proof standards in disparate impact cases, to provide for the promotion of using alternative resolution techniques in resolving disability complaints and to authorize an award of punitive and compulsory damages in certain cases.[6]

Disability—employer knowledge of disability prerequisite: A Federal District Court, interpreting Texas Disability Law, has ruled that a discharged employee's lawsuit against his employer, on the basis that the employer discharged him because of his disability (depression), was not actionable because the employee had never specifically communicated his depression to the employer.[7]

Sexual harassment—ratification of manager's conduct: The Fifth Circuit Court of Appeals, applying Texas law, has ruled that an employer ratified and approved sexual harassment conduct of a supervisor against an employee by not taking timely corrective action against the supervisor although the employer may have been otherwise exonerated in that the conduct was outside the course and scope of the supervisor's employment.[8]

Whistle-blowing—taking unfriendly political position: The Texas Supreme Court permitted a discharged employee's lawsuit, which alleged that her employer, the City of Laporte, had discharged her in retaliation of her taking an unfriendly political position, despite the City's contention that it had governmental immunity to such lawsuits. The Court ruled that the immunity argument could not prevail over the spirit of the Texas Whistle-Blowers Act.[9]

Service letters: A statute requiring Texas employers to provide former employees with service letters, stating the cause of the employee's discharge when requested, has been held to be unconstitutional.[10]

[115.06] PAYMENT UPON TERMINATION

Employees who are discharged from employment must be paid in full not later than the sixth day after the date of the employee's discharge.[11] Employees who leave employment other than by discharge must be paid in full not later than the next regularly scheduled payday.[12]

[115.06A] WELFARE AND BENEFITS LAWS

Insurance coverage for alcohol/drug abuse treatment: Texas laws require insurance policies to provide mandatory coverage for treatment of employees undergoing rehabilitation for alcohol and/or drug abuse.[13]

Insurance coverage for newborns: Texas statutes mandate that employee health-related insurance policies include coverage of newborns—including adopted children—of employees.[14]

Insurance coverage for mental health treatment: Texas statutes require insurance policies to provide an option to cover treatment for serious mental illness.[15]

State holidays: Texas statutes specify the following as state recognized holidays: New Year's Day, Martin Luther King's Birthday, Washington's Birthday, Memorial Day, July 4th, Labor Day, Veteran's Day, Thanksgiving Day, and Christmas Day.[16]

[115.08] UNEMPLOYMENT COMPENSATION LAWS

Aside from private sector employers generally subject to the coverage of Texas' Unemployment Compensation Laws, agricultural (with three or more employees), nonprofit, state government agencies, and employers of domestic employees also are subject to the unemployment laws.[17]

Texas law disqualifies individuals who are recipients of pension, retirement pay or other such annuities, recipients of unemployment benefits from federal and other state unemployment compensation funds, recipients of wages in lieu of notice, recipients of workers' compensation benefits, and recipients of old-age Social Security benefits from collecting unemployment compensation.[18]

Texas' unemployment compensation laws do not provide coverage to such employees as: persons self-employed; railroad employees; wholly commissioned insurance and real estate agents; persons employed by parent, spouse or child; patients and student nurses employed by hospitals; hospital interns; minor newspaper carriers; students providing employment services to schools, colleges, and universities, if under college work study program, and students at nonprofit or public education institutions who are in full-time work study programs.[19]

[115.10] EMPLOYMENT-AT-WILL DEVELOPMENTS

Implied contracts—handbook promises: A Texas Court of Appeals has held that a personnel policy manual, containing a provision that assured employees that no employee would be retaliated against because of his or her having filed a complaint under the employer's grievance procedure, modified the employee's "at-will" relationship with the employer and provided a basis for the employee's promissory estoppel, fraud and wrongful discharge cause of action, absent a legally enforceable disclaimer to that effect.[20]

[115.11] TORT ACTIONS

Intentional infliction of emotional distress: A Texas Appellate Court, rejecting the "reasonable woman" test in a claim for intentional infliction of emotional distress involving sexual harassment, has upheld the dismissal of the plaintiff's claim, ruling that a male's discussion of sexual conduct and sexual inquiries of the plaintiff did not meet the "extreme and outrageous" standards that are applied in emotional distress causes of action.[21]

Retaliatory discharge—workers' compensation: A Texas Court of Appeals, in upholding an award of $140,000 in actual and punitive damages to an employee who was discharged for filing a workers' compensation claim, concluded that there was sufficient evidence to support the trial court's decision.[22]

Negligence—failure to warn: A Texas Court of Appeals has overturned a jury verdict in favor of a widow who contended her husband's employer breached its duty to properly warn her or her husband of his termination from employment, which termination she contended resulted in her husband's suicide. The Court ruled that the company owed no duty of care to foresee such a suicide occurring as a result of an employee's dismissal.[23]

[115.12] TIME LIMITATIONS FOR FILING WRONGFUL DISCHARGE LAWSUITS

Texas statutes provide time limits for litigants to file wrongful employment lawsuits to be: one year for defamation, two years for discharge in violation of public policy, and four years for discharge in violation of implied contracts causes of action.[24]

SUPPLEMENTAL NOTES TO CHAPTER 115

1. Texas Statutes, Article 5221K, Section 7.01.
2. Texas Statutes, Article, 5221K, Sections 3.01, *et seq.*
3. Texas Statutes, Article 5221K, Section 7.01.
4. Texas Executive Order, MW-6.
5. *Central Power & Light Co. v. Bradbury*, No. 13-92-426CV (Texas Ct. App. 2-10-94).
6. L. 1993, Ch. 276.
7. *McIntyre v. The Kroger Co.*, (N.D. Tex., 2-25-94).
8. *Prunty v. Arkansas Freightways, Inc.*, No. 92-4338 (CA-5, 1993).
9. *City of Laporte Texas v. Barfield*, (Texas Sup Ct., 1995).
10. Attorney Gen. Opin. Nos. 0-3562 (1941) and WW-114 (1956); *St. Louis Southwestern Ry. Co. of Texas v. Griffin*, 171 S.W. 333 (Tex. Sup. Ct., 1914).
11. Texas Labor Code, § 61.014.
12. *Ibid.*
13. Texas Insurance Code Annotated, Article 3.51.9.
14. Texas Insurance Code Annotated, Article 3.51-6.
15. Texas Insurance Code Annotated, Article 3.51-14.
16. Texas Civil Statutes Annotated, Article 4591.

17. Texas Civil Statutes Annotated, Article 5221b-17.

18. Texas Civil Statutes Annotated, Article 5221b-2a, 5221b-3, 5221b-17.

19. Texas Civil Practices and Remedies, Sections 16.002 and 16.004.

20. *Vida v. El Paso Employees' Credit Union*, (Tex. Ct. App., 6-16-94).

21. *Garcia v. Mo-Vac Service Company*, (Tex. Ct. App., 1994).

22. *Acme Boot Company, Inc. v. Montenegro*, No. 08-93-00017-CV (Tex. Ct. of App., 1993).

23. *Shell Oil Co. v. Humphrey*, (Tex Ct. App., 6-16-94).

24. Texas Civil Practices and Remedies, Sections 16.002, 16.003 and 16.004.

116

Utah Labor and Employment Laws

[116.05] REGULATION OF EMPLOYMENT PRACTICES

Bona fide exceptions to prohibited employment practices: Utah statutes provide that bona fide seniority systems, bona fide occupational qualifications, and bona fide benefits programs are legally recognized exceptions to otherwise unfair employment practices.[1]

EEOC—certified deferral: Utah statutes provide that the Industrial Commission of Utah is to serve as a certified deferral agency of the Equal Employment Opportunity Commission relative to fair employment claims filed with the EEOC.[2]

Court review of agency decisions: Utah statutes permit claimants and respondents to adverse decisions by the Industrial Commission of Utah a right of review to applicable courts within the state.[3]

Affirmative action programs (state employment):   Utah law requires state agencies to adopt an affirmative action plan to identify persons with protected characteristics who are underutilized in their employment and establish affirmative action programs to overcome any such underutilization.[4]

AIDS testing: Utah law provides for certain rules governing HIV testing and disclosure of AIDS tests for the benefit of emergency medical service employees who are exposed to AIDS in the performance of their job duties.[5]

[116.06A] WELFARE AND BENEFITS LAWS

Insurance coverage for alcohol/drug abuse treatment: Utah laws require insurance policies to provide an option to cover treatment of employees undergoing rehabilitation for alcohol and/or drug abuse.[6]

Insurance coverage for newborns: Utah statutes mandate that employee health-related insurance policies include coverage of newborns—including adopted children—of employees.[7]

State holidays: Utah statutes specify the following as state recognized holidays: New Year's Day, Martin Luther King's Birthday, Washington's Birthday, Memorial Day, July 4th, Labor Day, Columbus Day, Veteran's Day, Thanksgiving Day, and Christmas Day.[8]

[116.08] UNEMPLOYMENT COMPENSATION LAWS

Aside from private sector employers generally subject to the coverage of Utah's Unemployment Compensation Laws, agricultural, nonprofit, state government agencies, and employers of domestic employees also are subject to the unemployment laws.[9]

Utah law disqualifies individuals who are recipients of pension, retirement pay, or other such annuities, recipients of unemployment benefits from federal and other state unemployment compensation funds and recipients of wages in lieu of notice, separation pay, or vacation pay from collecting unemployment compensation.

Utah's unemployment compensation laws do not provide coverage to such employees as: persons self-employed; railroad employees; wholly commissioned insurance and real estate agents; persons employed by parent, spouse or child; casual labor; patients employed by hospitals; students and spouses of students providing employment services to schools, colleges, and universities, if under college work study program and students at nonprofit or public education institutions who are in full-time work study programs.[10]

[116.12] TIME LIMITATIONS FOR FILING WRONGFUL DISCHARGE LAWSUITS

Utah statutes provide time limits for litigants to file wrongful employment lawsuits to be: one year for defamation and four years for discharge in violation of implied contracts causes of action.[11]

SUPPLEMENTAL NOTES TO CHAPTER 116

1. Utah Code Annotated, Sections 34-35-2, 34-35-6.

2. Utah Code Annotated, Sections 34-35-5, 34-35-7.1

3. Utah Code Annotated, Section 34-35-7.1.

4. Utah Code Annotated, Sections 17-33-3, 17-33-10.
5. Utah Code Annotated, Section 31A-22-715.
6. Utah Code Annotated, Section 31A-22-610.
7. Utah Code Annotated, Section 63-13-2.
8. Utah Code Annotated, Sections 35-4-22.2, *et seq.*
9. Utah Code Annotated, Sections 35-4-5, 35-4-22, *et seq.*
10. Utah Code Annotated, Sections 35-4-5, 35-4-22, *et seq.*
11. Utah Code Annotated, Sections 78-12-25, 78-12-29.

117

Vermont Labor and Employment Laws

[117.05] REGULATION OF EMPLOYMENT PRACTICES

Bona fide exceptions to prohibited employment practices: Vermont statutes provide that bona fide seniority systems, bona fide occupational qualifications, and bona fide benefits programs are legally recognized exceptions to otherwise unfair employment practices.[1]

EEOC—certified deferral: Vermont statutes provide that the Vermont Human Rights Commission is to serve as a certified deferral agency of the Equal Employment Opportunity Commission relative to fair employment claims filed with the EEOC.[2]

Available remedies for fair employment violations: Vermont statutes provide for punitive damages and compensatory damages, if appropriate, as well as back pay for claimants who prevail in claims before the Vermont Human Rights Commission.[3]

Sexual harassment guidelines: Vermont law requires employers to adopt a sexual harassment policy, the contents of which are to, *inter alia,* include (a) a statement that sexual harassment in the workplace is illegal, (b) a statement that it is unlawful to retaliate against an employee for filing a sexual harassment complaint or cooperating in an investigation of sexual harassment, (c) an outline of the consequences for committing sexual harassment behavior, (d) a description of what constitutes sexual harassment, (e) a statement of internal processes to address sexual harassment complaints, and (f) a statement specifying available processes and agencies to address sexual harassment complaints in a formal sense.[4]

AIDS testing: Vermont law prohibits employers to request or require applicants or employees to take HIV or AIDS tests as a condition of employment.[5]

[117.06A] WELFARE AND BENEFITS LAWS

Insurance coverage for alcohol abuse treatment: Vermont laws require insurance policies to provide mandatory coverage for treatment of employees undergoing rehabilitation for alcohol abuse.[6]

Insurance coverage for newborns: Vermont statutes mandate that employee health-related insurance policies include coverage of newborns of employees.[7]

Insurance coverage for mental health treatment: Vermont statutes require insurance policies to provide an option to cover treatment for mental health illness.[8]

State holidays: Vermont statutes provide that the following are state recognized holidays: New Year's Day, Martin Luther King's Birthday, Washington's Birthday, Lincoln's Birthday, Memorial Day, July 4th, Labor Day, Columbus Day, Veteran's Day, Thanksgiving Day, and Christmas Day.[9]

[117.08] UNEMPLOYMENT COMPENSATION LAWS

Aside from private sector employers generally subject to the coverage of Vermont's Unemployment Compensation Laws, agricultural, nonprofit, state government agencies, and employers of domestic employees also are subject to the unemployment laws.[10]

Vermont law disqualifies individuals who are recipients of pension, retirement pay, or other such annuities, recipients of unemployment benefits from federal and other state unemployment compensation funds, recipients of wages in lieu of notice, vacation pay, holiday pay, backpay award or settlement, and recipients of certain workers' compensation payments from collecting unemployment compensation.[11]

Vermont's unemployment compensation laws do not provide coverage to such employees as: persons self-employed; employees of commercial fishing vessels; railroad employees; wholly commissioned insurance and real estate agents; persons employed by parent, spouse or child; casual labor; patients employed by hospitals; students and spouses of students providing employment services to schools, colleges, and universities, if under college work study program and students at nonprofit or public education institutions who are in full-time work study programs.[12]

[117.10] EMPLOYMENT-AT-WILL DEVELOPMENTS

Implied contracts—handbook: The Vermont Supreme Court has reinforced the law in Vermont that an employee handbook or manual, as well as a hiring letter, on which the employer intends its employees to rely, can modify an employee's "at-will" relationship with the employer, the breach of which can provide the basis of a cause of action by the employee against the employer.[13]

[117.11] TORT ACTIONS

Negligent failure to disclose: The Vermont Supreme Court, in affirming a lower court decision, has held that a failure to disclose pertinent facts about the future of a work project for which the plaintiff was hired—particularly upon the plaintiff's request about the matter—provided a basis for an actionable "negligent failure to disclose" as well as a "negligent misrepresentation" lawsuit.[14]

[117.12] TIME LIMITATIONS FOR FILING WRONGFUL DISCHARGE LAWSUITS

Vermont statutes provide time limits for litigants to file wrongful employment lawsuits to be: three years for defamation, three years for discharge in violation of public policy, and six years for discharge in violation of implied contracts causes of action.[15]

SUPPLEMENTAL NOTES TO CHAPTER 117

1. Vermont Statutes Annotated, Title 21, Sections 495a, 495d, 495f.
2. Vermont Statutes Annotated, Title 9, Sections 2458, *et seq.*
3. Vermont Statutes Annotated, Title 3, Sections 1002, 1003; Title 8, Sections 2458, *et seq.*
4. 21 VT SA, Section 495h.
5. Vermont Statutes Annotated, Chapter 21, Section 495; Chapter 3, Section 961.
6. Vermont Statutes Annotated, Title 8, Section 4098.
7. Vermont Statutes Annotated, Title 8, Sections 4090, 4092.
8. Vermont Statutes Annotated, Title 8, Section 4089.
9. Vermont Statutes Annotated, Title 1, Section 371.
10. Vermont Statutes Annotated, Title 21, Sections 1301, *et seq.*
11. Vermont Statutes Annotated, Title 21, Sections 1301, 1343, 1344.
12. Vermont Statutes Annotated, Title 21, Section 1301.
13. *Taylor v. National Life Ins. Co.*, 652 A2d 466 (Vt. Sup. Ct. 1993).
14. *Pearson v. Simmonds Precision Products, Inc.*, 624 A2d 1134 (Vt. Sup. Ct., 1993).
15. Vermont Statutes Annotated, Title 12, Sections 511, 512.

118

Virginia Labor and Employment Laws

[118.05] REGULATION OF EMPLOYMENT PRACTICES

Bona fide exceptions to prohibited employment practices: Virginia statutes provide that bona fide seniority systems, and bona fide occupational qualifications are legally recognized exceptions to otherwise unfair employment practices.[1]

EEOC—certified deferral: Virginia statutes provide that the Virginia Council of Human Rights is to serve as a certified deferral agency of the Equal Employment Opportunity Commission relative to fair employment claims filed with the EEOC.[2]

Available remedies for fair employment violations: Virginia statutes provide for punitive damages, when deemed appropriate, as well as for backpay and compensatory damages for claimants who prevail in claims before the Virginia Council of Human Rights.[3]

Affirmative action programs (state employment): Virginia law requires state agencies to adopt an affirmative action plan to identify persons with protected characteristics who are underutilized in their employment and establish affirmative action programs to overcome any such underutilization.[4]

AIDS testing and confidentiality: Virginia law requires an informed consent from an individual prior to the administration of an AIDS test and prohibits a disclosure of the results of such test unless authorized by the person tested or otherwise required to be released to certain health care providers or agencies.[5]

[118.06A] WELFARE AND BENEFITS LAWS

Insurance coverage for alcohol/drug abuse treatment: Virginia laws require insurance policies to provide mandatory coverage for treatment of employees undergoing rehabilitation for alcohol and/or drug abuse.[6]

Insurance coverage for newborns: Virginia statutes mandate that employee health-related insurance policies include coverage of newborns—including adopted children—of employees.[7]

Insurance coverage for mental health treatment: Virginia statutes require insurance policies to cover treatment for mental health illness.[8]

State holidays: Virginia statutes provide that the following are state recognized holidays: New Year's Day, Martin Luther King's Birthday, Washington's Birthday, Memorial Day, July 4th, Labor Day, Columbus Day, Veteran's Day, Thanksgiving Day, and Christmas Day.[9]

[118.08] UNEMPLOYMENT COMPENSATION LAWS

Aside from private sector employers generally subject to the coverage of Virginia's Unemployment Compensation Laws, agricultural, nonprofit, state government agencies and employers of domestic employees also are subject to the unemployment laws.[10]

Virginia law disqualifies the following individuals from collecting unemployment compensation: aliens who are unlawfully within the state, recipients of pension, retirement pay or other such annuities, recipients of unemployment benefits from federal and other state unemployment compensation funds, and recipients of benefits to which the person was not entitled.[11]

Virginia's unemployment compensation laws do not provide coverage to such employees as: persons self-employed; employees of commercial fishing vessels; railroad employees; wholly commissioned insurance and real estate agents; persons employed by parent, spouse or child; casual labor; patients employed by hospitals; hospital interns; minor newspaper carriers; students providing employment services to schools, colleges, and universities, if under college work study program and students at nonprofit or public education institutions who are in full-time work study programs.[12]

[118.09] WORKERS' COMPENSATION LAWS

The Virginia Court of Appeals affirmed the Workers' Compensation Commission's decision that found an employer was required to pay for HIV and hepatitis B tests for a health care worker who sustained a needle-stick injury when treating a patient.[13]

[118.10] EMPLOYMENT-AT-WILL DEVELOPMENTS

The Fourth Circuit Court of Appeals, applying Virginia law, has held that a contractual disclaimer in an employee handbook was sufficient to defeat an employee's contention that the employer had violated its non-retaliatory provision regarding the use of its open door policy.[14]

[118.11] TORT ACTIONS

Discrimination claims actionable in tort—public policy violations: The Supreme Court of Virginia, in expanding the exceptions to the employment-at-will rule, has held that inasmuch as terminations of employment based on race or sex contravene employees' personal freedom from discrimination as protected under the Virginia Human Rights Act, such claims are actionable in tort for violation of public policy.[15]

[118.12] TIME LIMITATIONS FOR FILING WRONGFUL DISCHARGE LAWSUITS

Virginia statutes provide time limits for litigants to file wrongful employment lawsuits to be: one year for defamation, two years for discharge in violation of public policy, and three years for discharge in violation of implied contracts causes of action.[16]

SUPPLEMENTAL NOTES TO CHAPTER 118

1. Code of Virginia, Sections 51.1-101, 51.1-154.
2. Code of Virginia, Sections 2.1-717, *et seq.*
3. Code of Virginia, Sections 2.1-720.14, 2.1-725, 15.1-48.1.
4. Code of Virginia, Sections 2.1-37, *et seq.*
5. Code of Virginia, Sections 32.1, *et seq.*
6. Code of Virginia, Sections 38.2-3412.1.
7. Code of Virginia, Sections 38.2-3409, 38.2-3411.1.
8. Code of Virginia, Section 38.2-3412.1.
9. Code of Virginia, Sections 2.1-21, 2.1-21.1, *et seq.*
10. Code of Virginia, Sections 60.2-201, 60.2-210, 60.2-213, 60.2-214, 60.2-215.
11. Code of Virginia, Sections 60.2-219, 60.2-229, 60.2-604, 60.2-609, 60.2-612, 60.2-618.
12. Code of Virginia, Section 60.2-219.
13. *County of Fauquier Emergency Services v. Justice R. Clayton,* (VA Ct. App., 1993).
14. *Weinberger v. MCI Telecommunications,* No. 92-2550 (CA-4, 1-25-94).
15. *Lockhart v. Commonwealth Education Systems Corporation,* Nos. 921503, 930205 (Va. S. Ct., 1-7-94).
16. Code of Virginia, Sections 8.01-243, 246, 248.

119

Washington Labor and Employment Laws

[119.05] REGULATION OF EMPLOYMENT PRACTICES

Bona fide exceptions to prohibited employment practices: Washington statutes provide that bona fide occupational qualifications are legally recognized exceptions to otherwise unfair employment practices.[1]

EEOC—certified deferral: Washington statutes provide that the Washington State Human Rights Commission is to serve as a certified deferral agency of the

Equal Employment Opportunity Commission relative to fair employment claims filed with the EEOC.[2]

Court review of agency decisions: Washington statutes permit claimants and respondents to adverse decisions by the Washington State Human Rights Commission a right of review to applicable courts within the state.[3]

Available remedies for fair employment violations: Washington statutes provide for limited punitive damages, when deemed appropriate, as well as for back pay and limited compensatory damages for claimants who prevail in claims before the Washington State Human Rights Commission.[4]

Affirmative action programs (state employment): Washington law requires state agencies and higher education institutions to adopt an affirmative action plan to identify persons with protected characteristics who are underutilized in their employment and establish affirmative action programs to overcome any such underutilization.[5]

Sexual harassment—accidental discovery of sexual act constitutes no violation: A Washington Appellate Court has held that an accidental discovery by a janitorial employee of a supervisor masturbating in an unlighted and locked electrical room was not sexual harassment in that the supervisor did not intentionally perform the act in her presence and had no reason to suspect her entry into the area.[6]

Retaliatory action for complaining about overtime: The Supreme Court of Washington affirmed a jury award in favor of employees who had been harassed by their employer in retaliation for their seeking overtime. The Court held that the employer violated Washington's retaliation statute and that the lawsuit by the employees was not preempted by the National Labor Relations Act, as amended, on the basis that the employees were engaging in protected concerted activity.[7]

Disability—failure to accommodate: A Washington Appellate Court has ruled that an employee who receives workers' compensation benefits, as a result of a work-related injury, is not barred from bringing an action against the employer for failure to reasonably accommodate the employee's disability under the state's disability law, if such injury constitutes a recognized disability under the statute.[8]

Family medical leave: Washington law requires employers with at least 100 employees within a twenty-mile radius to provide up to twelve weeks of leave in a two-year period to those employees who have been employed full time for at least one year for the birth or adoption of a child or because of a terminal illness of a child under age 18 years of age; provided, also, that such employee must be reinstated to his or her regular or equivalent position upon his or her return from leave.[9]

AIDS—employer immunity from lawsuits: A Washington statute provides that employers are immune from civil damages arising from the transmission of HIV to others within their workplace, unless grossly negligent.[10]

[119.06A] WELFARE AND BENEFITS LAWS

Insurance coverage for alcohol/drug abuse treatment: Washington laws require insurance policies to provide mandatory coverage for treatment of employees undergoing rehabiliation for alcohol and/or drug abuse.[11]

Insurance coverage for newborns: Washington statutes mandate that employee health-related insurance policies include coverage of newborns—including adopted children—of employees.[12]

Insurance coverage for mental health treatment: Washington statutes require insurance policies to provide an option to cover treatment for mental health illness.[13]

State holidays: Washington statutes provide that the following are state recognized holidays: New Year's Day, Martin Luther King's Birthday, Washington's Birthday, Memorial Day, July 4th, Labor Day, Veteran's Day, Thanksgiving Day and Christmas Day.[14]

Smoking restrictions: Washington law bans smoking in all office environments in the State of Washington as well as in private sector workplaces, except for certain restaurants, bars and related businesses. Employers may arrange for designated "smoking areas" if properly vented and in compliance with other specified requirements.[15]

[119.08] UNEMPLOYMENT COMPENSATION LAWS

Aside from private sector employers generally subject to the coverage of Washington's Unemployment Compensation Laws, agricultural, nonprofit, state government agencies, and employers of domestic employees also are subject to the unemployment laws.[16]

Washington law disqualifies individuals who are recipients of pension, retirement pay, or other such annuities from collecting unemployment compensation.[17]

Washington's unemployment compensation laws do not provide coverage to such employees as: persons self-employed; railroad employees; wholly commissioned insurance and real estate agents; persons employed by parent, spouse or child; casual labor; patients employed by hospitals; minor newspaper carriers; newspaper distributors; students and spouses of students providing employment services to schools, colleges, and universities, if under college work study program and students at nonprofit or public education institutions who are in full-time work study programs.[18]

[119.10] EMPLOYMENT-AT-WILL DEVELOPMENTS

Management guide constitutes implied contract: The Washington Supreme Court, in rejecting the employer's argument that its "management guide" was to advise managers and supervisors of corporate policies, held that it was a question of fact for a jury to determine if the employer had discharged the plaintiff contrary to the provisions noted in the guidebook.[19]

[119.12] TIME LIMITATIONS FOR FILING WRONGFUL DISCHARGE LAWSUITS

Washington statutes provide time limits for litigants to file wrongful employment lawsuits to be: one year for defamation, three years for discharge in violation of public policy, and three years for discharge in violation of implied contracts causes of action.[20]

SUPPLEMENTAL NOTES TO CHAPTER 119

1. Revised Code of Washington, Section 49.80.180.
2. Revised Code of Washington, Sections 49.60.140, 49.60-230, *et seq.*
3. Revised Code of Washington, Sections 34.05, *et seq.*
4. Revised Code of Washington, Section 49.60.030.
5. Revised Code of Washington, Sections 28B.16.020, *et seq.*, 39.19.010, *et seq.*
6. *Coville v. Cobarc Services, Inc.*, (Wash. Ct. App., 1994).
7. *Hume v. American Disposal Co.*, (Wash. Sup. Ct., 9-22-94).
8. *Goodman v. Boeing Co.*, (Wash. Ct. App., 7-25-94).
9. Revised Code of Washington, Section 49.78.010-49.78.901.
10. Revised Code of Washington, Section 49.60.172.
11. Revised Code of Washington, Section 48.21.180.
12. Revised Code of Washington, Section 48.21.150.
13. Revised Code of Washington, Section 48.21.246.
14. Revised Code of Washington, Section 1.16.050.
15. WAC 296-62-12000, *et seq.* (effective 9-1-94).
16. Revised Code of Washington, Sections 50.04.90, 50.04.150, 50.04.155, 50.04.160, 50.44.010, 50.44.020, 50.44.030, 50.44.040, 50.44.060.
17. Revised Code of Washington, Sections 50.020.050–50-20.118, 50.44.037, 50.44.040.
18. Revised Code of Washington, Sections 50.04.100, 50.04.180, 50.04.230, 50.04.240, 50.04.270, 50.20.050, 50.44.037, 50.44.040.
19. *Burnside v. Simpson Paper Company*, (Wash. S. Ct., 1-6-94).
20. Revised Code of Washington, Sections 4.16.080, 4.16.100.

120

West Virginia Labor and Employment Laws

[120.05] REGULATION OF EMPLOYMENT PRACTICES

Bona fide exceptions to prohibited employment practices: West Virginia statutes provide that bona fide seniority systems, bona fide occupational qualifications, and bona fide benefits programs are legally recognized exceptions to otherwise unfair employment practices.[1]

EEO—certified deferral: West Virginia statutes provide that the West Virginia Human Rights Commission is to serve as a certified deferral agency of the Equal Employment Opportunity Commission relative to fair employment claims filed with the EEOC.[2]

Affirmative action programs (state employment): West Virginia law requires state agencies to adopt an affirmative action plan to identify persons with protected characteristics who are underutilized in their employment and establish affirmative programs to overcome any such underutilization.[3]

AIDS testing and confidentiality: West Virginia law regulates AIDS testing and under what circumstances test results may be disclosed.[4]

[120.06A] WELFARE AND BENEFITS LAWS

Insurance coverage for alcohol abuse treatment: West Virginia laws require insurance policies to provide an option to cover treatment of employees undergoing rehabilitation for alcohol abuse.[5]

Insurance coverage for newborns: West Virginia statutes mandate that employee health-related insurance policies include coverage of newborns of employees.[6]

Insurance coverage for mental health treatment: West Virginia statutes require insurance policies to provide an option to cover treatment for mental health illness.[7]

State holidays: West Virginia statutes provide that the following are state recognized holidays: New Year's Day, Martin Luther King's Birthday, Washington's Birthday, Lincoln's Birthday, Memorial Day, July 4th, Labor Day, Columbus Day, Veteran's Day, Thanksgiving Day, and Christmas Day.[8]

[120.08] UNEMPLOYMENT COMPENSATION LAWS

Aside from private sector employers generally subject to the coverage of West Virginia's Unemployment Compensation Laws, agricultural, nonprofit, state government agencies, and employers of domestic employees also are subject to the unemployment laws.[9]

West Virginia law disqualifies individuals who are recipients of pension, retirement pay, or other such annuities, recipients of unemployment benefits from federal and other state unemployment compensation funds, and recipients of wages in lieu of notice and certain workers' compensation payments from collecting unemployment compensation.[10]

West Virginia's unemployment compensation laws do not provide coverage to such employees as: persons self-employed; railroad employees; wholly commissioned insurance agents; persons employed by parent, spouse or child; patients employed by hospitals; students and spouses of students providing employment services to schools, colleges, and universities, if under college work study program and students at nonprofit or public education institutions who are in full-time work study programs.[11]

[120.10] EMPLOYMENT-AT-WILL DEVELOPMENTS

Public policy—wrongful discharge: The West Virginia Supreme Court has ruled that the discharge of an employee for the refusal to operate a vehicle with defective brakes constitutes wrongful discharge.[12]

Implied contracts—handbook disclaimers: The West Virginia Supreme Court has ruled that an employee handbook disclaimer must state that employees are employees at-will in order to be effective, holding that disclaimer statements to the effect that the information in a handbook is not to be construed as a promise or a contract or that the employer has the discretion to modify policies at its discretion, standing alone, are insufficient to establish a valid disclaimer in an employee handbook. To be a valid disclaimer, the Court implied the disclaimer language should inform employees that both parties are "at-will" and that the handbook is not a contract.[13]

[120.12] TIME LIMITATIONS FOR FILING WRONGFUL DISCHARGE LAWSUITS

West Virginia statutes provide time limits for litigants to file wrongful employment lawsuits to be: one year for defamation, two years for discharge in violation of public policy, and five years for discharge in violation of implied contracts causes of action.[14]

SUPPLEMENTAL NOTES TO CHAPTER 120

1. West Virginia Code, Section 5-11-9.
2. West Virginia Code, Sections 5-11-8, 5-11-9, *et seq.*
3. West Virginia Code, Section 29-6-20.
4. West Virginia Code, Sections 16-3C-1, *et seq.*
5. West Virginia Code, Section 33-16-3c.
6. West Virginia Code, Sections 33-6-32.
7. West Virginia Code, Section 33.16-3a.
8. West Virginia Code, Sections 2-2-1, *et seq.*
9. West Virginia Code, Sections 21A-1-3, 21A-2-16, 21A-5-3a, 21A-6-15.
10. West Virginia Code, Sections 21A-2-6a, *et seq.*
11. West Virginia Code, Sections 21A-1-2, 21A-6-3.
12. *Lilly v. Overnite Transportation Co.,* 425 SE2d 214 (W. VA. S. Ct., 1993).
13. *Dent v. Fruth,* (W. VA Sup Ct., 1994).
14. West Virginia Code, Sections 55-2-6, 55-2-12.

121

Wisconsin Labor and Employment Laws

[121.05] REGULATION OF EMPLOYMENT PRACTICES

Bona fide exceptions to prohibited employment practices: Wisconsin statutes provide that bona fide seniority systems, bona fide occupational qualifications and bona fide benefits programs are legally recognized exceptions to otherwise unfair employment practices.[1]

EEOC—certified deferral: Wisconsin statutes provide that the Wisconsin Department of Industry, Labor and Human Relations is to serve as a certified deferral agency of the Equal Employment Opportunity Commission relative to fair employment claims filed with the EEOC.[2]

Court review of agency decisions: Wisconsin statutes permit claimants and respondents to adverse decisions by the Wisconsin Department of Industry, Labor and Human Relations a right of review to applicable courts within the state.[3]

Affirmative action programs (state employment): Wisconsin law requires state agencies to adopt an affirmative action plan to identify persons with protected characteristics who are underutilized in their employment and establish affirmative action programs to overcome any such underutilization.[4]

Sexual harassment statute enlarged: The Wisconsin law prohibiting sexual harassment has been modified to include harassment by a member of the same sex as well as single instances of speech or conduct if sufficiently severe to create a hostile and intimidating work environment.[5]

Polygraph protection does not extend to honesty tests: A Wisconsin Court of Appeals has held that the Wisconsin law regulating polygraph tests does not prohibit the use of written honesty tests.[6]

[121.06A] WELFARE AND BENEFITS LAWS

Insurance coverage for alcohol/drug abuse treatment: Wisconsin laws require insurance policies to provide mandatory coverage for employees undergoing treatment for alcohol and/or drug abuse.[7]

Insurance coverage for newborns: Wisconsin statutes mandate that employee health-related insurance policies include coverage of newborns—including adopted children—of employees.[8]

Insurance coverage for mental health treatment: Wisconsin statutes require insurance policies to provide mandatory coverage for mental health illness.[9]

State holidays: Wisconsin statutes provide that the following are state recognized holidays: New Year's Day, Martin Luther King's Birthday, Washington's

Birthday, Memorial Day, July 4th, Labor Day, Columbus Day, Veteran's Day, Thanksgiving Day, and Christmas Day.[10]

[121.08] UNEMPLOYMENT COMPENSATION LAWS

Aside from private sector employers generally subject to the coverage of Wisconsin's Unemployment Compensation Laws, agricultural, nonprofit, state government agencies and employers of domestic employees also are subject to the unemployment laws.[11]

Wisconsin law disqualifies individuals who are recipients of pension, retirement pay, or other such annuities, and recipients of unemployment benefits from federal and other state unemployment compensation funds from collecting unemployment compensation.[12]

Wisconsin's unemployment compensation laws do not provide coverage to such employees as: persons self-employed; employees of commercial fishing vessels; railroad employees; wholly commissioned insurance and real estate agents; persons employed by parent, spouse or child; patients and student nurses employed by hospitals; hospital interns; minor newspaper carriers; newspaper distributors; students and spouses of students providing employment services to schools, colleges, and universities, if under college work study program and students at nonprofit or public education institutions who are in full-time work study programs.[13]

[121.11] TORT ACTIONS

Public policy—wage deductions: Despite a Wisconsin law that prohibits unauthorized wage deductions for stolen property, a Wisconsin Appellate Court refused to sustain a former employee's legal position that he had been wrongfully discharged because of his walking off the job in protest of being fined $10 for failing to return a company master key to its proper location, the court concluding that the discharge did not violate the fundamental spirit of the law.[14]

Defamation—conditional privilege: A Wisconsin Appellate Court dismissed a lawsuit by two employees who had been discharged for engaging in sexual harassment, the employees contending that the employer had defamed them by issuing a press release to the public about their discharge without specifically naming them. However, the Court held that the employer had a conditional privilege to issue the press release because its employees had a common interest with the employer in knowing its sexual harassment policy was being enforced.[15]

[121.12] TIME LIMITATIONS FOR FILING WRONGFUL DISCHARGE LAWSUITS

Wisconsin statutes provide time limits for litigants to file wrongful employment lawsuits to be: two years for defamation, three years for discharge in violation of public policy, and six years for discharge in violation of implied contracts causes of action.[16]

SUPPLEMENTAL NOTES TO CHAPTER 121

1. Wisconsin Statutes, Section 111.33.
2. Wisconsin Statutes, Section 111.39.
3. Wisconsin Administrative Code, Industrial Section 86.03.
4. Wisconsin Statutes, Sections 16.765, 230.01.
5. Wisconsin Act 427, (Effective 5-6-1994).
6. *Pluskota v. Roadrunner Freight Systems*, (Wisc. Ct. of App., 1994).
7. Wisconsin Statutes, Section 632.89.
8. Wisconsin Statutes, Section 632.895(5).
9. Wisconsin Statutes, Section 632.89.
10. Wisconsin Statutes, Section 895.20.
11. Wisconsin Statutes, Sections 108.02, 108.04, 108.14.
12. Wisconsin Statutes, Sections 108.02, 108.04, 108.05.
13. Wisconsin Statutes, Sections 108.02, 108.04.
14. *Evenson v. Fogan Chevrolet-Cadillac, Inc.*, No. 92-1764 (Wis. App. Ct., 12-2-93).
15. *Olsen v. 3M Company*, 523 NW2d 578 (Wisc. Ct. of App., 1994).
16. Wisconsin Statutes, Sections 893.43, 893.57.

122

Wyoming Labor and Employment Laws

[122.05] REGULATION OF EMPLOYMENT PRACTICES

Bona fide exceptions to prohibited employment practices: Wyoming statutes provide that bona fide seniority systems, bona fide occupational qualifications, and bona fide benefits programs are legally recognized exceptions to otherwise unfair employment practices.[1]

EEOC—certified deferral: Wyoming statutes provide that the Wyoming Fair Employment Commission is to serve as a certified deferral agency of the Equal Employment Opportunity Commission relative to fair employment claims filed with the EEOC.[2]

Court review of agency decisions: Wyoming statutes permit claimants and respondents to adverse decisions by the Wyoming Fair Employment Commission a right of review to applicable courts within the state.[3]

AIDS testing and confidentiality: Wyoming statutes regulate conditions in which AIDS tests may be given and under what circumstances the results of such tests may be disclosed to others.[4]

[122.06A] WELFARE AND BENEFITS LAWS

Insurance coverage for newborns: Wyoming statutes mandate that employee health-related insurance policies include coverage of newborns—including adopted children—of employees.[5]

State holidays: Wyoming statutes specify the following as state recognized holidays: New Year's Day, Martin Luther King's Birthday, Washington's Birthday, Memorial Day, July 4th, Labor Day, Veteran's Day, Thanksgiving Day and Christmas Day.[6]

[122.08] UNEMPLOYMENT COMPENSATION LAWS

Aside from private sector employers generally subject to the coverage of Wyoming's Unemployment Compensation Laws, agricultural, nonprofit, state government agencies, and employers of domestic employees also are subject to the unemployment laws.[7]

Wyoming law disqualifies individuals who are recipients of pension, retirement pay or other such annuities, recipients of unemployment benefits from federal and other state unemployment compensation funds, and recipients of severance payments, termination allowances, or earned vacation pay from collecting unemployment compensation.[8]

Wyoming's unemployment compensation laws do not provide coverage to such employees as: persons self-employed; railroad employees; wholly commissioned real estate agents; persons employed by parent, spouse or child; patients employed by hospitals; minor newspaper carriers; students and spouses of students providing employment services to schools, colleges, and universities, if under college work study program and students at nonprofit or public education institutions who are in full-time work study programs.[9]

[122.10] EMPLOYMENT-AT-WILL DEVELOPMENTS

Handbook disclaimer insufficient: The Wyoming Supreme Court has ruled that in order for a disclaimer to be sufficient to overcome contractual implications provided in an employee handbook, there must be a conspicuous disclaimer clarifying that the employment relationship is at-will; the court concluded that no such conspicuous disclaimer was present in the handbook in question.[10]

[122.11] TORT ACTIONS

Bad faith discharge: The Supreme Court of Wyoming has stated that it would recognize a tort of implied covenant of good faith and fair dealing but only in cases in which a special relationship "of trust and reliance" has been created between the employee and the employer, such as by the existence of separate considerations or rights accruing as a result of length of service years with the employer.[11]

[122.12] TIME LIMITATIONS FOR FILING WRONGFUL DISCHARGE LAWSUITS

Wyoming statutes provide time limits for litigants to file wrongful employment lawsuits to be: one year for defamation and six years for discharge in violation of implied contracts causes of action.[12]

SUPPLEMENTAL NOTES TO CHAPTER 122

1. Wyoming Statutes, Section 27-9-105.

2. Wyoming Statutes, Section 27-9-106.

3. Wyoming Statutes, Section 27-9-107, 27-9-108.

4. Wyoming Statutes, Section 35-4-132.

5. Wyoming Statutes, Section 26-20-101.

6. Wyoming Statutes, Sections 8-4-101, *et seq.*

7. Wyoming Statutes, Sections 27-3-103, 27-3-105, 27-3-107, 27-3-501, 27-3-502.

8. Wyoming Statutes, Sections 27-3-102, 27-3-106, 27-3-307, 27-3-313.

9. Wyoming Statutes, Sections 27-3-102, 27-3-107, 27-3-108, 27-3-313.

10. *Sanchez v. Life Care Centers of America, Inc.*, No. 92-25 (Wyo. S. Ct., 7-15-93).

11. *Wilder v. Cody County Chamber of Commerce*, 868 P.2d 211 (Sup. Ct. Wyo., 1994).

12. Wyoming Statutes, Section 1-3-105.

CUMULATIVE INDEX

Supplement page numbers are preceeded by the letter "S": e.g., S8.

Utah (cont'd)
ments, 1090; employment practices, 1085-88, S205; labor relations laws, 1084, 1095; mediation and arbitration laws, 1085; newborns, insurance coverage for, S206; safety and health laws, 1089; state holidays, S206; strikes, picketing, and boycott laws, 1084-85; time limitations for filing wrongful discharge lawsuits, S206; unemployment compensation laws, 1089, S206; union activities, regulation of, 1085; Utah Labor Relations Act, 1084; wage and hour laws, 1088-89; welfare and benefit laws, S206; workers' compensation laws, 1090; wrongful discharge lawsuits, S206

V

Vacation pay:
Alabama, 568; Delaware, 656; Idaho, 709; Iowa, 744; Louisiana, 778; Maine, 790-91; Massachusetts, 818; Nebraska, 890; New Hampshire, 912; North Carolina, 959; North Dakota, 971; Oregon, 1006; Tennessee, 1066; Vermont, 1099; West Virginia, 1131; Wisconsin, 1144
Vacations, as noncompensable working time, 392
Vermont, 1093-1102, S207-9
AIDS testing, S207; alcohol abuse treatment, insurance coverage for, S208; EEOC-certified deferral, S207; employment-at-will developments, 1100, S208-9; employment practices, 1096-98, S207; implied contracts, S208-9; labor relations laws, 1095; mediation and arbitration laws, 1096; mental health treatment, insurance coverage for, S208; negligent failure to disclose, S209; newborns, insurance coverage for, S208; safety and health laws, 1099; sexual harassment guidelines, S207; state holidays, S208; strikes, picketing, and boycott laws, 1095-96; time limitations for filing wrongful discharge lawsuits, S209; tort actions, 1101, S209; unemployment compensation laws, 1099, S208; union activities, regulation of, 1096; Vermont Labor Relations Law, 1095; Vermont Municipal Labor Relations Act, 1095; wage and

hour laws, 1098-99; welfare and benefits laws, S208; workers' compensation laws, 1100; wrongful discharge lawsuits, S209
Veterans' reemployment rights, 334-40, S37-S40
administration/enforcement, 335; automatic promotions, 337; background/coverage of, 335; bonuses, 337; claims processing, 338; conditions of reemployment, 335-36
other than temporary position upon departure, 336; qualified to perform, 335- 36; seniority privileges, 336; timely application, 336; veterans' intent upon departure, 336
employer obligations, 337-38; general wage increases, 336; holiday pay, 337; insurance, 337; pension and retirement benefits, 337; severance pay, 337; sick leave credits, 337
Vietnam Era Veterans Readjustment Assistance Act (1974), 345
Violence, threats of: District of Columbia, 663; Mississippi, 855
Virginia, 1103-12, S210-12
adoptive baby insurance, S210; affirmative action programs, S210; AIDS testing and confidentiality, S210; alcohol/drug abuse treatment, insurance coverage for, S210; Coal Industry Seizure Act, 1106; discrimination claims, S211; EEOC-certified deferral, S210; employment- at-will developments, 1109-10, S211; employment practices, 1106-8, S210; labor relations laws, 1105; mediation and arbitration laws, 1106; mental health treatment, insurance coverage for, S210; newborns, insurance coverage for, S210; Public Utilities Seizure Act, 1105; safety and health laws, 1109; state holidays, S210; strikes, picketing, and boycott laws, 1105-6; time limitations for filing wrongful discharge lawsuits, S212; tort actions, 1110-11, S211; unemployment compensation laws, 1109, S211; union activities, regulation of, 1106; wage and hour laws, 1108-9; welfare and benefits laws, S210; workers' compensation laws, 1109, S211; wrongful discharge lawsuits, S212

Voice stress analyzers:
Pennsylvania, 1017; South Carolina, 1043; Texas, 1075
Volunteer firefighters protection:
California, 612; Colorado, 628; Connecticut, 642; Indiana, 731-32; Nevada, 899; Pennsylvania, 1018
Volunteer public service protection, Maryland, 801
Voting:
Alabama, 567; Alaska, 578; Arizona, 587, 589; Arkansas, 599; California, 616; Colorado, 630; Delaware, 656; Georgia, 688; Hawaii, 699; Indiana, 732; Iowa, 743; Kansas, 755; Kentucky, 766-67; Maryland, 802; Minnesota, 845; Nebraska, 890; Nevada, 901; New York, 946; Ohio, 980; Oklahoma, 992; South Dakota, 1055; Tennessee, 1065; Texas, 1076; Utah, 1088; Wisconsin, 1144; Wyoming, 1154

W

Wage advancement, fraudulent receipt of:
North Carolina, 956 North Dakota, 968
Wage assignments:
Alabama, 568; Tennessee, 1066; Texas, 1077
Wage attachments, as noncash item includible in wages, 394
Wage claims protection:
Alabama law, 567; North Dakota, 970
Wage disclosure protection, California, 616
Wage and hours laws, federal, S51-S56
Fair Labor Standards Act, S53-S56
child labor laws, S55; overtime pay requirements, S54; overtime for public sector employees, S54; special arrangement as basis of payment, S53-S54; "working time," compensable, S53
Wage reduction, Missouri, 866
Wages:
disparity in, 51-52; protests over, 60
Wage withholding:
California, 616; Colorado, 630; Connecticut, 645; Delaware, 657; District of Columbia, 666; Hawaii, 700; Illinois, 721; Iowa, 744; Kansas, 756; Kentucky, 767; Maine, 791; Maryland, 803;